THE
BMW
STORY

Also from Veloce Publishing –

www.veloce.co.uk

First published in 2003, this updated second edition published April 2019 by Veloce Publishing Limited, Veloce House, Parkway Farm Business Park, Middle Farm Way, Poundbury, Dorchester DT1 3AR, England.
Fax 01305 250479 / Tel 01305 260068 / e-mail info@veloce.co.uk / web www.veloce.co.uk or www.velocebooks.com.
ISBN: 978-1-787113-58-9 UPC: 6-36847-01358-5

THE
BMW
STORY
SECOND EDITION

PRODUCTION AND RACING MOTORCYCLES FROM 1923 TO THE PRESENT DAY
IAN FALLOON

VELOCE PUBLISHING
THE PUBLISHER OF FINE AUTOMOTIVE BOOKS

CONTENTS

Following on from the R90S and R100S, the R100CS incorporated the attributes of the early S models, with the technical improvements of the post-1981 boxers. *Ian Falloon*

INTRODUCTION & ACKNOWLEDGEMENTS

Over nearly 100 years, BMW motorcycles have provided a unique alternative to those of other manufacturers. Some motorcycles may have been faster, certainly others were cheaper, but, with their emphasis on quality and reliability, none has emulated the practicality of BMWs. With its commitment to ease of serviceability, the BMW motorcycle has become the preferred choice for hundreds of thousands of motorcyclists around the world.

Although built in Berlin since 1969, the BMW motorcycle tradition began in Munich, the capital of Bavaria in Southern Germany. Situated in the shadow of the Alps, the design of BMW motorcycles was suited to the twisting roads of the Bavarian countryside and the nearby Alps. When Schorsch Meier, winner of the 1939 Senior TT on a 500 Kompressor, was asked how he could lap the Isle of Man at more than 90mph with virtually no track experience, he replied that it reminded him of the roads around his home in Bavaria. When motorcycle production recommenced after World War II, BMW continued this tradition of building motorcycles that excelled in the back roads, the Alps, or the Autobahn: a tradition that continues today. With the establishment of the dual-purpose GS (Gelände/Straße), the parameters widened to include off road use.

BMW motorcycles are built to be ridden, and if the journey includes a mixture of straight roads, corners and dirt trails, there is no better motorcycle. Factor in the best range of factory luggage and accessories available, and the success of BMW motorcycles isn't surprising. Ownership of a BMW was also generally a long-term affair. Because of long model runs, the designs were so well developed there seemed little need to update on the whim of fashion. But, as the motorcycle rider ages and becomes increasingly affluent, this is changing. Electronic aids are improving every year, as is safety. Unlike in earlier times, BMW now promotes desuetude, new models providing significant improvement over their predecessors.

My own experience with BMW motorcycles extends from many wonderful long rides on a friend's early model R100RS, to long-term ownership of a K100RS.

Advancing age has seen a reversion to the traditional boxer twin, currently a 1976 R90S. Over the years, I have had the fortune to sample a wide range of BMW motorcycles, although I must admit to finding the huge size of some of the newer examples intimidating.

While I have endeavoured to document every road and racing BMW motorcycle since 1923, I have also tried to provide an insight into the people responsible for the designs. Without Max Friz, Rudolf Schleicher, Alfred Böning, Alexander von Falkenhausen, Hans-Günther von der Marwitz, and Stefan Pachernegg, BMW motorcycles wouldn't be what they are.

Compiling this book would have been impossible without the help of many friends, colleagues, and enthusiasts. I have endeavoured to find as many previously unpublished photographic material as possible, and for this am indebted to Fred Jakobs of the BMW Historical Archive in Munich. Brian J Nelson contributed wonderful images of older BMW motorcycles from collections in the US, and BMW Group Press provided the more recent images. While the majority of the material appeared in the 2003 edition of this book, the sheer number of additional models since then has made this second edition quite a challenge. Every new Model Year brings a series of updates and the rate of replacement models is accelerating. In 1969 BMW released the /5 series, and for 1970 the model range included only three boxer twins, the R50/5, R60/5 and R75/5. Fifty years later, not only are there multiple models of singles, parallel twins, boxer twins, fours and sixes, the range of options for customisation is virtually endless.

My thanks go to Rod Grainger and his Veloce team, and the tireless hours spent researching and writing this book wouldn't have been possible without the wonderful support from my wife Miriam, and two sons, Benjamin and Timothy.

Ian Falloon
January 2019

The R32 of 1923. With its boxer engine and shaft drive, it established a layout that would epitomise most BMW motorcycles for the next 80 years. *Cycle World*

1BEGINNINGS
FROM AIRCRAFT TO MOTORCYCLES

In the company's register in the Munich District Court, there is an entry in copperplate handwriting for 7 March 1916, listing the Bavarian Aircraft Works, a company to manufacture and market aircraft. One of the six investors listed was Gustav Otto, an engineer, pilot, flying instructor, and entrepreneur. Gustav came from an illustrious background and his father, Nikolaus August Otto, was the creator of the four-stroke petrol engine. When Gustav was only eight years old, in 1891, Nikolaus died, but he would follow his father's footsteps into engineering and when he saw Louis Blèriot flying in 1909, he was captivated.

In 1910, Gustav formed his own aircraft manufacturing works in Munich and by 1912 he was one of Germany's most prominent air pioneers. Unfortunately, just like his father, Gustav was a poor businessman and the only financial partnership he could arrange was with the German military. Even war couldn't save Gustav and during 1915 his relationship with the German War Ministry disintegrated following a disagreement with one of Germany's leading generals, von Brug. Forced into bankruptcy, Gustav spent some time in a mental hospital, then he sold the Otto Works and the premises in Oberwiesenfeld. These premises, at 76 Neulerchenfeld Street, later renamed Lerchenauer Street, are still the site for Plant 1 at BMW AG. Although he then severed all ties with the new company, ultimately shooting himself in 1926, Gustav Otto is credited as being BMW's founding father. Yet, this is only where half of the BMW story began.

The other half commenced in another corner of Oberwiesenfeld, in 1912, when Karl Rapp established a Munich subsidiary of the Aachen-based Flugwerke Deutschland to manufacture aircraft engines. Unlike Otto, Rapp couldn't boast an illustrious ancestry, but he came at a time when Germany suddenly discovered they were falling behind France in the development of military aviation. Kaiser Wilhelm II established an Imperial Prize for an aviation engine, but Rapp's entry failed. The firm went into receivership and Rapp managed to raise 200,000 marks to establish the Rapp Motor Works in the same premises at 288 Schleiflheim Street, on 28 October 1913.

With six workers, Rapp again prepared an engine for the Imperial Prize. This time, it was a six-cylinder, but, plagued with excessive vibration, the engine was not completed on time. The outbreak of war gave Rapp

Max Friz, the father of the BMW boxer
motorcycle. *Stefan Knittel*

MAX FRIZ

Born in Urach in 1883, Max Friz was apprenticed at
the age of 15 to the Kuhn steam engine company
in Cannstatt. In 1902, he went to the Royal Building
Trade School in Stuttgart-Esslingen and from 1906
worked in the design office of the Daimler-Motoren-
Gesellschaft. Here, he made a significant contribution
to the design of the racing engine for the 1914
Mercedes Grand Prix car that won the French Grand
Prix. Between 1912 and 1913, Friz designed the first
German aircraft engine with separate cylinders on
the crankcase, and an overhead camshaft driven
by a vertical shaft and bevel gears. Following the
release of the R32 motorcycle, Friz became a director
of BMW AG, and from 1925 until 1937 was their
first chief designer. He was general manager of the
Munich plant from 1935 until 1937, and then held a
similar position at Eisenach until 1944. Friz retired in
1945 and died in 1966.

a reprieve and he soon produced V8 and V12 aero
engines. Unfortunately, these also vibrated and they were
rejected by the Prussian military command in Berlin.
Like the Otto Works down the road, Rapp's company
also suffered from poor business management and his
new commercial director, Max Wiedmann, steered the
company towards the brink of disaster. The workforce
grew to 370, but by the autumn of 1916, the Austrian
military ceased to be a customer because of the poor
reputation of Rapp's engines. Wiedmann befriended a
Vienna-based financier (and notorious war profiteer)
Camillo Castiglioni who already controlled Austro-
Daimler in Austria. Austro-Daimler didn't have the
capacity to supply the new Ferdinand Porsche-designed
350bhp engine and this led to a contract in October
1916 for the Rapp Motor Works to produce 224 engines
worth 10 million marks. Because of Rapp's dubious
reputation for quality, the Austrian War Ministry insisted
on appointing a supervisor to oversee the production.

This supervisor was Franz Josef Popp, a 30-year-
old Austrian Lieutenant, and qualified engineer.
Popp was initially dismayed at the sight of only three
wooden sheds for the works, but after a week was
convinced that Rapp and his loyal workers could
produce the engines. This coincided with a dramatic
turn of events. With America's entry into the war
the Prussian military administration requested more
aircraft. They didn't want the 350bhp engines Rapp
was building, but required six-cylinder engines for
fighters. Rapp's reputation was so tainted that Popp,
now technical manager, decided the only solution to
ensure survival was to remove Rapp's name from the
company. Thus, on 20 July 1917, the Rapp Motor
Works became the Bavarian Motor Works, and on 5
October 1917, Popp registered the rotating-propeller
trademark at the Imperial Patents Office. With the
creation of BMW, Rapp immediately left, although he
had earlier retired through illness. Despite a precarious
business environment, Popp was intent on expansion,
purchasing 25 hectares of land on Moosach Street on
the northern end of Oberwiesenfeld one month after
forming BMW. At this time, there was no merger with
the Bayerische Flugzeug-Werke (Bavarian Aircraft
Works and formerly Otto Works). This continued to
coexist happily with BMW until 1922.

On 2 January 1917, Max Friz joined Rapp Motor
Works. He had known Rapp when they worked
in the design department of Daimler together, but
had resigned from Daimler when his request for a
50-mark pay rise was declined. Friz wrote to Rapp
asking for a job and he brought along a design for a
high-altitude carburettor that incorporated an inlet
fitting that opened at an altitude of 2,000m (6,500ft),
but which remained closed at lower levels. The dour
Rapp was sceptical, but Popp decided Friz's idea was

worth investigating. When the Austro-Daimler engine contract was cancelled in May 1917, Popp sent Friz off to redesign Rapp's problematic six-cylinder engine. The result was an engine that no longer vibrated, and produced 160bhp at 3,000m (1,000ft), considerably more than the comparable Daimler unit. Friz convinced the authorities in Berlin of the advantages of his new engine, the IIIa, and by the end of 1917, had tested it successfully in the air. So superior was the IIIa that by the middle of 1918, the Prussian military ordered 2,000 engines. Popp's gamble on expansion was vindicated, but the company was soon in trouble.

It was one thing to have a superior product, but another to be able to produce it. Food and material shortages in Munich in 1918 severely affected worker morale and engine production slumped. With 1,744 workers, the costs associated with building the new premises at Moosach Street, as well as Wiedmann's extravagant lifestyle, the only solution was to convert BMW from a limited to a public company. So, on 13 August 1918, BMW became a public company, with one of the main investors the same Camillo Castiglioni. This allowed the expansion of the workforce to 3,400, and engine production to 150 per month by October 1918.

Although Ernst Udet achieved 30 victories with his BMW IIIa-powered Fokker D.VII fighter plane, and new BMW II and IV engines were about to enter production, it was too late. The end of the war arrived on 11 November and by 6 December production at BMW had ceased. Somehow, Popp managed to reopen the factory on 1 February 1919 enabling further development of the BMW IV engine, a development of the IIIa. Zeno Diemer used this engine on 9 June 1919 to reach an altitude of 9,760m (32,023ft), a world record that wasn't ratified by the international authority, the FAI, as Germany was a defeated power. Only eleven days after Diemer's repeat flight on 17 June, and just as Popp believed this record would set the company on a new path, the Treaty of Versailles was signed. Germany was now forbidden to be involved in the manufacture of aircraft and engines until mid-1920. Popp was now in a dilemma as to what BMW could manufacture.

While Friz was designing engines for boats and trucks out of the remains of aero-engines in the cellars, salvation appeared from experienced foreman, Martin Stolle. Stolle was a committed motorcyclist who had won third prize in a race from Vienna to Munich on a 1913 model English Douglas in 1914. Stolle joined BMW in 1917 and, impressed by the reliability of the Douglas flat-twin, he persuaded Popp to sanction the development of a similar motorcycle engine.

Orders for the M2 B15 were too small to sustain the company so Popp negotiated a contract with Knorr Bremse AG in Berlin to supply 10,000 compressed-air

Martin Stolle astride the Victoria KR1 with the BMW M2 B15 engine. *Mick Woollett*

THE M2 B15

Early in 1920, Stolle acquired a 1914–15 Model B 500cc Douglas motocycle and stripped it down on Friz's workbench. Every part was measured and drawn up reluctantly by Friz, an innovator used to designing every part, and loath to copy something else. From these drawings, Stolle built six test engines before installing one in the Douglas chassis and riding over to the Victoria Works in Nuremberg. Victoria then fitted the engine in their frame and marketed it as the Victoria KR1. Essentially, the M2 B15 ('2' for two cylinders and 'B' for boxer) was a copy of the 494cc Douglas, sharing the side-valve layout and 68 x 68mm bore and stroke, but with a BMW trademark on the crankcase. Friz incorporated enclosed valves and force-fed gear lubrication. With an exposed flywheel and non-detachable cylinder heads, the engine weighed only 31kg (68lb), and with a single carburettor produced a modest 6.5bhp at 3,000rpm. Positioned in the frame longitudinally like the Douglas, with either belt or chain final drive, the M2 B15 soon found its way into other motorcycles besides the Victoria. This included Corona, SMW, Bison, RS Bayerland, Heller, and later the Bayerische Flugzeug-Werke Helios, motorcycles. On 28 March 1921, Stolle entered a Victoria KR1 in the 370km (230-mile) Bavarian Motorcycle Derby.

During 1920, Bayerische Flugzeug-Werke produced the two-stroke Flink under contract for Karl Rühmer. *Stefan Knittel*

After BMW moved into the BFW premises during 1922, they inherited a number of Helios motorcycles with the BMW M2 B15 engine. *Rainer Schwinge*

THE FLINK AND HELIOS

By 1917, BFW was producing 200 aircraft a month and had a workforce of 2,400. Then, a fire in November 1917 reduced the works to ashes, from which BFW never really recovered. The buildings weren't rebuilt, and as BFW was prohibited from aircraft manufacture following the Versailles Treaty, it was engaged initially in building office furniture out of leftover wooden aircraft mountings. Shortly afterwards, an engineer, Karl Rühmer, contracted BFW to produce a simple motorised bicycle that he had designed. Rühmer undertook to manage the sales and marketing and the Flink was born. With a 1½bhp 143cc single-cylinder two-stroke engine bought from Carl Hanfland in Berlin, the Flink weighed 40kg (88lb) and had a top speed of around 50km/h (31mph). The cylinder was angled forward with fins parallel to the ground, while the magneto bolted to the back of the crankcase to

form a 'V' shape. The engine was mounted in Rühmer's simple loop frame with sprung forks and drove the rear wheel directly by belt. At the same time, Gustav Otto, BMW's founder, was also engaged in the production of a motorised bicycle. Otto's Flottweg featured a 1bhp four-stroke engine driving the front wheel through an epicyclical gear.

The success of the Flink during 1920 and into 1921 saw BFW decide to compete with the Victoria. After building a prototype Helios with a Douglas engine in October 1921, Rühmer used the BMW M2 B15 engine for production examples. The chassis of the Helios was similar to the Flink, and was not sufficient for the heavier engine. This was no match for the Victoria in the depressed days of 1922, and only 1,015 examples of the Helios were produced, the last one in November 1923.

brakes for the Bavarian Railways Board. In May 1920, Knorr Bremse bought Castiglioni's BMW shares and set up production in Moosach Street. Over the winter of 1920–21, production of the M2 B15 commenced, continuing alongside brakes. However, by 1922, the German mark was virtually worthless due to rampant inflation and the board of directors instructed Popp to concentrate purely on brake production. But Popp wasn't about to give up engine production. He already had plans to produce a small, 1,100cc car (the Sasha) and again approached Castiglioni. Castiglioni suggested they bought back the name BMW from Knorr Bremse, along with the construction facilities not required for brakes. Popp then went to Knorr with 75 million Marks and came away with the BMW name and symbol, and on 20 May 1922, the contract was ratified. Knorr Bremse remained in Moonbach Street,

the name changing to Südbremse AG in July 1922. All BMW needed now were new premises.

Coincidentally, in nearby Neulerchenfeld Street, the Bayerische Flugzeug-Werke was close to bankruptcy. Castiglioni had acquired a majority shareholding in BFW in November 1921, and on 5 June 1922, BFW became Bavarian Motor Works. Camillo Castiglioni was listed as the only shareholder, remaining on the board until October 1929 when he was forced to relinquish his shareholding under mysterious circumstances.

When BMW moved into the BFW premises they inherited the small-scale Helios motorcycle production line and a considerable number of unsold examples. Popp commissioned Friz to modify the Helios to allow the remaining stock to be sold. Although Friz was a competent and enthusiastic motorcyclist, he was reluctant to work on the Helios. However, he repositioned the engine in the frame to improve steering and handling. Popp then instructed Friz to consider designing a completely new motorcycle, the R32. The main reason for this was that there was no longer a market for the M2 B15 engine as Victoria, BMW's main customer, was now using an engine from WSM (Wilhelm Sedlbauer Munich). Martin Stolle created this engine, but had left BMW in 1922 because BMW had refused to pay 100 marks in expenses for a trip. Stolle's overhead valve engine produced 8bhp, and powered the most successful sporting motorcycle in Germany at the time, the Victoria KR2. It also proved superior to the new BMW R32 at Solitude in June 1923, where none of the three special overhead valve BMWs finished.

THE R32

Friz retired to his home at 34 Riesenfeld Street near the BMW factory, working uninterrupted from the guests' room. As BMW already had a 500cc horizontally opposed twin-cylinder engine, Friz took this as a basis for his new motorcycle. The rear cylinder tended to overheat on the Victoria and Helios, so he decided to mount the engine transversely, adding a shaft drive. The rigid frame meant the driveshaft didn't require a universal joint, and a rubber disc (Hardy) was sufficient as a shock absorber. Although the English Sopwith ABC motorcycle of 1919 also featured a transverse twin-cylinder engine (without shaft drive), according to Friz he was unaware of the ABC at the time. Later, there were accusations from Granville Bradshaw, a designer at ABC, that the BMW was a copy of their motorcycle, but there were too many detail differences for this to be substantiated. Within four months, in December 1922, Friz completed the drawings.

The side-valve engine, a development of the M2 B15, was known as the M2 B33 or M33a, and was uprated to produce 8.5bhp. While this power output wasn't particularly outstanding, it was the execution of the design which set the R32 apart. Here was a motorcycle designed with reliability and ease of maintenance foremost. The engine, including the valve timing system, was fully encased, there were no chains requiring adjustment, and there was a hand-operated side lever for a three-speed, grease-filled gearbox. The ignition was by a magneto generator and a rather complicated set of handlebar controls.

Friz installed this engine in a closed twin-loop tubular steel frame, with the petrol tank underneath the upper frame tubes. The frame was brazed and sleeved, and as the workers lacked experience in brazing, fractures on the solder joints were a problem until the introduction of pressed-steel frames in 1929.

The side-valve R32 engine was a development of the M2 B15, and every component was encased.
Cycle World

The front suspension consisted of a short swinging fork with a cantilever plate spring beneath the steering stem. Initially, there were no front brakes, a block brake on the rear being operated by the rider's heel, but by 1925 there was also a 150mm drum front brake. The R32 ('R' for Rad meaning cycle, but the '32' remains a mystery), not only offered a top speed of around 90km/h (56mph), but the low centre of gravity promised safe and manageable handling for a touring motorcycle on the poor quality roads of the day. In May 1923, Friz himself tested the R32, finishing a club outing through the Bavarian mountains without incurring any penalties. The R32 was launched at Berlin in September 1923, one month before the Paris Car Show where it was a star attraction. It established a boxer-twin shaft-drive format that would characterise BMW motorcycles through until the present day, but the initial response was mixed. Sceptics feared the engine could be easily damaged in a fall, others felt it was underpowered, but no-one could deny the compact engine and transmission unit was a brilliant design and beautifully executed.

The release of the R32 coincided with stability of the German mark, but at 2,200 marks (or 2,600 marks with a light, horn, pillion seat and speedometer) it still represented a significant investment. However, the motorcycle market was flourishing in Germany as cars were for the wealthy few and with the demand for motorcycles strong, BMW managed to sell 1,500 R32s by the end of 1924.

One of the most important figures in the history of BMW motorcycles, Rudolf Schleicher, with his first creation, the R37. *Stefan Knittel*

Below: Schleicher's 1934 R37 has been restored and is in a private collection in Bavaria. The cylinders were different to the production version, with the valve covers held by a single bolt. *Ian Falloon*

RUDOLF SCHLEICHER

Rudolf Schleicher was born in Basle, Switzerland, in 1897 of German parentage, graduating from the Munich College of Advanced Technology after the First World War. Schleicher was an enthusiastic motorcyclist and went to work for BMW in September 1922 under Friz and Martin Duckstein. As well as working on the design of the R37 Schleicher gave BMW their first motorsport success, at the 1924 ADAC Winter Rally in Garmisch-Partenkirchen. In April 1927, following a disagreement with Friz over supercharging and the viability of two-stroke engines in cars, he went to work for Horch in Zwickau as manager of the experimental engine department. There, Schleicher was involved in the development of Horch eight-cylinder engines with Fritz Fiedler. Returning to BMW in 1931, he became chief of the experimental department for cars and motorcycles, and from 1932 was in charge of motorcycle design. Schleicher also developed BMW's first six-cylinder passenger-car engine. He remained head of motorcycle development until 1945 and at the end of the Second World War set up Schleicher Fahrzeugteile KG, repairing cars and manufacturing camshafts. The company was later taken over by his sons Rolf and Hans, with Rudolf returning to BMW AG's development and experimental department from October 1956 staying through to his retirement in 1960.

THE R37

After the humiliation at Solitude in 1923, BMW returned the following year with a revised machine designed by Schleicher. Overheating of the steel cylinder and monoblock head was the main problem with the M35a overhead valve engine and it was only reliable when the ambient temperature was extremely low. At Garmisch early in 1924, Schleicher and the M35a were successful, but it was obvious that there was no real competition future with this design.

Shortly after joining BMW, Schleicher drew up a light alloy cylinder head with fully enclosed and lubricated overhead valves set at an included angle of 90°. This was quite a radical development as the valves were usually exposed to dust and water and often required manual lubrication of the rocker shafts. To achieve improved cooling, Schleicher incorporated (and patented) circumferential cooling fins with cooling passages around the valves. The cylinders were turned from a billet of steel and as Friz was once again involved in aircraft engine design (the BMW VI V12), it was left to the young Schleicher to develop the M2 B36 (M36a) for Solitude. The chassis was similar to the R32, and the new machine was given the designation R37.

Schleicher headed a team of three at Solitude, being joined by Franz Bieber and Rudi Reich. The three

The R37 was the first sporting BMW, but was extremely expensive in its day. *Ian Falloon*

new R37s produced a claimed 22hp and won three categories, with Reich setting the fastest time of the day. This success continued in the Eifel Mountain Race, the German Grand Prix, the Avus Race in Berlin, while Bieber took the German Road Championship. The R37 then went into limited production during 1925, albeit at a price of 2,900 marks, making it the most expensive German motorcycle available. With a new, three-slide 26mm BMW carburettor the power was 16hp at 4,000rpm, enough to propel the R37 to 115km/h (71mph).

It wasn't until 1926 though that the R37 managed to capture the attention of those outside Germany. Schleicher and his friend Friz Roth ventured to England on production R37s as private entrants in the Six-Day Race. Not realising that off-road tyres were necessary, and unable to source any, they fronted with conventional tyres and low pressures. Almost laughed out of the race when they arrived, Schleicher crossed the finishing line with a gold medal. The British press

sat up and took notice, and Professor A. M. Low wrote in the Auto-Cycle Union magazine: 'After the toughest days in the field we could not find a single oil leak, the machine was beautifully quiet, and seemed to possess great reserves of power. From a design point of view it is miles ahead of any British machine.'

THE R42 & R47

The R32 established BMW as a manufacturer of quality motorcycles, but after two years a replacement was needed. At the end of 1925, a redesigned touring twin appeared alongside the R32, and replaced it during 1926. Although still a side-valve 500, the R42 incorporated a number of developments, including a wedge-shaped combustion chamber to improve combustion. Designated the M43a, there were new cylinders with the cooling fins set across the barrel, and the beautifully sculptured alloy cylinder heads were detachable. With a BMW Special two-valve 22mm carburettor the power was increased significantly, to 12bhp at 3,400rpm. The three-speed gearbox also incorporated a speedometer drive, but the top speed of 95km/h (59mph) represented no improvement over the R32.

Accompanying the engine development was a new frame with straight downtubes placing the engine further rearwards for better weight distribution. This improved the rather top-heavy feeling of the R32 and led to more secure handling. The heel-operated driveshaft brake that appeared on the R39 single also featured on the R42. There was now a sidecar mount offered on the rear driveshaft housing and the overall weight of 126kg (278lb) was up slightly on the R32. By 1926, BMW was expanding, and a reduction in price of the R42 to 1,510 marks saw it as one of BMW's most successful motorcycles of the 1920s.

A year later, an overhead valve version, the R47, replaced the R37. Not purely a racing machine like its predecessor, the R47 used an identical chassis to the touring R42, complete with sidecar option. Developments of the engine, designated the M51a, included cast-iron, rather than steel, barrels, and valve covers retained by a single bolt. The three-slide carburettor made way for a standard BMW type and the power increased slightly to 18hp. The top speed was a little less than the R37, at 110km/h (68mph), but because the price was reduced significantly, to 1,850 marks, 1,720 R47s were produced in one series. A sports variant of the R47, with an Sp.M51a engine, was also available, providing 31bhp.

Below: The R42 replaced the R32 during 1926. The side-valve engine featured a new cylinder head design and longitudinal fins. *Brian J. Nelson*

Opposite: In addition to the R42, there was a sporting overhead valve R47 for 1927. This replaced the R37. *BMW Mobile Tradition*

THE R52, R57, R62, & R63

By 1928, BMW was established as a premier manufacturer of touring motorcycles and four new models were released using the same chassis (designated the F56a). The two 500cc models were joined by 750cc versions, but these were new designs with a pressed-up crankshaft instead of the earlier one-piece type. There was also a redesigned lubrication system and the side-valve engines now featured a longer, 78mm stroke, while the overhead valve engines retained the earlier, 68mm stroke.

The R52 touring side-valve 500 (designation M57a) had a 63 x 78mm bore and stroke, with the side-valve 750 R62 (M56a) a square 78 x 78mm. There was a new mounting system for the side-valve cylinder heads but they were visually similar to before. The overhead-valve R57 (M59a) 500 remained square at 68 x 68mm, with the overhead-valve R63 750 (M60a) featuring almost modern oversquare dimensions of 83 x 68mm.

The power of the R52 and R57 was the same as the earlier R42 and R47, while the 750 R62 produced 18bhp and the R63 now gave 24bhp at 4,000rpm. This appeared to be very conservative as the R63, with its equally modest claimed top speed of 120km/h (75mph), was one of the fastest machines available at the time. It also came at the premium price of 2,100 marks so it wasn't surprising that only 794 were produced. As with the R47, there was also a sporting version of the R63 available. With an Sp.M60a engine, the power was 36bhp. BMW also produced a 40bhp 749cc racing machine during this period.

All four new models came with a magneto-generator electrical system, with optional Bosch lights until 1929 when they became standard. There was a stronger three-speed gearbox with oil instead of grease, and a new hand-change mechanism. Underneath the gearbox was a useful toolbox, with a hinged door. Also for the first time, the kickstart was side-mounted, kicking out to the side, which was to be a BMW feature for many

years to come. The clutch was also originally a single-plate but was changed during production to a twin-plate. The F56 chassis followed the form of the R42 and R47, but with a larger front brake (200mm) and a six-leaf spring for the front forks, rather than a five-leaf. The weight was increased considerably through, and even the R52 weighed 152kg (335lb). All these models were distinguished by the triangular fuel tank mounted between the engine and the top frame tubes, with the majority being side-valve examples.

As the BMW still lacked the handling finesse of the British competition, racing versions were supercharged from 1928. Supercharging was initially instigated by Rudolf Schleicher during 1927, and was continued by Friz after Schleicher left BMW. Friz installed a French Cozette centrifugal supercharger, and later a Zoller rotary-vane type, mounted horizontally above the engine and gearbox where it was driven by an oil-bathed chain from the crankshaft. This was extremely effective, providing the racing R57 with around 55bhp and the R63 with 75bhp, and during 1929, the racing BMWs were virtually unbeatable in German competition. Hans Soenius won three German championships and Ernst Henne was another of BMW's outstanding riders. Convinced he could also take the world speed record away from the British riders Oliver Baldwin and Bert Le Vack, Henne persuaded Friz to prepare a short-stroke supercharged 750. On 19 September 1929, on the narrow tree-lined Ingolstädter road near Munich, Henne raised

the absolute motorcycle world speed record for the mile to 134.78mph (216.9km/h). The BMW was unfaired but Henne wore a streamlined helmet and tail attached to his riding suit. Because the FIM refused to acknowledge his kilometre record, as he should have attempted this before the mile, Henne returned a few days later and did it again.

Henne's records set off a competition between BMW, Brough Superior, and Gilera for the world speed record that would last throughout the next decade, and were the culmination of an extremely profitable period for BMW. Not only were nearly 20,000 motorcycles produced during the 1920s, but also aircraft engine manufacture was well underway again. Production of the type VI V12 began during 1926 and 7,000 units were sold by the mid-1930s. In 1928, BMW signed a licence agreement with the American company Pratt & Whitney to produce radial aircraft engines.

Perhaps the most significant development during 1928 was the purchase of the Eisenach car plant near Frankfurt, along with the licence to build a copy of the British Austin Seven called the 'Dixi'. BMW then also became a car manufacturer, with vehicles manufactured at Eisenach throughout the 1930s while motorcycle and aircraft engine production remained at Munich. Despite this new emphasis, motorcycle production remained pivotal to the company, and during 1929, BMW released two new 750cc models with totally revised frames. These were the R11 and R16, machines that would serve until 1934.

Opposite top: The BMW twin grew to 750cc with the R62 of 1928. *BMW Mobile Tradition*

Opposite bottom: One of the fastest motorcycles available at the end of the 1920s was the short-stroke overhead valve 750cc R63. *BMW Mobile Tradition*

Right: Ernst Henne gave BMW their first world speed record in 1929 on a supercharged 750, but also set 500cc records. This is in April 1932, on the way to setting a new flying kilometre record. *Mick Woollett*

After the war, Meier resurrected the
500 Kompressor, and raced it
in German events until 1951.
Ian Falloon

2 HIGHS AND LOWS:
THE 1930s, THE SECOND WORLD WAR, AND POST-WAR RECONSTRUCTION

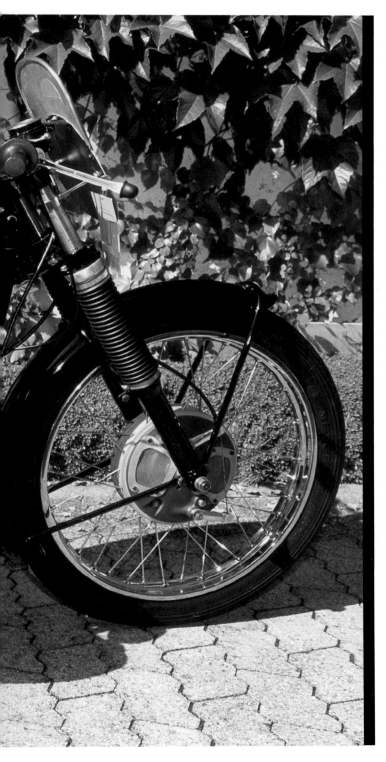

Ernst Henne ushered in the new decade with his world speed record, but this was short lived and he lost it soon afterwards to Joe Wright on the JAP-powered OEC Temple. Henne then set about regaining it, and on 30 September 1930, raised the record to 221.539km/h. Records were significant, both for BMW's importance as a world marque, and for national pride. Economically this was a difficult time, and motorcycle sales were directly related to Henne's achievements. After losing the record again to Wright, who raised it to an astonishing 242.568km/h (390.292mph) in November 1931, at Cork in Ireland, Henne attempted to regain it during 1932. After several failed attempts on the Neunkirchener Allee, a long straight road south of Vienna, there was a slump in motorcycle sales. Production slipped from 6,681 in 1931 to 4,652 in 1932.

Salvation for Henne and BMW came with the return of Rudolf Schleicher. During 1930, Henne persuaded Popp to entice Schleicher back from the troubled Horch company, and with Sepp Hopf, Schleicher designed a new multi-plate supercharger. On 3 November 1932 in Tata, Hungary, in front of a full military line-up and the Governor of Hungary, Admiral Horthy, Henne beat Wright's record and achieved 244.399km/h (393.238mph). Two years later, in October 1934 in Gyon, Hungary, Henne went slightly faster at 246.069km/h (395.925mph), and in 1935 gave the supercharged ohv 750 its final record. On the new Frankfurt–Darmstadt autobahn he reached 256.040km/h (411.968mph), and things were looking up again.

THE R11 & R16

Although the four-model range released in 1928 was selling well, problems with frame fractures and collapsing front forks (particularly when adapted for a sidecar) prompted the release of two new 750s for 1929, the R11 and R16. The side-valve engine of the R11 was carried over from the R62, while the R16 used the overhead-valve R63 engine, and apart from having larger carburettors, these were unchanged. It was the riveted pressed-steel frame that set the new machines apart, and although undeniably stronger, the frame was also heavier, and in the eyes of many, was ugly, scarring Friz's creation.

Rudolf Schleicher and Ernst Henne, the
two main proponents in the setting of
the series of motorcycle world speed
records during the 1930s.
BMW Mobile Tradition

ERNST HENNE

One of BMW's most successful riders, Ernst Henne, was born
in 1904 in Weiler (Allgäu). At the age of 15 he became an
apprentice motor mechanic in Ravensburg, and entered
his first race riding a Megola in Mühldorf, Bavaria, in 1923.
In 1925, he switched to an Astra, and after taking sixth
place in the European Grand Prix, at Monza in 1926, was
signed up as a factory rider by BMW. He was 500cc and
750cc German champion, in 1926 and '27 respectively and
also won the 1928 Targa Florio in Sicily, all on supercharged
machines. From 1932 to 1936 Henne was a member of the
German national team for the International Six-Day Trial
in England; the first win coming in 1934. Henne also raced
cars during the 1930s, and was badly injured in a Mercedes
in testing on the Nürburgring. Later he drove the 2-litre
BMW 328 sports car to victory in the 1936 Eifel Race and
again in the 1937 Grand Prix des Frontières in Chimay,
Belgium. Henne then pursued a successful business career
as a Mercedes dealer in Munich, but is best remembered for
his 76 motorcycle speed records for BMW. He was a tough
man and in 1929 he narrowly escaped death when the front
wheel spindle came out of the forks while he was travelling
at over 130mph (210km/h). Managing to bring the machine
to a standstill Henne later commented: 'Fate was kind to
me that day.' A few months later, early in 1930, he went
to Ostersund in Sweden with spiked tyres and managed
198.2km/h (123.2mph) for the kilometre on a frozen lake in
minus 14°C temperatures. Henne set this speed immediately
before crashing and sliding 500m (550yd) along the ice.

The F66 chassis of the R11 and R16 consisted
of two loops in a single pressing, joined by cross
members. These strengthening sheets were also riveted
at the front and to the fork blades. The only welding
was at the front where the two halves joined together
over the steering head. The trailing link front forks
were also pressed steel, with nine-leaf-spring front
suspension. The fuel tank was almost hidden by
the heavy gusseting around the steering head. The
result was a machine which conveyed a solidity and
robustness that appealed to commercial and military
interests, but was hardly a sporting mount. The
weight was around 10kg (22lb) more than the R62
and R63, and while the R16 was capable of 120km/h
(75mph), the R11 struggled to better 100km/h
(62mph).

After production was delayed during 1929 due
to some front fork problems, the pressed-steel
models replaced the tubular steel framed versions
in the following year. Only the sporting overhead-
valve 500cc R57 remained through 1930, while the
side-valve R52 disappeared altogether. The R11 and
R16 were then developed through five series until
1934.

SERIES 2

The Series 2 R11 and R16 appeared during 1930. The
engine was designated the M56 S2 for the R11 and
M60 S2 for the R16. A stronger thrust bearing was
added to the twin-plate clutch, there was an additional
bearing in the rear drive, and the rear driveshaft brake
shoes were increased to 55mm (from 37mm). For this
series, the Bosch headlamp changed from the older
drum style to a more modern cup shape.

SERIES 3

New carburettors appeared on the M56 S3 and
M60 S3 engines for 1932. The R11 carburettor was
now a SUM CK3/500 F1 from Berlin, with pre-
heated secondary air drawn through a tube on the
exhaust manifold. On the R16 the compression ratio
was increased to 7:1, and twin one-inch Amal type
6/011 carburettors (made under licence by Fischer in
Frankfurt) bolted directly on the intake manifolds of
each cylinder head. This was enough to see the power
increase quite dramatically to 33bhp and the top speed
to 126km/h (78mph).

Above: The pressed-steel frame of the 1936 sporting R17 may have been old fashioned, but the telescopic front forks were innovative. The heavy styling mimicked the contemporary German cars. *Ian Falloon*

Left: Although it still used the long-stroke 750cc side-valve engine of the R42, the R11 featured a new pressed-steel frame and trailing link forks. *BMW Mobile Tradition*

SERIES 4

With the M56 S4 and M60 S4 engines for 1933 came new, single-row caged roller big-end bearings instead of the earlier twin-row rollers. The gearchange mechanism was moved to a gate underneath the knee rubber on the right, while the saddle now had extension springs. Battery ignition was also offered on the R16.

SERIES 5

For the final series of 1934, the M56 S5 and M60 S4 received a roller timing chain instead of gears, to drive the camshaft from the front of the crankshaft. The M56 S5 featured battery and coil ignition for the first time on a BMW motorcycle. There was also a revised and more effective fishtail silencer and the R11 now had twin Amal carburettors (6/406 SP and 6/407 SP). The power rose to 20hp, but there was also an R11/5 RW single-carburettor version specifically for the army. A few R11/6 motorcycles were also built with a three-shaft four-speed gearbox as a precursor to the R12.

THE 500 KOMPRESSOR

In January 1933, Hitler became Chancellor of Germany and the Nazis were well aware of the boost to morale associated with competition success. As part of their nationalistic propaganda programme they encouraged German manufacturers to embark on racing, which resulted in a new, 500cc supercharged BMW twin that would eventually inspire a range of production models.

Instead of developing the existing overhead valve design, the 500 Kompressor was a purpose-built grand prix racer. Back in 1928, drawings were made for an overhead camshaft engine (M61a), and considerable time was spent investigating bevel-gear-driven overhead camshaft systems, through until 1932. There were four versions: 500cc (M250/1, M255/1) and 600cc (M260/1, M265/1) with or without a supercharger. The bore and stroke of the 500 was 66 x 72mm, and 72.2 x 72mm for the 600, with the valves operated by bevel-gear-driven twin-overhead camshafts in the cylinder head. Each pair of camshafts was geared directly to each other and opened the valves through short rockers. The Zoller multi-cell vane-type supercharger was now spline-driven from the front of the crankshaft, with a single 27mm Fischer-Amal side-mounted carburettor on the right.

Where the new Kompressor was superior to earlier examples was in the design which now included long induction ports under each cylinder to the rear intakes that ensured the mixture was adequately cooled. Because the supercharger ran at engine speed

Wiggerl Kraus debuted the 500 Kompressor at Avus in 1935, and during 1936 rode it to victory in German events. *Mick Woollett*

it provided boost of around 15psi, and its position improved weight distribution. The power delivery was very smooth, and the Kompressor would pull cleanly from as low as 2,500rpm. Many of the castings were lightweight electron magnesium, including the crankcases and gearbox housing and for the first time for BMW, there was a four-speed gearbox with a positive foot gearchange.

Rather than the pressed-steel frame of the production models at the time, the Kompressor used Schleicher's electrically arc-welded tubular steel frame, and incorporated his own design of oil-filled 28mm telescopic forks. This was the first time oil-damped telescopic forks appeared on a motorcycle, but the rigid rear end remained.

The Kompressor debuted at the high-speed banked Avus circuit near Berlin in June 1935. Ridden by Ludwig 'Wiggerl' Kraus, it was beaten by Ragnar Sunqvist on the Swedish Husqvarna V-twin at an

The rigid-framed Kompressor was also used for the ISDT of 1935 and 1936. *Mick Woollett*

Henne on the Frankfurt autobahn in November 1937, about to set another world speed record. *Mick Woollett*

average speed of 170km/h (106mph). There were no more outings that year except for the International Six-Day Trial where the German trophy team rode detuned Kompressors to victory.

For the 1936 season, Otto Ley and Karl Gall received works Kompressors, Ley taking second in the Swiss Grand Prix behind Jimmy Guthrie on a Norton. Despite its superior power, the Kompressor was a handful and difficult to ride. Ley managed another second at Assen before the Kompressor achieved its first victory in Sweden, on 30 August. Ley and Gall finished first and second ahead of the Norton, FN, and DKW works teams.

In the meantime, the world speed record was lost to Eric Fernihough on the Brough Superior, so Schleicher prepared a fully streamlined 500cc Kompressor. In October 1936, on the Frankfurt–Darmstadt autobahn, Henne went at 272.006km/h (169.025mph). BMW now looked optimistically towards the 1937 season, along with Alexander von Falkenhausen's new rear suspension. Faced with reluctance by the riders to race with, Falkenhausen had proved the superiority of his rear suspension by successfully riding the machine himself in the International Six-Day race at Füssen. The plunger rear suspension featured straight guide sleeves in vertical tubes, and the driveshaft required a universal joint.

In the hands of Ley and Gall, the fully sprung Kompressor now proved a match for the British machines. Gall outpaced the Nortons at the Dutch TT to take the victory, also winning the German Grand Prix at the Sachsenring, after Guthrie was killed on the last lap. Ley won the Swedish TT and Jock West

the Ulster, giving BMW four out of seven Grand Prix victories in 1937. Jock West also rode a solitary Kompressor at the Isle of Man, finishing a creditable sixth, and Gall won the German Championship. The year ended with Henne responding to Fernihough and Piero Taruffi's new world speed records. With wind tunnel-tested streamlining, on 28 November 1937, Henne achieved 279.503km/h (173.683mph) on the 90bhp 500cc. The record would last until 1951 as Fernihough was killed at Gyon in April 1938 trying to beat it.

The Isle of Man was the first event for 1938 and BMW fielded a three-man team. Developments saw the power up to 55hp at 7,000rpm running on petrol-benzol, and larger, full-width brakes. With the Nazi decree that a German should win on a German machine, Georg (Schorsch) Meier replaced Ley, alongside Gall, while West filled out the team. It was West who was fastest, while Gall crashed during practice and Meier was unable to remove the soft warm-up spark plugs on the start line. West finished fifth, Harold Daniell winning on the works Norton. Meier than went on to win the Belgian Grand Prix, the Dutch TT, and the German Grand Prix to take the European Championship. West again won the Ulster Grand Prix.

With war clouds looming, Norton withdrew from racing for 1939, leaving BMW to battle with Gilera for 500cc honours. Meier, Gall, and West went to the Isle of Man in June, Gall crashing at Ballaugh Bridge during practice, dying four days later. Despite this setback, Meier won the Senior TT at 89.38mph (143.81km/h), with West second, more than two

Schorsch Meier on his way to winning the 1939 Senior TT at the Isle of Man. *Mick Woollett*

minutes behind. Meier followed his TT victory with wins at the Dutch TT and the Belgian Grand Prix. Here, he lapped at 161.96km/h (100.63mph), the first time a 'ton' lap was achieved in a classic event. A crash in Sweden saw Meier out of the German Grand Prix due to injury and the outbreak of war ended the season after Ulster. The final Kompressor was a formidable machine, if somewhat of a beast to ride. When weighed after the TT, Meier's machine was found to be the lightest finisher at only 137kg (302lb).

During the Second World War, all the factory racing machines were transferred to Berg on Lake Starnberg for safe keeping, but Meier managed to retrieve the Isle of Man machine in 1943, having hidden it away in a hay barn on the Karsfeld estate at Allach. When he wheeled it out for a demonstration race against

the NSU at Solitude in 1947 hundreds of thousands of spectators turned out to watch. After this, the 500 Kompressor (M250/2) was further developed. There were redesigned superchargers (some two-stage), aluminium cylinders, and lighter reciprocating parts, producing as much as 95bhp on occasion.

THE R12 & R17

Motorcycle production more than doubled in 1934, from 4,734 in 1933 to 9,689, encouraging the development of two new 750cc models. These were the side-valve R12 and overhead-valve R17, which were first displayed at the Berlin Motor Show in February 1935. The engines were based on the earlier R11 and R16, but with a four-speed gearbox, and while the

The side-valve R12 with a single
carburettor was extremely
popular with the German military, and
was produced until 1942.
Brian J. Nelson

pressed-steel frame was retained, what set the new
machines apart from earlier models, were Rudolf
Schleicher's oil-damped telescopic forks. These had first
appeared on Alfred Böning's R7 prototype of 1934
and were the first modern-style hydraulic forks fitted
to a motorcycle. The R12 and R17 were a curious
combination of the old and the new, retaining a rigid
rear end when many British motorcycles featured rear
suspension. Even Hitler expressed his surprise at this
as he passed the BMW stand at the 1935 Berlin Motor
Show when he asked Schleicher: 'and when are we
going to get rear suspension?' Schleicher later admitted
he was filled with embarrassment and consternation by
Hitler's question, but it would still be two years before
rear suspension appeared. Schleicher already had
Böning's rear suspension design based on the Norton,

but he was unhappy with it. He then had Falkenhausen
design a new system, with sliding tubes housing the
driveshaft with springs at the frame ends.

The R12 and R17 four-speed engines featured
stronger crankshafts, but retained the hand-change
through a gate on the right side. The R12 (M56 S6
or 212) also came with a choice of a single Sum CK
25mm carburettor or two Amal 6/406/407 carburettors
and the power was identical to the two versions of
R11. As the flagship of the range, the R17 (M60) only
came with twin Amal 76/424 carburettors, but revved
up to 5,000rpm to produce 33bhp. This was enough
to provide an impressive 140km/h (87mph), but the
F66 chassis was still the same as the R12 workhorse,
suitable for military and sidecar duties. The rear brake
was now a 200mm drum instead of the driveshaft

GEORG 'SCHORSCH' MEIER

After joining the Bavarian State Police in 1929, Georg, known as 'Schorsch', Meier soon attracted attention for his ability on a motorcycle, and the fact that he rode too fast on the Bavarian country roads. However, these roads were similar to those of the Isle of Man so this stood him in good stead ten years later. By 1933, Meier was a member of the police team for the 2,000km (1,242-mile) cross-Germany run, immediately setting the fastest time in his class. Along with Josef Forster and Fritz Linhardt, he made up the successful 'cast-iron' cross-country team riding BMW R4s.

Born in 1910, Meier grew up in Mühldorf am Inn, where he was an apprentice motor mechanic from the age of 12. He always wanted to be either a racing motorcyclist or a policeman and when the Bavarian State Police force was wound up in 1935, Meier joined the German Army. This allowed him to continue riding in competitive events. He was German Army Champion in 1935 and 1936, and substituted for an ill Henne in the 1937 International Six-Day Trial at Donington in England. Meier won a gold medal, earning a ride in the BMW team. After his successful racing year on the 500 Kompressor during 1938, Meier was approached by Auto Union to race cars. Following the death of their leading driver, Bernd Rosemeyer, Auto Union needed a German driver so Meier came to an agreement with Schleicher to race cars and motorcycles on alternate weekends. At the Belgian Grand Prix he vainly tried to save Popp's son-in-law Dick Seaman from his burning Mercedes, while Meier's best result was a second in the French Grand Prix. Because he

spent seven months in hospital after the Swedish motorcycle Grand Prix, Meier ended as a driver to Admiral Canaris and head of the Abwehr (Military Intelligence) transport section during the war. From June 1945 to March 1948, he was a plant security officer in Allach, the US Army's Karsfeld Ordnance Depot. Meier then set up a motorcycle dealership in Munich, continuing to successfully race the Kompressor in German events and winning five German Championships between 1947 and 1953.

type, enabling the front and rear 19in wheels to be interchangeable. Although they were revolutionary for 1935, the telescopic forks were decidedly underdeveloped with only meagre one-way damping and 75mm of movement.

It was also difficult to disguise the heavy, pressed-steel frame, and for 1936, the R12 and R17 received sweeping mudguards imitating the styling of contemporary luxury German cars. While the R12, at 1,630 marks, would become the most popular pre-war BMW motorcycle, the princely sum of 2,040 marks for the R17 meant it was for the fortunate few. The most expensive German motorcycle available in its day, only 434 were produced. If viewed as a comfortable touring machine for straight smooth roads, rather

than as a sporting motorcycle, the R17 was successful. It epitomised the best German attributes: solidity, and efficiency, but by 1936, the time was right for a completely new machine. This was the R5, which not only looked much more modern, but was significantly lighter than the R17, and cost only 1,550 marks. BMW had made their sporting flagship obsolete.

THE R5 & R6

When the R5 was released at the Berlin Motor Show in February 1936, it drew heavily on the 500 Kompressor racer, and was the most advanced motorcycle available at that time. Designed by Leonhard Ischinger, it was

One of the finest motorcycles produced during the 1930s was the overhead valve R5. This 1937 version has the air filter incorporated in the gearbox housing. *Ian Falloon*

the first 500cc ohv production BMW since the demise of the R57; the engine (designation M254/1) was all-new, with the crankcase a one-piece tunnel-type similar to that of the singles. The crankshaft was inserted from the front and there were now two chain-driven camshafts instead of one, positioned over the crank to allow for shorter tappets and pushrods. The timing chain also drove the Bosch generator on top of the crankcase, with the ignition coil and distributor positioned inside the front cover. The included valve angle was reduced to 80°, and there were now double hairpin valve springs to provide safety at higher rpm. The rocker arms pivoted in needle roller bearings.

The four-speed gearbox was foot-operated by a linkage on the left, although the right-hand lever was retained primarily as a quicker way to select neutral. Carburation was by twin Amal 5/423 carburettors, each with a small ear-type air filter. These proved unsatisfactory and for 1937, were replaced by a central wire mesh air filter built into an extension of the gearbox casing. Although the power output of 24bhp at 5,800rpm was less than that of the R17, the R5 was a much more sporting motorcycle because of its electrically arc-welded tubular-steel duplex frame, similar in design to that of the 500 Kompressor. Schleicher used the same oval-section conical tubing and not only did the frame impart a more modern appearance, but the weight of the R5 was a svelte 165kg (364kg).

Completing the improved chassis specification was

an external damping adjustment for the telescopic forks. It was only the rigid rear end that limited the ride quality, but this was compensated through a softly sprung Pagusa rubber seat. The R5 provided exceptional sporting performance for the mid-1930s with a top speed of around 135km/h (84mph) and many enthusiasts rated the handling of the rigid-frame R5 superior to the later R51. The R5 was a milestone motorcycle for BMW, finally challenging the British in performance and handling. It also provided the basis for BMW twins for the next 20 years.

Joining the R5 for 1937 was a side-valve 600, the R6. Side-valve engines were considered better suited for motorcycles fitted with sidecars and BMW were optimistic for sales of the new R5 and R6 to the German military. There optimism proved unfounded, as the German army authorities were more interested in the proven, pressed-steel frame R12. The chassis of the R6 was identical to that of the sporting R5, but the engine (designation M261/1) was new. Instead of twin camshafts, there was single, central camshaft driven by spur gears as in the earlier engines. With twin Amal M75/426/S carburettors the power was an unremarkable 18hp and the top speed was barely 125km/h (78mph). Even the good torque of the long-stroke motor that made it suitable for sidecar use couldn't save the R6 which only lasted in production for one year.

Apart from the sprung rear end, the R61 was very similar to the R6. *Brian J. Nelson*

THE R51, R61, R71 & R66

As the works Kompressor racers successfully used Falkenhausen's plunger rear suspension during 1937, the release of a new range of fully sprung models at the Berlin Show in February 1938 wasn't unexpected. The R51 replaced the R5, and the R61 the R6, while there were two new models: the R66 and R71. The R71 was a 750cc side-valve sidecar machine, ostensibly to replace the R12 that was by now only a single-carburettor version and produced purely for the military. The 600cc ohv R66 assumed the position as the top-of-the-range sportster, with a list price of 1,695 marks.

Apart from a slightly lower compression ratio for the R61 there were few changes to the engines for the R51 (254/1) and R61 (261/1). As chrome was in short supply, and earmarked for gun barrels the mufflers, were generally painted black. The plunger telescopic rear suspension set the new machines apart, all sharing the 251/1 chassis, accompanied by an increase

Above: The final side-valve BMW motorcycle was the 750cc R71. This 1938 model has black-painted mufflers, indicating a shortage of chrome at that time. *Brian J. Nelson*

Right: The sporting R66 of 1938 combined the narrower side-valve 600cc single camshaft crankcases, with overhead valve cylinder heads. *Brian J. Nelson*

in weight to 182kg (401lb) for the R51 and 184kg (406lb) for the R61.

The R71 engine (designation 271/1) was based on the R61, the capacity increase to 745cc being achieved through a bore increase to 78mm. BMW's last side-valve model, with twin Graetzin G 24mm slide-type carburettors the R71, produced 22hp at 4,600rpm. Setting the R71 apart from the smaller R61 were the older style cylinders heads, but otherwise it looked identical. Undoubtedly the most exciting of the new models was the R66. Instead of using the R5/R51 twin camshaft engine with its long camchain as a basis, the 600cc R66 engine (266/1) featured the side-valve crankcases with one central gear-driven camshaft and a wider cylinder base to incorporate the pushrod tubes. The cylinder heads with hairpin valve springs came from the R51, but unique to the R66, were cylinders and heads tilted 5° forwards to provide more foot room. With a 69.8mm bore and larger, Amal 6/420 S

carburettors, the power was exceptional for an ohv twin at the time; 30bhp at 5,300rpm was enough to propel the R66 to 145km/h (90mph), and even with a sidecar it was good for 115km/h (71mph). Production of the four models lasted well into the war years, finally ending in 1941 although the last R51 appeared in 1940.

During 1939, new, 350cc (M231/1) and 500cc (M252/1) twins were considered, but development was halted in preference to the R75. By 1942, these projects were reinstated, and now incorporated many features from the R75, such as the split-valve covers. The 350 had a bore and stroke of 60 x 61mm and both versions featured battery and coil ignition. The generator, single carburettor, and airbox were all enclosed in a cover above the engine, but these models never made it to the production line.

THE MILITARY R75

As the German Army rolled relentlessly across Europe in 1940 their principal BMW motorcycle was still the rigid pressed-steel frame side-valve R12. Production of the R12 continued through until 1942, but as early as the winter of 1937–38 both Zündapp in Nuremberg and BMW were commissioned to design new 750cc military motorcycles. BMW decided to adapt the side-valve R71 engine with a split bolted tubular steel frame to allow easy engine installation and removal, with a rigid rear end. Zündapp developed their KS750 and this proved superior to the BMW. Designated the R72, the 800cc side-valve engine overheated at slow speeds, and a fan-cooled version was tested. Although BMW then considered licensed production of the

Zündapp, during 1939 they undertook development of a new design, the R75.

The most important design features of the R75 were its suitability for sidecar use, and the ability to sustain a marching speed of 3km/h (2mph) without overheating. Thus, it included sidecar wheel drive, a locking differential, and cross-country and reverse gears. The engine (designation 275/2) had overhead valves with the camshaft, a Noris generator, and a magneto driven by aluminium gears. Underneath the two-piece rocker covers were separately bolted rocker posts, unlike earlier twins with integrally cast posts. Twin Graetzin Sa 24mm carburettors fed the engine, with the air cleaned by a single moist felt air filter, with an oil strainer and sump pre-filter to ensure no dust entered the engine. This was initially positioned above the gearbox, but during June 1942 (after number 757201) it was moved to the top of the fuel

As head of motorcycle development, Alexander von Falkenhausen was involved in testing the R75. Here, he is with Hans Sachs at Groflen Donbogen during 1941.
BMW Mobile Tradition

Only a few R51RS catalogue racers were produced in 1939, and they were the closest a privateer could get to the factory Kompressor. *BMW Mobile Tradition*

THE R5SS, R51SS AND R51RS

While the double overhead camshaft 500 Kompressor always remained a factory racer, in 1937 a small number of R5SS (Super Sport) production racers was made available for selected riders. Although not offered to the public, the R5SS was essentially a modified R5, without lights or mufflers, and outside rather than inverted handlebar levers. The power output was around 4bhp more than the R5, achieved through different valve timing, polished ports and stronger valve springs, and carburettors with velocity stacks. The top speed was around 160km/h (99mph). Prior to the release of the sprung-frame R51 there was also an R51SS introduced during 1937, limited production of which continued into 1938, and a higher performance R51RS for 1939. The R51SS featured a special gearbox with higher ratios, a higher compression ratio of 8:1, and 6/432 Amal/Fischer 24mm carburettors. The power was 28bhp and the R51SS retained head and taillights. With a similar tank and seat to the works racers, the R51RS (Rennsport or Racing Sport) had 21in and 20in wheels and brakes with stiffening ribs. Although the engine was based on the pushrod R51, the long camshaft timing chain was replaced by spur gears and the cylinder barrels were the R66 type. With an output of 36bhp, the R51RS was capable of around 180km/h (112mph). Only 17 of these machines were produced.

tank, underneath a metal helmet-like cover. The power was 26bhp at 4,000rpm, with the emphasis on low-end torque, and the magneto provided automatic ignition advance. To overcome cooling problems in North Africa, Schleicher also developed a fan-cooled engine during 1942.

The four-speed transmission included a dog clutch and four lower ratios for off-road use, and the power-dividing crown wheel differential at the rear equalised any varying speeds of the two driven wheels. This allowed the R75 to perform as well as a four-wheeler and reduced tyre wear. The rear wheels, on stub axles, used the same, 4.50 x 16in tyres as the VW Kübelwagen and featured hydraulic brakes. Up front, the double-action hydraulic telescopic forks were a strengthened version of earlier BMW types, and the frame (275/1) was a lattice-girder type with a strong central box-section that could be dismantled into individual parts for easy repair.

Another design criteria for the R75 (and Zündapp KS750) was load capacity. Experience with the R12 in field conditions led to the Wehrmacht requesting a

By 1942, the R75 was in active service, as here in North Africa with the Afrikakorps. *BMW Mobile Tradition*

load of 500kg (1,100lb), corresponding to the weight of three soldiers and their equipment. However, the tyre suppliers set the maximum load at 270kg (595lb), well under the Wehrmacht's requirements. To avoid any bureaucratic problems there were two maximum total weights stated for the R75; an official figure of 670kg, and a Wehrmacht figure of 840kg (1,852lb). Most R75s were overloaded and rear tyre life was only around 3–6,000km (2–4,000 miles). As tyre supply was restricted, the delivery of bikes was also sporadic.

Development of the R75 was concluded in February 1941, with the first motorcycle leaving the production line in July 1941. After the construction of 6,000 examples, more space was required in Munich for aircraft engine manufacture and production moved to Eisenach from July 1942 (against Popp's recommendation). The GBK (Bike Select Committee) also decided that the Zündapp KS750 was a better machine than the R75, and by August 1942, instructed BMW to cease R75 manufacture in favour of the KS750. The R75 was proving too expensive to produce, and the front forks too weak for the heavy loads. The GBK also requested the R75 to be equipped with the KS750 parallelogram fork, but because BMW still had 5,000 telescopic forks in stock, this did not happen. Not surprisingly perhaps, but BMW was also reluctant to embark on the production of a competitor's motorcycle on the command of the Wehrmacht.

The R75 earned a reprieve and production continued at Eisenach, but this stalled initially because German workers were reluctant to move from Munich, as they would lose their reserved occupation status and were likely to be called up for military service. BMW therefore requested foreign workers, and around 1,000 Russian prisoners of war were trained to manufacture R12s and R75s. As a result, R75 production numbers were considerably below expectations, with around 2,000 less than was anticipated by the end of 1942.

Circumstances changed during 1943. A shortage of raw materials saw the aluminium castings sourced from outside with a resulting loss in quality. Combined with foreign workers who lacked training and motivation, production costs escalated as it now took a further two hours to repair defects on each machine after the first test drive. At a cost of 2,000 Reich marks each, the Wehrmacht placed their final order of 2,000 machines during 1943 and it was inevitable that R75

production would then cease. Not only was the R75 complicated, expensive, and considered inferior to the KS750, but also the army now preferred the cheaper, mass-produced four-wheeled VW Kübelwagen. Despite some export orders (to unspecified armies), the initial target was to cease R75 production in May 1944 (with chassis number 770200) to release the workers for aircraft manufacture. This was later amended to the end of December 1944 when it became clear this goal couldn't be met.

By the end of March 1944, 17,635 machines had been delivered, but air raids in July began to interrupt production. After three more raids production ended on 18 October 1944, and when US troops occupied the factory in April 1945, 60 per cent of the buildings were destroyed. Eisenach subsequently became part of East Germany and 98 R75s were produced out of spare parts during 1946 and delivered to Russia. Although the EMW factory began developing an updated R75 military motorcycle during 1952, this never reached the production stage.

At around the same time as the air raids on Eisenach, the Allies began bombing BMW in Bavaria in earnest. There were now two plants, one in Allach and are in Milbertshofen at Oberwiesenfeld. Allach was to the north west of Munich, close to the concentration camp at Dachau, and was largely spared allied bombing, but the RAF bombed Milbertshofen as early as September 1940. There was another RAF raid in March 1943, but the most damage was sustained when the US Air Force began their bombing on 9

Although around 18,000 R75s were produced, most were destroyed during the war and only a few have survived. This is an R75 in original Wehrmacht trim at the 1976 Lion Rally in Zolder, Belgium. *Damien Cook*

June 1944. After eight air offensives, through until 22 September 1944, more than half of the Milbertshofen works was destroyed. Although stripped and looted, the undamaged Allach works became a US Army supply and transport depot.

Earlier, in June 1942, Popp resigned as chairman of the board after differences of opinion with the Reich's Aviation Ministry, but remained a member of the Supervisory Board of BMW AG until 8 May 1945. Popp was always wary of the Nazis, maintaining his loyalty to BMW rather than the Third Reich, something he reiterated in the denazification court of 1947. On 11 April 1945, Hitler issued his 'scorched earth' policy that required the destruction of all military assets, including BMW, but Albert Speer thwarted this on the grounds that, 'we should not destroy what generations have built up before us.' This still didn't save BMW as the company was on the

Allies' blacklist, probably due to its development of the 003 jet engine. On 1 October 1945, the order came for the levelling of BMW factories 1 and 2, and it looked unlikely that the company would survive.

This was where Kurt Donath, Milbersthofen works manager since 1942, and non-Nazi party member appointed by the Allies in 1945, intervened. He managed to save the works and initiate the manufacture of saucepans, agricultural machinery, and bicycles. But a stroke of luck enabled BMW to rebuild as a motorcycle manufacturer. Currency reform and a relaxation of economic restraints during 1948 meant confiscated assets suddenly became 'free', and it was discovered that the Reich owed BMW 63.5 million marks from Deutsche Bank cheques dating back to 28 April 1945. Donath now had the money to get the company rolling again, and just as BMW did after the First World War, he decided to build motorcycles.

Many examples of the R25/3 of
1954 came factory-fitted with a
sidecar. *BMW Mobile Tradition*

3 SINGLE CYLINDERS

As the R32 twin was sold as a premium motorcycle, production levels were necessarily low and the profitability in difficult times was dubious. BMW's management though, wanted to expand aircraft engine production and develop a car, and they insisted the motorcycle operation should become profitable. This required building a lower priced model to supplement the R32, opening the door to a wider range of buyers. Development of a single-cylinder model began in April 1924, and the R39 made its first appearance at the Berlin Motor Show at the end of the year. The R39 was the first of a range of single-cylinder models that lasted through until 1966. However, despite often displaying an advanced specification, the singles always only provided adequate performance and have never garnered the following of the twins, particularly outside Germany. Within Germany though, the singles often outsold the more expensive boxers, especially during the 1930s and 1950s. In the two decades, from 1948 through until 1969, 62 per cent of BMW motorcycles produced were singles.

THE R39

Tyre supply problems saw production of the R39 delayed until September 1925, and while it was intended as a budget model, the specification was surprisingly high. Like the boxer twins, the 250cc engine (designation M40a) was mounted longitudinally in the frame, but with a vertical cylinder, and shaft drive. The three-speed gearbox was bolted directly to the crankcase and driven through a single-plate dry clutch mounted to the flywheel. The alloy overhead-valve cylinder head came from the sporting R37, and provided the R39 with a conservative 6.5bhp at 4,000rpm.

The R39 frame was a twin-tube design like the R32, but the rear brake was an external shoe acting on a drum on the driveshaft, rather than the earlier wedge-shaped brake block. With a Bosch magneto-generator lighting set and speedometer the R39 cost 2,150 marks, almost as much as an R32. The performance for a 250cc was outstanding, with a top speed of around 100km/h (62mph) – more than the R32. Sepp Stelzer rode an R39 to victory in the 1925 250cc German road racing championships, but while sales were initially strong they dwindled following reports of problems

The first BMW single was the R39, and while the performance was excellent for a 250 single it was too expensive. Few were manufactured and only a handful has survived. This example is in a private collection in Bavaria. *Ian Falloon*

with cylinder bore wear and excessive oil consumption. Production ended in 1926 but the R39 was offered well into 1927.

THE R2

The failure of the R39 deterred BMW from producing another single until 1931. By this time however, the economic circumstances and registration requirements in Germany were quite different. After 1 April 1928 the registration rules were amended so that motorcycles under 200cc could be used without road tax and ridden without a licence. This saw DKW produce large numbers of mass-produced two-strokes, and while BMW wasn't initially interested in competing in this market, they were forced into it following the deteriorating economic climate after the Wall Street Crash of October 1929.

Unlike the R39, BMW managed to find the right formula with the R2. It was no easy feat, trying to combine traditional BMW four-stroke quality and a price people could afford, but BMW managed to do this. Also retaining shaft drive, the 198cc R2 engine (M67a) was mounted longitudinally in the frame, with a three-speed gearbox bolted behind. The overhead valves were exposed and the crankcase a one-piece tunnel design, a feature of all later air-cooled BMWs. Ignition was by battery and coil and the power was an acceptable 6bhp which was enough to propel the rather heavy (130kg/287lb) R2 to around 95km/h (59mph), with excellent fuel economy.

The F57 pressed-steel frame and nine-plate cantilever forks followed the lines of the R11 and R16, but the engine was offset to the right to allow for a direct driveline in top gear, from the crankshaft, to minimise power loss. One improvement made was the inclusion of an internally expanding rear drum brake instead of the earlier driveshaft brake. The R2 was designed with practicality and ease of ownership in mind, even including a front stand to assist with

New registration requirements led to the 200cc R2 for 1931. *BMW Mobile Tradition*

wheel removal. Although it sold for 975 marks, three times the cheapest DKW, the R2 proved immediately successful.

SERIES 2A & 2/33

For 1932, the R2 engine (M67 S II) received enclosed valve gear, a SUM type K5/250 carburettor, and a new gearlever. There was a second Series 2 for 1933, 80 examples having an Amal carburettor, but the main changes were to the F67 S II 33 chassis which, from June 1933, incorporated a friction damper with scissors on the front fork.

SERIES 3

All M67 S III engines for 1934 received the Fischer-made Amal push-in carburettor and a revised camshaft to increase the power to 8bhp. The 6-volt, 30-watt generator on the left side of the engine was now under

an aluminium cover. The wheelbase was also reduced slightly, to 1,303mm.

SERIES 4

For 1935 (M67 S IV engine, F67 S IV chassis), there was a reshaped, smaller, and longer fuel tank, and a new type of Bosch headlamp. A rubber saddle also replaced the leatherette type.

SERIES 5

The final R2 of 1936 (M67 S V engine, F67 S V chassis) featured an Amal type 74/412S carburettor, a revised driveshaft, and a wider rear wheel mudguard and numberplate. With over 15,000 produced, the R2 was one of BMW's motorcycle production mainstays between 1931 and 1936. The R2 may now seem an insignificant model, but it was pivotal to the survival of the company in the early 1930s.

The R2 Series 2a of 1932 featured enclosed valve gear. *Brian J. Nelson*

THE R4 & R3

Following the demise of the 500cc R52 and R57 in 1930 there was a gulf in the line-up between the 200cc R2 and 750cc R11 and R16. Rather than build another expensive twin, BMW opted for expediency, creating the 400cc R4 single out of the R2 for 1932. The 78 x 84mm engine (M69 S1) was based on the R2, but always featured enclosed valves. The kickstart was on the right and the engine produced 12bhp, enough for 100km/h.

Although the chassis (F69 S1) was essentially the same as the R2, the pressed-steel forks featured additional strengthening steel strips, the front mudguard was valanced, and the tyres were a slightly larger section. From July 1932, the forks incorporated a friction damper, but this was largely ineffective.

SERIES 2

For 1934, the M69 S2 engine received a four-speed gearbox, there was a new gear lever and starter (no longer sideways), and a copper-wool air filter for the Sum CK 3/500 Fr carburettor. The F69 S2 chassis incorporated some styling revisions, an extender spring saddle, and new rubber-covered footrests in place of the alloy boards.

SERIES 3

A new cylinder head for the M69 S3 of 1934 saw the power up to 14hp, with the generator on the left now under a cover. The toolbox was also incorporated in the gearbox casting. Chassis changes (F69 S3) included a larger fuel tank (12 litres), with the gearshift now in a gate near the fuel tank, as on the R11 from 1933.

A 400cc single, the R4, was available from 1932, lasting until this final Series 5 version appeared in 1936. *Brian J. Nelson*

SERIES 4

The toolbox was now integrated into the crankcase (M69 S4) for 1935, with the generator on top of the crankcase driven by a V belt from the crankshaft, and the battery in a separate box near the gearbox. The F69 S4 chassis received a new headlamp and the forks had twin friction dampers.

SERIES 5

For 1936–37 (M69 S5), the gearcase was changed, with new gears, and the oil riser moved. The chassis (F69 S5) was much as before, and this final series was produced in relatively large numbers for military use.

As the R4 wasn't able to compete with the more powerful ohv 500s it was an alternative to the more mundane side-valve models. The price of 1,150 marks

also deterred it from younger buyers but it soon earned a reputation for ruggedness and reliability that saw it become the standard training and dispatch model for the military and police. It was also used in trials events and was offered for a while as an off-road sports model, albeit without any modifications from standard.

Joining the range of singles for 1936 was a small-bore version of the R4, the R3. The long-stroke 305cc single (M203/1) produced 11bhp, but not having the performance of the R4 or the tax and licence advantages of the R2, it was discontinued after only one year.

THE R35, R20, R23

The final pressed-steel frame single was the R35, replacing the R4 during 1937. A reduction in the cylinder bore to 72mm gave 342cc, but the power

Opposite top: The final
pressed-steel frame single was the
R35 of 1937, now with telescopic
forks. *BMW Mobile Tradition*

Opposite bottom: The more
modern R20 single replaced
the R2 for 1937, followed by
this 250cc R23 for 1938.
BMW Mobile Tradition

output of the M69a-derived engine (M235/1), with a SUM CK 9/22 carburettor, remained at 14bhp. New for the R35 was a set of telescopic forks, although these were rather rudimentary in design and didn't incorporate the hydraulic damping of the R5. The R35 was very much an anachronism at this time of technical innovation at BMW, but despite this, it was very popular with the German military which bought it in large numbers, just as they had the R4. Although the main production ended in 1940, more were produced from 1947 at the Eisenach plant, now in East Germany, to use up stocks of parts. The EMW (Eisenacher Motorenwerke) R35 and R35-3 (with plunger rear suspension) remained in production through until 1955. Of the 80,000 examples completed, only a handful ever made it to the West.

During 1937, BMW also envisaged 500cc and 350cc singles, the R36 (M236/1). This design had both inlet and exhaust ports facing the rear of the engine, and the engine was rubber mounted. Following delays from the military, development was suspended in mid-1939.

More modern than the R35 was the R2 replacement, the R20 with its tubular steel frame, also introduced for 1937. The ohv engine (M220/1) was an all-new design, with dimensions of 60 x 68mm, producing 8bhp. There was a foot-change for the three-speed gearbox and the generator was now driven from the crankshaft and positioned in front of the timing cover. The frame of the R20 consisted of butted-end tubes bolted together, and the telescopic forks were the undamped R35 type. After June 1938, new traffic regulations in Germany no longer exempted 200cc machines and there was now a restricted licence for motorcycles up to 250cc. BMW then responded by creating the 250cc R23 by boring the R20 engine to 68mm (M223/1). The power went up to 10hp and apart from a toolbox which was now incorporated inside the fuel tank, the R23 was identical to the R20. Large numbers of both the R20 and R23 were produced, but the outbreak of the Second World War saw the demise of production.

THE R24, R25, R25/2 & R25/3

When BMW decided to recommence motorcycle production after the Second World War, Allied requirements restricted the displacement to 250cc. Also, all the drawings for all BMW products were requisitioned by the Americans so a pre-war R23 was stripped down and minutely measured. The plans were complete by Summer 1947, but a complete machine took a further year to materialise. When the R24 was first shown at the Geneva Show in March 1948, most of the basic components were missing (but represented by wooden mock-ups), although at the Export Fair in Hanover in May, it was only minus a gearbox, gearwheels and crankshaft. There was an overwhelming response to the R24, with 2,500 advance orders, but material shortages delayed commencement of production until December 1948.

Although largely based on the R23, the R24 engine (M224/1) featured a new cylinder head, strongly influenced by the design of the wartime R75. The valve angle was changed, the rockers worked in bolted-on pillars rather than cast bosses, and the pushrods were led in through tunnels in the cylinder head. Like the R75, the valve covers were in two pieces, held by a clamp with a single bolt. The compression ratio was increased slightly, to 6.75:1, and with a Bing AJ1/22/140b 22mm carburettor the power was up to 12bhp at 5,600rpm. The electrical system was from Noris in Nuremberg, with the battery ignition incorporating a centrifugal advance. Also new was a four-speed gearbox. The chassis was similar to the R23, with a bolted, rigid tubular steel frame and telescopic forks.

With a chromed fishtail exhaust and trim embellishments on the mudguards, the finish and appearance were of high quality. The R24 was also the most expensive German motorcycle, but undoubtedly Schorsch Meier's exploits on the 500 Kompressor boosted sales, and 9,400 were sold in 1949. Production continued through until 1950 when the R25 replaced it.

During the early 1950s, singles like
this R25/3 were extremely popular
in Germany with production
considerably outstripping twins.
Ian Falloon

Opposite: Earles forks and a rear
swingarm graced the R26, which
was the most popular BMW
motorcycle in the late 1950s.
BMW Mobile Tradition

There were only a few developments for the R25 engine (M224/2), including a stronger crankshaft, 2mm larger inlet valve, and a Bing 1/22/28 24mm carburettor. More significant was the welded tubular steel frame that was suitable for sidecar attachment, and plunger rear suspension for the first time on a BMW single. Also setting the R25 apart was the deeply valanced front mudguard.

The similar R25/2 appeared during 1951, the engine (M224/3) reverting to the earlier R24 specification. Either a Bing 1/22/44 or SAWE K22F 22mm carburettor was fitted and there were only detail changes to the cycle parts (designation 225/1). For the R25/3 of 1953 the engine (M224/4) there was a higher compression ratio (7:1), with improved intake and exhaust system, and a 24mm Bing 1/24/42 or SAWE K24F carburettor for a power increase to 13bhp at 5,800rpm. The chassis (225/3) included hydraulically damped forks, full hub width brakes, 18in alloy

wheels, and a larger fuel tank that incorporated the induction pipe. During the early 1950s, the R25 singles proved extremely popular in Germany. This was a period where cheap transportation was in demand, and while the BMW 250s only provided barely adequate performance, they were quality machines, built to last. However, circumstances had changed by 1955. The domestic market had reached saturation and a more modern motorcycle was required for export.

THE R26 & R27

Following on from the R50 and R69 of 1955 (see Chapter 4), the 250cc single also received Earles-forks and a rear swingarm for 1956. The new model was the R26, and while motorcycle sales were generally extremely depressed during the latter half of the 1950s, the R26 proved surprisingly popular, particularly for export markets in Third World countries. More than

The final shaft-drive BMW single was the R27, now with a rubber-mounted engine to isolate the vibration.
BMW Mobile Tradition

BMW R 27

BMW R 27
Antrieb:
Motorleistung 18 PS, bei Drehzahl 7400 U/min
Hubraum 247 ccm, höchstes Drehmoment 1,85 mkg
Bohrung und Hub 68 mm/68 mm, Verdichtungsverhältnis 8,2:1
Kraftübertragung:
Getriebeübersetzung I 5,33 II 3,02 III 2,04 IV 1,54
Hinterachsübersetzung solo 4,5:1, wahlweise 4,16:1, mit Beiwagen 5,2:1
Bereifung: 3.25 – 18
Bremsen:
Leichtmetall-Vollnabenbremsen, vorn Duplex-, hinten Simplex-Bremse
Gewichte: größte Breite 660 mm, größte Länge 2090 mm, Sattelhöhe 770 mm
Gewichte: fahrfertig solo 162 kg, zulässiges Gesamtgewicht solo 325 kg
Lichtanlage: 6 Volt/60 – 90 Watt
Tankinhalt: 15 Liter
Kraftstoff-Normverbrauch: 3,9 l/100 km
Höchste Geschwindigkeit: solo 130 km/h

BMW R 50
Antrieb:
Motorleistung 26 PS bei Drehzahl 5800 U/min (Sonderwunsch: mech. Drehzahlmesser-antrieb), Hubraum 494 ccm, höchstes Drehmoment 3,5 mkg
Bohrung und Hub 68 mm/68 mm, Verdichtungsverhältnis 7,5:1
Kraftübertragung:
Getriebeübersetzungen solo   I 4,171 II 2,725 III 1,938 IV 1,54
                              m. Beiwagen   5,33   3,02   2,04   1,54
Hinterachsübersetzung solo 3,13:1, wahlweise 3,58:1, mit Beiwagen 4,33:1
Bereifung: 3.50 – 18, mit Beiwagen hinten 4.00 – 18
Bremsen: Leichtmetall-Vollnabenbremsen, vorn Duplex-, hinten Simplex-Bremse
Abmessungen: größte Breite 660 mm, größte Länge 2125 mm, Sattelhöhe 725 mm
Gewichte: fahrfertig solo 195 kg, zulässiges Gesamtgewicht solo 360 kg
Lichtanlage: serienmäßig 6 V/60–90 W. Behörden und Polizei 12 V/100–150 W
Tankinhalt: 17 Liter
Kraftstoff-Normverbrauch: 5,1 l/100 km
Höchste Geschwindigkeit: solo 140 km/h

BMW R 60
Antrieb:
Motorleistung 30 PS bei Drehz
antrieb), Hubraum 594 ccm, hö
Bohrung und Hub 72 mm/73 m
Kraftübertragung:
Getriebeübersetzung solo
                         m. Beiwa
Hinterachsübersetzung solo 3,
Bremsen: Leichtmetall-Vollnab
Abmessungen: größte Breite 6
Gewichte: fahrfertig solo 198
Lichtanlage: serienmäßig 6 Vo
Tankinhalt: 17 Liter
Kraftstoff-Normverbrauch: solo
Höchste Geschwindigkeit: solo

Änderungen von Konstruktion und Ausstattung im Interesse der technischen Weiterentwicklung vorbehalten · Bayerische Motoren Werke AG, München   Printed in

BMW R 69 S
Antrieb:
Motorleistung 42 PS bei Drehzahl 7000 U/min (Sonderwunsch: mech. Drehzahlmesser-
antrieb), Hubraum 594 ccm, höchstes Drehmoment 4,45 mkg
Bohrung und Hub 72 mm/73 mm, Verdichtungsverhältnis 9,5 : 1
Kraftübertragung:
Getriebeübersetzungen I 4,171 II 2,725 III 1,938 IV 1,54
Hinterachsübersetzung 3,13 : 1
Bereifung: 3.50 S 18
Bremsen:
Leichtmetall-Vollnabenbremsen, vorn Duplex-, hinten Simplex-Bremse
Abmessungen: größte Breite 722 mm, größte Länge 2125 mm, Sattelhöhe 725 mm
Gewichte: fahrfertig 202 kg, zulässiges Gesamtgewicht solo 360 kg
Lichtanlage: serienmäßig 6 V/60-90 W. Behörden und Polizei 12 V/100-150 W
Tankinhalt: 17 Liter
Kraftstoff-Normverbrauch: 5,3 l/100 km
Höchste Geschwindigkeit: solo 175 km/h

half the motorcycle production between 1956 and 1960 comprised the R26.

The R26 chassis (226/1) was very similar in layout to the R50, providing improved handling and comfort over the old plunger-frame R25/3. The weight was also increased slightly, so the engine (M224/5) was uprated. No longer painted black, the cylinder head had larger cooling fins, a higher compression ratio (7.5:1), and a larger, Bing type 1/26/46 carburettor to produce 15bhp at 6,400rpm. There was also an aluminium con-rod, with the big-end running directly on the rod journal. Tests with the aluminium con-rod had begun back in 1951, but later, BMW returned to the steel con-rod and roller bearing big-end. During 1956, an engine with an overhead camshaft driven by a vertical shaft was considered, with another designed by Ludwig Apfelbeck in 1959. Both these designs were deemed too expensive.

During the restructuring of BMW in 1960, the R26 was developed, becoming the R27. Although essentially similar, the engine (226/2) now produced 18bhp, at a considerably higher 7,400rpm. The compression ratio was increased to 8.2:1, and there was a new camshaft. The contact breaker was positioned on the front of the crankshaft, and there was a spring-loaded tensioner for the timing chain. The most significant development though was the engine which was now rubber mounted to quell the increased vibration. The engine and gearbox were supported by rubber mounts in four locations in the duplex frame, along with a rubber cylinder head bracket and two fore and aft rubbers on the front and rear to limit longitudinal movement. In all other respects though the chassis (226/2) was identical to the R26.

The R27 was intended to be the biggest seller in the revamped motorcycle range of the early 1960s, but it was too expensive and still only offered barely adequate performance. After production ended in 1966, efforts were made to secure an order from the German Federal Armed Forces for a revamped model, the R28. During 1967, various prototypes with a new duplex frame and a variety of forks (including telescopic) were tested, but BMW's bid failed and the contract was awarded to Hercules.

Production of BMW singles numbered more than 230,000 over their 41-year lifespan, and they served a useful purpose in providing reliable and inexpensive transport. However, by the end of the 1960s, motorcycling was increasingly becoming a leisure activity, and buyers demanded more performance. It looked as if the days of single-cylinder BMWs were over, but times change, and 27 years later it was resurrected in the form of the F650 which soon followed the R25 and R26 in eclipsing the twins to become the best-selling model in the BMW motorcycle line-up.

Klaus Enders and Ralf Engelhardt
on their way to winning the 1972
Dutch TT, and the Sidecar World
Championship. *Mick Woollett*

4 POST-WAR TWINS

During the summer of 1949, the Allied force's restriction on motorcycle displacement was lifted for German motorcycle manufacturers, opening the door for the reintroduction of the 500cc boxer twin. As there was still little money for development, the 500 twin was initially based on a pre-war design, in this case the 1938 R51. BMW was fortunate that the R51 was an advanced design for its day, and although its foundations went back to the even earlier R5, the R51/2 proved immediately popular when it was released in 1950.

THE R51/2

Apart from the split valve covers (similar to those of the R75), and Bing 1/22/39 and 1/22/40 carburettors, the engine of the R51/2 (M254/3) was virtually identical to the pre-war R51. There were new cylinder heads with coil valve springs, but the roller-less chain-driven twin camshaft set-up was the same. Ignition was still by battery and coil, and the R51/2 retained the exposed generator with its distinctive finned clamp on top of the engine. There was now a coil spring damper on the gearbox mainshaft, and a revised lubrication system with pressurised oil to the camshaft bearings. Although the frame (251/2) was the same as the final R51 of 1941, with two additional strengthening tubes, the telescopic forks gained two-way damping. Finally, the old-style inverted pivot control levers gave way to the more usual pivot type. The R51/2 certainly re-established BMW as a prominent motorcycle manufacturer, but as a pre-war design, it was always only going to be a stopgap. After only a year, BMW released the R51/3, with a new engine.

THE R51/3, R67, R67/2 & R67/3

Apart from slightly different pinstriping on the front mudguard, the R51/3 of 1951 looked almost identical to the R51/2. Despite the power output of 24hp remaining the same, inside the redesigned engine cases was a completely new engine (M252/1) that would power all twins through until 1969. The crankshaft was still a built-up type, with two ball bearings at the

The first post-war twin was the R51/2, which was essentially the same as the pre-war R51 but the split valve covers were new.
Ian Falloon

Opposite top: Although it looked similar to the R51/2, the engine was new for the R51/3 of 1951.
BMW Mobile Tradition

Opposite bottom: The 600cc R67 was sold primarily for sidecar use, but was never especially popular.
Ian Falloon

front and a ball bearing at the rear. The con-rods also ran on roller bearings. Replacing the twin camshafts and long timing chain that was always susceptible to whipping, was a single camshaft above the crankshaft. Driven by helical gears, this allowed for a much narrower crankcase, with a Noris magneto driven from the crankshaft and a contact breaker and automatic advance from the front of the camshaft. A third gear drove the oil pump and as everything was encased in smooth new covers the engine appeared to be much more modern. Gone too were the two-piece valve covers, and there were new cylinders and heads. The 34mm and 32mm valves retained the 80° included valve angle. The paper-element air filter was also now mounted in a special casing above the gearbox.

The engine may have looked more up-to-date, but the chassis (251/3) was almost identical to that of the R51/2. For 1952 (251/4) there was a duplex 200mm front brake, and rubber gaiters for the front forks,

while for 1954, the front brake was a full-width duplex type. Also, for 1954 there were alloy wheel rims, a fully covered air filter, and new mufflers.

Alongside the R51/3 for 1951 was the similar R67. A bore and stroke of 72 x 73mm provided 594cc, but the R67 (M267/1) was intended mainly as a sidecar machine rather than a sportster like the pre-war R66. A power output of only 26bhp provided sedate performance, and for 1952 and the R67/2 (M267/2) this was increased marginally to 28bhp. The R67 chassis was identical to that of the R51/3, and the R67/2 received the 1952 R51/3 improvements. The R67/3 of 1955–56 was the final BMW twin to retain the plunger rear end, and with its 4.00 x 18in rear tyre was even more suitable for sidecar haulage. However, the new Earles fork models were more appropriate for sidecar attachment and the R67/3 remained a relatively unpopular budget model.

Alfred Böning, one of the most important BMW motorcycle engineers for more than 40 years, pictured in 1960.
BMW Mobile Tradition

Opposite: One of the most coveted post-war BMW motorcycles is the high performance, and rare, R68.
Ian Falloon

ALFRED BÖNING

Involved in the design of nearly every BMW motorcycle for over four decades, Alfred Böning was one of BMW's most significant engineers. Böning was born of German parents in Salerno, Southern Italy, in 1907, moving to Esslingen in Southern Germany in 1917. He graduated from engineering school in 1930, and after working at NSU, Böning went to BMW in November 1931. One of the few senior engineers to remain with BMW immediately after the war, Böning ended up staying with the company until 1972. Initially employed as a motorcycle engineer, Böning designed frames, gearboxes and rear-wheel drives for motorcycles, and was responsible for the R12, R5, and R75. During 1943, he became manager for aircraft engines, including supervising the design of rocket and jet engines.

In May 1945, Kurt Donath, director of the Munich plant, instructed Böning to rebuild the development department away from the factory, which was still in ruins. He was subsequently responsible for all the first post-war motorcycles, and also the Isetta 600 and 700 cars. After handing over the design department to von Falkenhausen in 1960, Böning remained a senior engineer, and in 1968, became director of the development of car and motorcycle chassis and transmissions.

THE R68

As motorcycle production continued to climb, from 9,400 in 1949 to 25,101 in 1951, BMW needed a sporting flagship to compete with the new 100mph British Triumph and BSA twins. Their response was the R68, first displayed at the Frankfurt Motorcycle Show at the end of 1951. Here was the first real sporting BMW motorcycle since the R66, and it has rightly earned a place as one of the most desirable post-war production models. Not only did the R68 look far more purposeful than the R67, it also provided improved performance, with a claimed top speed of 100mph (161km/h).

The uprated 594cc R68 engine (designation 268/1) included 8:1 pistons, 38mm and 34mm valves, a fiercer camshaft, rockers pivoting on needle rollers under the new twin-rib valve covers, and a barrel-shaped roller bearing for the rear of the crankshaft. With Bing 1/26/9 and 1/26/10 carburettors, the power was increased to 35bhp at 7,000rpm. The initial show bike featured an upswept two-into-one exhaust system resembling that of the 1951 Varese International Six-Day Trial factory R51/3 racers of Meier, Zeller, and Kraus. This exhaust system didn't make it to the 1952 production R68 that wore standard fishtail exhausts, but the 2-1 remained an optional accessory. Also setting the R68 apart were finned exhaust clamps.

Although the R68 chassis (251/4) was essentially identical to the R67/2, it was distinguished by several features. The front mudguard was narrower, with a steel brace, and an optional sprung pillion pad was available, although this was primarily to allow the rider to adopt a more prone riding position. The claimed top speed was 160km/h (100mph), and the brakes were the same 200mm duplex of the 1952 R51/3.

There were few changes for 1953. By late 1952 rubber gaiters appeared on the front forks, and the mufflers were now non-finned. After July 1953, a sidecar mount was provided on the frame, and later that year the 100,000th BMW motorcycle rolled off the production line. There were more developments for 1954. Along with light alloy wheel rims, the front brake was full width and there was a larger headlamp. At a price of DM3,950, the R68 continued a BMW tradition that made it available only to a fortunate few, and with only 1,452 produced, the R68 remains one of the rarest post-war BMW motorcycles.

THE RS54

As soon as the FIM allowed Germany to compete in the World Championship in 1951, Leonhard Ischinger created a new racing engine (M253a) strongly based on the pre-war Kompressor, but without the supercharger and with twin carburettors. This retained telescopic forks and the plunger rear end, but with only 43bhp at 8,000rpm was never going to provide international glory. Although Walter Zeller won the 1951 German Championship, BMW decided to produce a motorcycle suitable to promote racing and provide German riders with an affordable competitive machine. The M253b followed during 1952, with the M253c for 1953. After experimenting with square, 68 x 68mm dimensions (as on the production R51/3), and a narrower 60° included

valve angle, the M253c eventually retained many of the basic features of the Kompressor. This included the 66 x 72mm bore and stroke, a wide included valve angle of 82°, the close-coupled twin overhead camshafts driven by bevel gears, and only two main crankshaft bearings. As the cylinders were offset, the bevel drive lined up with the exhaust camshaft on the right and the inlet on the left, the second camshaft coupled directly to the driven shafts. The cams were too close together to actuate the valves directly, so rockers were used, resulting in the wide valve angle. The power was around 50bhp at 8,500rpm.

A small M253 production series was also offered during 1953. These were the RS54 (Rennsport), and

Only a few RS54 500cc racers were produced, and they were extremely expensive and not very competitive in standard trim.
Ian Falloon

were so expensive to produce that the factory lost almost as much on each machine as it made. At around DM6,000 each, only 24 were manufactured. The catalogue engine had a low, 8:1 compression ratio and with two Fischer-Amal 30mm carburettors produced 45bhp at 8,000rpm. The RS54 also had a new frame, with an oval section top tube, duplex loops, and a pivoted fork at both ends. At the front was an Earles-pattern leading link type, and for the first time the driveshaft was enclosed in the right fork arm. There was a twin leading shoe front brake, and because the RS54 weighed only 130kg (287lb), the performance was surprisingly good.

During 1953, there was experimentation with fuel injection on the works M253, the first stage

spraying through the sides of the inlet tracts, with the second featuring axial sprays into the air trumpets. This featured on Walter Zeller's 253 at the Isle of Man in 1953. Zeller crashed on the second lap but it was evident the 253 wasn't yet competitive in the solo 500cc category. It was another story altogether in sidecar racing, and Wilhelm Noll and Fritz Cron showed that even by simply attaching a Steib sidecar to the RS54 solo machine it was competitive. Already the engine layout was proving ideal for sidecar racing, the low, wide engine facilitating safe drifting and the shaft drive an asset rather than a hindrance. Encouraged by the performance of the works 253 racers, during 1953 the plans were laid for a 500cc four-cylinder boxer engine with direct fuel injection. Titled the

Walter Zeller's factory RS racers generally featured fuel injection, and took him to second place in the 1956 500cc World Championship. *Ian Falloon*

Haufenmotor, or 'heap engine', the rear cylinders were angled 20° upwards for better cooling. There were also plans for an even more complicated twin-crankshaft engine, but neither was built.

On the works M253, the fuel injection was further developed for 1954, with fuel now pumped directly into the cylinder heads through nozzles opposite the spark plugs. Valve sizes were 40mm and 36mm, and a high-domed four-ring piston provided 10.2:1 compression. As there were still only two main bearings the safe maximum revs were 9,000rpm. Zeller won the German Championship but didn't achieve any spectacular international results. Noll and Cron's works sidecar racer now featured streamlining, and with three victories, they easily won the Sidecar World Championship.

In October 1954, Alex von Falkenhausen returned to head the competition department and there was more development for 1955. Carburation was either by Dell'Orto carburettors or fuel injection, and Zeller won the German Championship, finished second at the German Grand Prix, and 10th in the 500cc World Championship. One of von Falkenhausen's developments was to patent a pivoted rear-wheel drive housing by Helmut Werner Bönsch. Zeller's machine from 1955 thus featured a modified drive system with external drive shaft, and his performances during 1955 prompted the factory to further develop the machine and contest the entire World Championship the following year. Willy Faust and Karl Remmert headed a display of complete

Fritz Hillebrand and Manfred Grünwald at the Isle of Man, 1957 where they won the TT and went on to take the Sidecar World Championship. *Mick Woollett*

Opposite top: Geoff Duke (20) and Dickie Dale (standing on the right) before the start of the 1958 Isle of Man Senior TT. *Mick Woollett*

Opposite bottom: Dickie Dale on the RS at the Austrian Grand Prix at Salzburg, 1958. *Mick Woollett*

BMW dominance in the sidecar class during 1955 with their BMW/Steib.

For 1956, the works racers (M253f) had a bore and stroke of 70 x 64mm, and a five-speed gearbox. Depending on the circuit, Dell'Orto carburettors or fuel injection were used, the engine producing 58bhp on carburettors and 61bhp with injection, although low-speed response was inferior. Handicapped by a decision not to run a fairing due to the high winds, Zeller managed fourth at the Isle of Man, but followed this with second places in Holland and Belgium. Zeller failed to win a Grand Prix but finished second to John Surtees in the 500cc World Championship. That year, former World Champion Fergus Anderson also rode the RS, but was killed on one at Floreffe in Belgium. BMW again dominated sidecar racing in 1956, the fully streamlined 'Barquette' RS of Noll and Cron, now with an integral BMW sidecar and 16in wheels, taking out the World Championship.

With the Gilera fours back to full strength, the BMWs struggled in the 1957 500cc World Championship, although Ernst Hiller and Zeller managed some respectable results. Fritz Hillebrand and Manfred Grünwald continued BMW's dominance of the sidecar championship. Zeller retired at the end of 1957 and Geoff Duke and Dickie Dale were provided with works machines for 1958, but without official support. Dale had some reasonable results, finishing second in the Swedish Grand Prix and fourth overall in the World Championship, while Duke never managed to come to terms with the idiosyncratic BMW.

Later in 1958, a 250cc boxer twin (M207) was constructed which was a resurrection of a 1933 design for a prototype R7. With a vertically split magnesium crankcase it featured a centre crankshaft bearing and revved safely to 11,500rpm. A desmodromic cylinder head was also produced for the 500cc (M253/d), but both projects were abandoned due to financial

Alexander von Falkenhausen astride an R90S in 1975. *BMW Mobile Tradition*

ALEXANDER VON FALKENHAUSEN

Alexander von Falkenhausen masterminded BMW's domination of sidecar racing until 1964, but his influence on the general technical development of BMW motorcycles was even wider ranging. Born in 1907, von Falkenhausen graduated from the Munich College of Advanced Technology in 1934 and went directly to BMW as a motorcycle frame and suspension designer, with a contract as an off-road competition rider following his success during 1933 on a British Calthorpe motorcycle. By 1936, he was in charge of motorcycle gearbox design, and in 1937 became head of motorcycle experimental development. From 1943 until 1945, von Falkenhausen was manager of engine development. Before the war, he was a successful competitor, winning three gold medals in the 1936 ISDT before changing to cars. With his private BMW 315, von Falkenhausen took 35 victories, switching to a BMW 328 that took him to more than 100 race wins through until 1953.

After the war, von Falkenhausen established his own company AFM (Alex. von Falkenhausen, Munich), building sports and racing cars. He won the 1948 German Sports Car Championship in a 1500cc AFM, but also continued to race his BMW 328. Soon after rejoining BMW in 1954, he oversaw the preparation of Wilhelm Noll's RS54 speed record sidecar. With a fully streamlined machine, Noll set a new absolute sidecar world speed record of 280.20km/h (174.12mph) in 1955. In 1966, von Falkenhausen took to the wheel himself, setting two world records in a BMW Formula 2 racing car over a quarter-mile and 500m. From 1957 he was again in charge of BMW engine development, until retiring in 1975.

considerations. Dale rode the RS again during 1959, finishing eighth in the World Championship, and while the Japanese rider Fumio Ito rode the BMW during 1960, this was the end for the RS. Not only was BMW restructuring, but the adherence to the Earles-type fork with its high steering inertia also limited the RS's competitiveness as a solo racer.

It remained a different situation in sidecar racing where the Earles fork was ideally suited. Walter Schneider and Hans Strauss won the Sidecar World Championship in 1958 and 1959. As the development of the racing sidecar proceeded towards lower outfits, only the BMW engine, driveline and suspension was retained. In 1960, Helmut Fath and Alfred Wohlgemuth won the championship on a private machine, while Scheidegger built his first kneeler outfit in an attempt to offset the power differential between his and the factory engines. The factory outfit of Max Deubel and Emil Hörner that gave them four consecutive world championships between 1961 and 1964 persisted with a conventional sitting position and the fuel tank above the engine. Scheidegger's machine on the other hand was a generation removed. By 1962, each wheel had a disc brake, and for 1964, he fitted 10in magnesium Mini car wheels at the front and side. When the factory withdrew from competition at the end of 1964, Scheidegger and John Robinson took their first World Championship, repeating this in 1966.

Even though the RS engine had long ceased production and spares dwindled, BMWs dominated the sidecar grids. After Scheidegger was killed at Mallory Park early in 1967, Klaus Enders (with Ralf Engelhardt and Wolfgang Kalauch) went on to win World Championships in 1967, '69, '70, '72, '73, and '74. With engines prepared by Dieter Busch, Enders final BMW kneeler outfit produced around 65bhp, featured a wide rear car tyre, and used a very short steering column with a U-link pivoted front fork. After 21 years and 19 World Championships, the RS monopoly ended, and the two-strokes took over. Although not exceptionally powerful, the RS BMW engine proved incredibly reliable and ideally suited to sidecar racing. Ironically, its era ended just as BMW was entering a new age of profitability, but von Falkenhausen wouldn't consider producing a two-stroke racer.

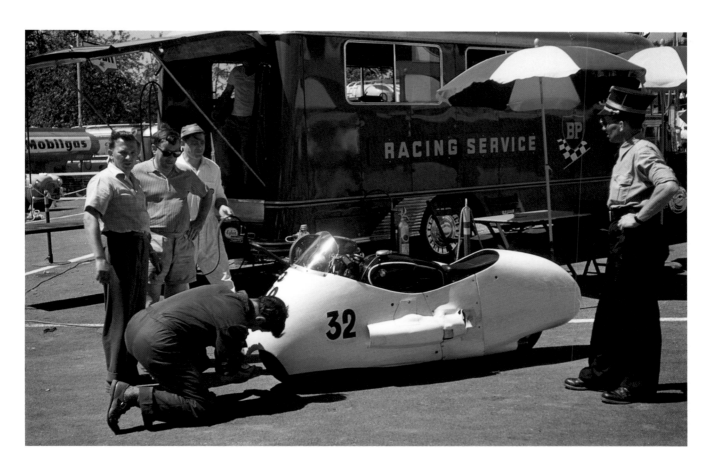

THE R50, R69 & R60

Production peaked in 1954 with 29,699 motorcycles manufactured, but already it was evident that the short-travel pre-war plunger frame was struggling to harness the moderate power of the R68. A new chassis was needed, and this arrived with the R50 and R69 of 1955. Unfortunately, the release of the R50 and R69 also coincided with a dramatic slump in motorcycle sales as cars became more affordable. Many of BMW's competitors (Horex, Adler, Ardie, and DKW) had vanished by the end of the decade, and BMW too was fortunate to survive. After dropping to 23,531 in 1955, and 15,500 in 1956, by 1957 production had crumbled to only 5,429, and most of these were for export markets.

The R50/R69 frame (245/1) was derived from the RS54 racer of 1953. This not only incorporated a swingarm rear suspension, but following racing experience the driveshaft housing connected to the swingarm. The front suspension was a development of the leading link swingarm type developed by Englishman Ernie Earles. By the early 1950s, swingarm rear suspension was considered de rigueur for a sporting motorcycle, but Earles-type forks were not as popular, except for sidecar use. Earles forks did possess the advantage of not diving under braking,

but they also put handling at a disadvantage because of the increased unsprung weight and steering inertia. Manufactured by BMW under licence from Earles, two tubes were angled back from the steering head to behind the front wheel. A swingarm pivoted on a fixed axle was attached to these tubes, with two hydraulic dampers connecting the swingarm to the lower fork crown. There were tapered roller bearings for both the front and rear swingarm pivots. Despite the addition of swingarm rear suspension the frame still resembled the earlier plunger type, but with supports for the swingarm and steel cups locating the tops of the shock absorbers. Like the RS54, the driveshaft was enclosed in the right side of the swingarm, with the universal joint moved to the gearbox end of the driveshaft. The wheels were also now 18in, and the toolbox was hidden in the left side of the fuel tank.

The engine of the R50 (M252/2) was essentially that of the R51/3, but with four-ring (rather than five-ring) pistons providing a slightly higher compression ratio (6.8:1), and two Bing 1/24/45 and 46 carburettors. The previous I-section con-rods now had sword-shaped shanks. The power was up slightly to 26bhp while the R69 (268/2) retained the higher-performance R68 engine, along with the barrel-shaped rear crankshaft roller bearing. New for both was the

The R50 incorporated the Earles fork and rear swingarm of the RS54, but the engine was very similar to the R51/3's.
BMW Mobile Tradition

Opposite: One of the classic BMW twins of the post-war era was the sporting R69S. *Ian Falloon*

gearbox and clutch. There was no external hand lever and the four-speed gearbox featured an improved input shaft shock absorber. There were also two sets of gearbox ratios available, one for solo use and another for sidecars.

With two Boge hydraulic dampers, the Earles-fork R50 and R69 offered improved ride over earlier models, and for 1956, these forks were adopted over the entire range. The R60 replaced the R67/3 as a sidecar hauler, sharing the same 28bhp engine (M267/4), but with slightly different 24mm Bing

carburettors. Because of the deepening sales crisis, there was virtually no development between 1955 and 1960. A bigger taillight appeared in 1957, but that was the extent of progress.

The main reason for the stagnation of motorcycle development was due to the spiralling losses caused through the manufacture of the expensive eight-cylinder 502, 503 and 507 cars. Although the small Isetta was selling in reasonable numbers, profits on these weren't enough to offset the loss of around DM5,000 on each large car. In an effort to improve

profitability, the Austrian distributor Wolfgang Denzel produced the prototype of a 700cc car based on the Isetta chassis, during 1958. Unlike the Isetta, this was a conventional car, with a 697cc fan-cooled version of the boxer motorcycle engine. Although it was received positively, with 30,000 advance orders, by the end of 1959 BMW faced bankruptcy. At a shareholder meeting on 9 December 1959 Denzel forestalled a management decision to sell BMW to Daimler-Benz. Denzel found that the development costs of the 700

had been written off illegally and didn't appear in the balance sheet. Two shareholders, Eric Nold and Friedrich Mathern, managed to obtain 10 per cent of represented share capital to adjourn the meeting, and the deadline for the sale to Daimler Benz elapsed.

With the fate of the company now in the hands of the shareholders, attention turned to the major shareholder Herbert Quandt. The Quandts were one of Germany's richest industrial families, but Herbert's interest in keeping BMW alive was more than financial.

There was little development of the R50 and R60 after 1955, but a slightly revised R60/2 was released for 1960. *Ian Falloon*

THE R50/2, R60/2, R50S & R69S

Improvements to the R50/2 and R60/2 were primarily aimed at increasing reliability. While they looked similar to their predecessors, inside the engine (M252/2 and M267/5) had stronger bearing housings, clutch, crankshaft, and improved crankcase ventilation. The new three-ring pistons provided a 7.5:1 compression ratio and a slight increase in power for the R60/2 to 30bhp at 5,800rpm. While many examples were fitted with an old-fashioned solo pan-type saddle, a dual seat was also available, and Hella bar-end turn signals were fitted as standard.

Replacing the R69 was a more sporting R69S, joined also by the R50S. Developments to the engine (M252/3 and M268/3) included even higher compression pistons (9.5:1), rockers pivoting on needle bearings under two-rib valve covers, larger inlet ports, Bing 26mm carburettors, and larger volume air filters and mufflers. The four-speed gearbox now featured closer ratios, and there was a hydraulic steering damper to quell instability at the rather optimistic claimed top speed of 175km/h (109mph), for the R69S. With 42bhp at 7,000rpm, the R69S was the strongest performing production BMW twin up to that time, but with this performance came reduced reliability.

It did not take BMW long to respond to reliability problems and by 1962 there were new cylinders and pistons, and from September 1963, a rubber-mounted vibration damper was incorporated on the front of the crankshaft. While the anti-vibration damper now meant the R69S could run all day at high rpm, it was a source of irritation for owners as it required frequent maintenance. The high revving R50S (35bhp at 7,650rpm) placed even more demands on the crankshaft, despite the sports models featuring a stronger rear spherical roller main bearing, and by 1962, it was dropped from the range. The chassis of both S models (245/2) remained robust and heavy, and at 202kg (445lb) the R69S was hardly a true sporting motorcycle. The Earles forks also contributed to slow and ponderous steering, and from early 1965, stiffer springs were specified for solo use to improve the handling.

During the late 1950s and 1960s there were occasional racing successes for the Earles-fork twins,

Impressed by the commitment shown by the smaller shareholders, workers, and dealers, he decided to personally supervise the restructure of BMW. Entrusting his personal legal advisor, Wilcke, with the responsibility, the aircraft division was sold off and there were now limited resources for development of new products. Although motorcycles were lower on the priority than cars, the existing motorcycle range was improved and expanded.

The R69S lasted from 1960 through to 1969, this being the 1962 version. *Ian Falloon*

primarily in endurance events where their reliability gave them an advantage. London BMW dealer MLG entered an R69 in the 1958 Thruxton 500-mile (800km) race, and a fourth place encouraged further competition. In the hands of Peter Darvill and John Lewis, their R69 won the following year. Darvill and Bruce Daniels then pulled off a more amazing victory by winning the Barcelona 24-hour race at the twisting Montjuich circuit. They narrowly failed to win at Montjuich in 1960, but with factory assistance, the MLG R69 won again in 1961. Even by 1964, the BMW twin was competitive, with Darvill and Norman Price coming second this year. The success of the MLG racer led to them setting a 24-hour record at Montlhéry, near Paris, during 1961. A team of four riders, Sid Mizen, Ellis Boyce, George Catlin, and John Holder, covered 4,220km (2,622 miles) at a speed of nearly 176km/h (109mph), the record standing for 16 years.

Compared to British motorcycles of the 1960s, the BMW R69S appeared to be an anachronism. Instead of a tiny fuel tank and slim seat, the R69S offered a 17- or 24-litre tank, small solo saddle, or wide dual seat. Only available in black or other colours to special order they remained expensive and exclusive. Ultimately, the conservatism of the R69S counted against it during the 1960s. While the Earles forks undoubtedly assisted in its suitability for sidecar attachment, sidecars went out of fashion during the 1960s. As the automotive side of the company expanded motorcycle sales stagnated, and BMW's response was to release a series of three motorcycles exclusively for the US market, all with telescopic forks.

THE R50US, R60US & R69US

The impetus for fitting telescopic forks came from BMW's experimentation with them on the ISDT bikes following their tentative re-entry into off-road competition in 1958. A factory 246GS was produced during 1963, based on the R69S but with a higher mounted engine and telescopic forks. This led to Manfred Sensburg and Sebastian Nachtmann riding similar ISDT machines during 1965 and 1966. They were outclassed by the lighter two-strokes, but BMW

learnt how to successfully produce long travel telescopic forks. For the US models of 1967, these forks were simply grafted on to the existing R50/2, R60/2 and R69S, although the sidecar lugs on the frames (245/3) were removed, as the telescopic forks were considered unsuitable for such an attachment. The engines were unchanged for the US versions, and all came with a 4.0 x 18in rear tyre.

For their day, the leading axle telescopic forks were very sophisticated, with progressive rebound and compression damping achieved through a tapered hydraulic metering rod. The only change from the ISDT fork was stiffer springing, and they provided a considerable, 214mm of travel. Compared to the Earles fork the telescopics were lighter, offered improved high-speed performance on bumpy roads, but heavier low-speed steering. They also increased the wheelbase slightly. The telescopic forks certainly presented a more modern image, but it was only a stopgap. Production levels gradually decreased and by 1969, only 4,701 motorcycles were manufactured.

By the end of the 1960s, the R50/60/69S didn't appeal to the average motorcyclist who demanded more power, noise and flashiness, even if it did mean putting up with vibration and a lot of maintenance. BMW's stood apart from the mainstream. Not only did the market require a new machine, the 18-year-old engine, with its built-up crankshaft, expensive ball and roller bearings, and gear-driven camshaft, was uneconomic to produce in quantity. To make more power would also require considerable modification to maintain reliability, so an easier solution was to create an all-new engine. The R69 engine's demise on 13 May 1969 coincided with the end of motorcycle production at Munich.

This 1979 R100S continued the tradition of the classic R90S, but featured cast-alloy wheels and a rear disc brake. *Ian Falloon*

5 A NEW GENERATION OF BOXERS

During the 1960s, car production increased, while motorcycle sales stagnated and BMW could have elected to cease motorcycle manufacture and concentrate on ventures that were more profitable. There had been little development on their motorcycle range for a decade although the motorcycle market had changed dramatically during this period. Not only had the European motorcycle market collapsed, but the Japanese manufacturers had begun producing powerful, reliable, and sophisticated, larger displacement machines. Against this background of pessimism, the technical director, Helmut Werner Bönsch, then managed to launch a new series of motorcycles.

Bönsch knew that for BMW to remain a viable motorcycle producer they had to expand their market for quality, luxury touring motorcycles, and saw the future as being with the development of the traditional flat-twin. Aimed at the rider who placed a premium on comfort and convenience, the new /5 series was the most radical motorcycle design in BMW's history, and would grow to become one of the most successful.

All that was needed for the production of the /5 was a suitable factory, and BMW decided to convert their repair and machine work facility in Spandau, West Berlin. Siemens & Halske had set up an aircraft engine factory at Spandau in 1928, and in 1936, it became Brandenburgische Motorenwerke (Bramo). In 1939, Bramo merged with BMW to become BMW Flugmotoren-Gesellschaft. After the war, the works became BMW Maschinenfabrik Spandau, and from 1958 it was involved in the manufacture of vehicle components. Motorcycle production commenced at Spandau in September 1969 with the R60/5. A month later, the R75/5 joined it, and in November, the R50/5 completed the line-up. By the end of the year, 1,205 motorcycles had left the Spandau works.

THE R50/5, R60/5 & R75/5

Von der Marwitz may have adhered to the traditional 'boxer' layout, but the engine (designation M04*) was all new. Three displacements were offered, 498cc, 599cc, and 745cc, all sharing the same 70.6mm stroke and basic architecture. There were a number of

Below: Hans-Gunther von Der Marwitz.

HANS-GÜNTHER VON DER MARWITZ

Continuing the tradition of Rudolf Schleicher and Alexander von Falkenhausen, Hans-Günther von der Marwitz was an enthusiastic motorcyclist. Hailing from a distinguished family, von Marwitz was born in 1927 and joined BMW in 1964 from Porsche. He was used to racing around on an AJS 7R, and was dismayed at the handling of the Earles-fork BMW. When entrusted with the design of the new BMW motorcycle, von der Marwitz wanted it to handle as well as a Manx Norton.

significant departures from the earlier engine. Inside the one-piece aluminium, internally reinforced tunnel housing crankcase was a one-piece forged crankshaft (without a centre bearing to minimise cylinder offset) running in plain bearings. As was envisaged back in 1932 with the M205 to M208 designs, the camshaft was now underneath the engine. A duplex chain drove this from the front of the crankshaft. Many components came straight off the automotive production line; the automatic tensioning camchain was from the rally-winning sports saloons, and the three-layer plain bearings for the crank and con-rods from the six-cylinder cars.

As the bearings required high-pressure lubrication, an Eaton trochoidal oil pump was fitted at the rear of the camshaft. At the front of the crankshaft was a three-phase 180-watt alternator to power the new 12-volt electrical system. The earlier magneto went in favour of battery and coil ignition with an automatic advance, and above the engine (on the R60 and R75 – optional on the R50) was an electric starter motor. As the flywheel and single-plate dry clutch were an automotive type the electric start was a simple and effective addition.

Although the valve actuation system retained pushrods, with the pushrod tubes now underneath the cylinders the engine looked more modern. Aluminium was used extensively to minimise the effect of the heavy starting system, including alloy instead of steel cylinder barrels, with a cast-iron sleeve bonded to the cylinder through the Al-Fin process. This contributed to increased cooling efficiency.

The cylinder heads were also new, with a much shallower included valve angle of 65°. The R75/5 had large, 42mm and 38mm valves, and a more radical camshaft than the R50/5 and R60/5. The R75/5 also had 32mm Bing constant velocity carburettors as opposed to the Bing 26mm concentric carburettors on the smaller versions. All this contributed to 50bhp at 6,200rpm for the R75/5, although the R50/5 and R60/5 made a very modest 32bhp and 40bhp respectively.

The four-speed, three-shaft gearbox bolted on the rear of the engine, and apart from strengthening, the drivetrain was similar to the previous model. What was new was the backbone-type, double-loop frame designed exclusively for solo riding. There were no sidecar lugs, and the frame was constructed of variable section tapered and oval tubing with a bolted-on rear subframe. BMW also claimed to have incorporated some controlled longitudinal flexing at the steering head to improve handling. The weight of the frame was reduced from 17.5kg (38.6lb) to 13kg (28.7lb) and further weight saving extended to the wheels and brakes. There were light alloy wheel rims (a 19in on the front), and narrower (200 x 30mm) drum brakes with special linings which had been developed for the last Porsche cars to have drum brakes.

Suspension included the telescopic forks of the earlier US versions, providing a generous, 208mm of travel, with twin shock absorbers at the rear giving 125mm of travel. Practical features extended to a large, 24-litre fuel tank and a good-sized dual seat. With a host of lightweight features extending to glass-fibre mudguards, the new /5 series were also reasonably light for their class, the R75/5 topping out at 210kg (463lb).

The /5 certainly vindicated Bönsch's optimism. The R75/5 may not have been as powerful as the new Honda 750 Four, but it was no longer a staid and stodgy motorcycle only for the initiated diehard. For a rider interested in long distance, comfortable high-speed travel there was simply no other contender in 1969. Here was a motorcycle that could reliably cruise all day at 160km/h (100mph), with all the conveniences expected of modern machinery. Offering excellent handling, and respectable performance, the new boxer, especially the R75/5, was immediately successful.

As it was an all-new model there were many developments to the /5 series over the next three years. For 1971, there was a lower final drive ratio (10:32 instead of 11:32) to aid fourth gear performance, and the carburation was altered to quell low-speed running problems. More careful assembly of the long-travel front fork, with closer tolerances, also alleviated some of the criticism of head shaking and wobbles.

Styling changes were the most evident development for 1972. For this year, there was the controversial 17-litre 'toaster' tank with chrome panels, and chrome-plated side panels to hide the battery. Primarily for the US market and so-called because of its apparent similarity to a kitchen appliance, this styling was attributed to then BMW sales director Bob Lutz, an American, but also a motorcycle enthusiast. It proved unpopular and for 1973, the smaller tank was standard, without the chrome panels. The 24-litre tank was now an option. More colour schemes were available as the years went by, culminating in six colours by 1973. The days of black-only BMWs were now long gone.

The R75/5 was the first official post-war BMW 750. This 1973 version had a longer swingarm than previous examples.
Ian Falloon

Also new for 1972 was a wider rear wheel rim (WM3), longer and stronger front fork springs, stronger crankshaft and bearings, and new rocker shaft supports to reduce noise. The most important development occurred in January 1973 when the swingarm was lengthened by 50mm to improve the handling. This also allowed for a longer seat and room for a larger battery. Although the /5 series, and in particular the R75/5, re-established BMW as one of the world's leading motorcycle manufacturers, by 1973 the /5 needed updating. Certain features, such as the four-speed gearbox, drum front brake, and instruments in the headlight, harked back to an earlier era. On 28 July 1973, only three days after the 500,000th BMW motorcycle (an R75/5) came off the production line, the last /5 left the Spandau factory. The time was ripe for a BMW Superbike.

THE R90S

When the new /6 series was unveiled in September 1973, all the expected improvements were incorporated, but the new top-of-the range sporting R90S took the world by storm. Out of the R75/5 BMW created a cutting-edge sporting motorcycle, and the R90S proved unsurpassed on the road performance, as well as setting new aesthetic standards.

The engine was shared with the rest of the /6 series, incorporating a five-speed gearbox with a revised gearshift mechanism, and stronger crankcases. This required reducing the size of the front counterweight to pass through the strengthened tunnel so tungsten plugs were inserted in the crank webs to restore the balance. The R90S featured higher compression, 90mm pistons (9.5:1), and feeding the engine was a pair of the new generation of 38mm Dell'Orto slide carburettors

The spectacular R90S was initially painted a beautiful Smoke Black, this being continued through to this 1975 model. *Ian Falloon*

with accelerator pumps. There were black cylinders for improved heat dissipation, but otherwise the engine was identical to the R90/6, itself very similar to the R75/6 except for the larger pistons, and 40mm exhaust valves (up from 38mm). These few modifications had a significant effect on the power output, and the R90S produced 67bhp at 7,000rpm. In the space of only four years, the power of the top-sporting boxer had increased by 63 per cent. The R90S was also easier to live with, a 280-watt alternator and larger battery providing more reliable starting.

It wasn't sheer power that set the R90S apart. The Kawasaki Z1 was more powerful, but the R90S was the first production motorcycle to feature a factory-fitted fairing as standard equipment. Designed by Hans Muth, the small cockpit fairing incorporated full instrumentation, including a clock and voltmeter,

and complemented a beautifully styled fuel tank and seat. Each bike was hand-painted in Smoke Black so no two were identical. The R90S was also the first BMW to feature dual stainless-steel 260mm front disc brakes, although the floating single-piston ATE brake calipers lacked ultimate power. To tidy the cockpit the front brake master cylinder was also located under the tank, as was a three-way adjustable hydraulic steering damper. While the frame was essentially identical to that of the long wheelbase R75/5, there was additional gusseting around the steering head. With its shaft drive and long-travel suspension, the R90S may have lacked the sharpness and handling precision of a comparable Ducati or Laverda, but more than made up for it in civility. It was on the road that the R90S excelled, and for its day it was a genuinely fast motorcycle, capable of 200km/h (125mph).

Helmut Dähne in action on a
semi-works R75/5-based Formula
750 racer in the 1973 Imola 200.
Mick Woollett

RACING /5s

Although the R69S had isolated success in long-distance racing during the 1960s, the R75/5 was a much more suitable basis for a racer. The R69S was difficult to set up for racing and required a specific riding approach to attain its best. Von der Marwitz may not have succeeded totally in creating a motorcycle that handled as well as a Manx Norton but it was surprisingly close, and by 1971, Helmut Dähne was achieving some good results in production racing in Germany. Hans-Otto Butenuth rode a special racer in the 1971 Production TT, finishing a creditable fourth, Dähne repeating this in 1972 and 1973. With the advent of Formula 750 in 1972, Butenuth, Dave Potter, and Dähne rode F750 machines in the Imola 200, Dähne finishing 13th. He campaigned the F750 bike during 1973, finishing 14th in the Imola 200.

On the other side of the Atlantic, Butler & Smith, the US distributor, decided to allow their service manager Helmut Kern to prepare a racing R75/5. Sales of the R75/5 were rather slow in the USA, and with some backdoor help from contacts at the factory, Kern was able to obtain many special engine parts, such as titanium valve covers. The modified R75/5 engine was placed in a special German GP-style frame prepared by Volker Beer and Kurt Liebmann raced it on the East Coast and in Canada during 1972. Then, at the instigation of ex-patriot British rider Reg Pridmore on the West Coast, Kern approached Rob North to build a frame similar to those of the factory Triumph three-cylinder racers.

North built two frames, and the 745cc engine featured bigger valves, and 36mm racing Mikuni carburettors. With Ceriani forks and later, Lockheed disc brakes, Pridmore and Liebmann campaigned the Butler & Smith racers throughout 1973 and 1974. Weighing around 140kg (309lb) and capable of 265km/h (165mph), the handling was impeccable, but as they were running against two-stroke 750s in AMA racing, there were no race victories. This would change with the advent of Superbike racing and the R90S.

Below: Kurt Liebmann rode this /5-based racer in the 1972 Daytona 100-mile Junior race, but didn't finish. *Mick Woollett*

Below: At Daytona in 1973, Reg Pridmore (84) joined Liebmann (57) on the Butler & Smith racers. *Mick Woollett*

Bottom: Pridmore in action on the outclassed Rob North-framed racer in the 1974 Daytona 200. *Mick Woollett*

Opposite: Few motorcycles have garnered the following of the R90S, and it is well deserved. This is the author's 1976 example.
Ian Falloon

Following on from the R75/5 was the R75/6, with a front disc brake and five-speed gearbox.
Ian Falloon

So good was the R90S there were very few developments for 1975. New switches, a faster action twist grip, and drilled discs complemented the choice of either Smoke Black or Daytona Orange. The pinstriping was now hand-painted instead of the tape as on earlier models. Early gearbox shifting problems were rectified through revised shifting forks, and there was a more powerful starter motor. More modifications were incorporated for 1976, most as a prelude for the /7 series released later that year. To improve intake flow and exhaust heat dissipation, the included valve angle was reduced slightly. There were aluminium pushrods and shorter and re-angled rockers. A stiffer camshaft spindle resulted as the diameter was increased from 12mm to 20mm, and the crankcases and front

main bearing were upgraded. A deeper sump also kept the oil further away from the crankshaft, reducing oil drag. The front fork travel was reduced slightly (to 200mm), with a firmer action. The swingarm was now pressed and welded around its entire section for additional strength and the front brake calipers and master cylinder received larger pistons.

More than any other model, the R90S created a performance aura for BMW that previously didn't exist, even with the R75/5. With nearly 17,500 manufactured, they weren't exactly a rare limited edition, but the R90S was BMW's first Superbike, and one of the most beautifully styled and balanced of all the boxer twins. Many dreamed of owning an R90S in the early 1970s, but it was one of the most expensive

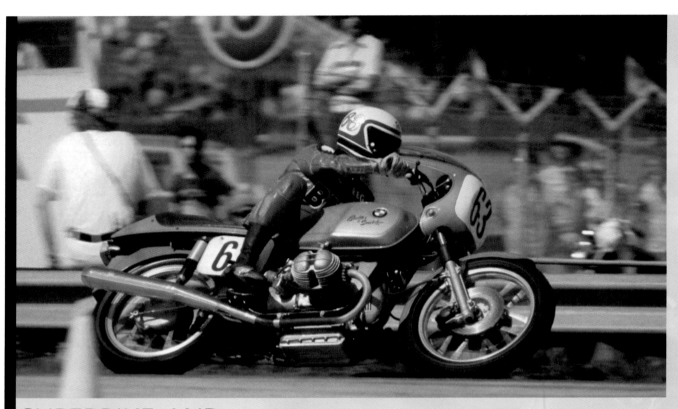

SUPERBIKE AND PRODUCTION RACING

Many of the performance developments of the R90S emanated from the specially developed R75/5 campaigned by Helmut Dähne. Dähne and the BMW were particularly suited to the Isle of Man. In 1974, he came third in the Production TT and was leading the race in 1975 until a stone punched a hole in the well-worn rocker cover. Dähne finally gave BMW a victory in 1976, when sharing a factory-assisted machine with Butenuth, he won the ten-lap 1,000cc Production TT.

As production-based racing grew in the USA during 1974, Reg Pridmore rode one of the new R90Ss. After narrowly failing to win at Laguna Seca, when an ignition coil wire broke, Pridmore gave BMW their first production race-win, at Ontario. He was so far in front of Yvon DuHamel's second-placed Yoshimura Kawasaki that DuHamel assumed he had dropped out. Although Pridmore also campaigned the R90S during 1975, finishing 31st in the Daytona 200, the creation of the Superbike class for 1976 opened a new door for the R90S.

Superbikes allowed for much more engine modification, but retained standard frames. As the Japanese bikes were powerful, but ill handling, the regulations played into the hands of the European manufacturers, particularly BMW. Butler & Smith had the bikes (R90S), the budget, and the experience to produce an unbeatable Superbike. They may have looked like stock R90Ss, but the 1976 Butler & Smith Superbikes were extraordinary racers.

In Norwood, New Jersey, Udo Gietl, assisted by Todd Schuster and Tom Woods, looked closely at the regulations and stretched the boundaries to the limit. The engine was modified to not only increase horsepower, but also improve ground clearance. Borrowing from the factory ISDT engines, shorter rods and barrels were possible through short, 95mm Venolia pistons with the gudgeon pin inside the ring grooves, and with 10mm shorter Carrillo con-rods. This enabled the engine to be 28mm shorter on each side. With 995cc, the compression ratio was 12.2:1. Kenny Augustine worked the cylinder head with 46mm and 39mm valves, and twin spark plugs, while Sig Erson ground a special camshaft. With the Dell'Orto carburettors bored out to 40mm, the eventual power was around 100bhp at 8,300rpm.

The engine may have used standard American hot-rod technology, but Gietl really stretched the regulations by extensively strengthening the swingarm and changing the twin shock absorber set-up to incorporate a single Koni Formula One car damper. Further chassis modifications involved moving the engine and driveshaft to the right to allow for a racing slick tyre, and moving the engine forward by 30mm and up by 10mm for improved weight distribution and ground clearance. Weighing 204kg (450lb), the top speed was in the region of 235km/h (146mph).

At the opening Superbike race at Daytona the appearance of the three Daytona Orange Butler & Smith BMWs left the opposition stunned. Nicknamed the 'Bavarian Murder Weapons' by Schuster, in the hands of three of the best Superbike riders in America, Reg Pridmore, Steve McLaughlin and Gary Fisher,

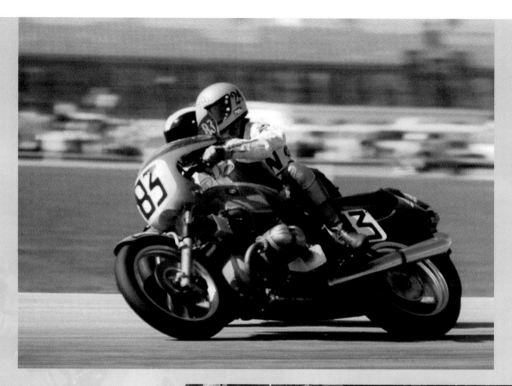

Left: Steve McLaughlin, side-by-side with Reg Pridmore, on the special Butler & Smith R90S monoshock Superbike. McLaughlin, here on his way to victory in the 1976 Daytona Superbike race, headed a BMW one-two. *Mick Woollett*

Below: This is McLaughlin's 1976 Daytona-winning R90S Superbike, one of the most successful of all BMW racers. *Mick Woollett*

Opposite: Reg Pridmore rode this stock-looking R90S in the 1975 Daytona 200-mile race. *Mick Woollett*

the BMWs ran away with the Superbike race. In a photo finish, McLaughlin narrowly beat Pridmore, who had reverted to a twin-shock set-up for the race. With victories at Laguna Seca and Riverside, Pridmore went on to give BMW their first and only AMA Superbike Championship.

Butler & Smith withdrew from racing after Daytona 1977, and Gietl and Schuster took up the racing programme independently. Superbike regulations for 1977 banned the monoshock, and although there were now dual-piston Lockheed brakes and engine developments increased the power by around 6bhp, the BMWs were outclassed. More development for 1978 though, saw the BMW almost take out the AMA Superbike Championship. Gietl worked his magic on the still R90S-based racer and in the hands of John Long it finished third at Daytona. Consistent results throughout the season, and a win at Mosport, ended with Long finishing a close second in the championship. Although this represented the end of competitive racing in Superbike, the boxer twin continued to hold its own in the Battle of the Twins series, with Stuart Beatson winning in 1983.

motorcycles available and unaffordable for many. Now it is a much sought-after model, and rightly so, as an R90S still provides a wonderful riding experience. Later twins may be functionally superior, but the R90S has rightfully earned its status as the classic BMW motorcycle of the modern era.

THE R60/6, R75/6 & R90/6

Alongside the R90S was a revamped /6 series for 1974. The underpowered and unpopular 500 was dropped altogether, and the range expanded upwards to include the R90/6. Compared with the R90S, the R90/6 engine featured lower compression (9:1) 90mm pistons, and Bing 32mm constant-velocity carburettors. The power was down to 60bhp at 6,500rpm. Almost identical to the earlier R75/5 and R60/5, but for the five-speed gearbox, were the smaller R75/6 and R60/6. They all shared similar styling to the final /5 series, but there were individual instruments and the R90/6 and R75/6 received a single front disc brake. The /6 series models continued the BMW tradition of offering superb touring ability and useable, if moderate, power. As the /6 series soon earned a reputation for outstanding build quality and reliability, sales were strong. For 1975 the larger models received a drilled disc, there was new switchgear, and for 1976, they shared the developments of the R90S. Although overshadowed by the R90S, the /6 series represented superior value for money, and sold in greater numbers. The /6 series were exceptional motorcycles, and many examples have covered hundreds of thousands of miles with few problems.

In 1976, coinciding with the new engine developments, there was a reorganisation of BMW's motorcycle division into a company separate from the cars. The introduction of the successful /6 series resulted in production accelerating from 15,078 in 1973, to 23,160 in 1974, and 25,566 in 1975. Despite losses in the USA, exports were increasing, particularly in Britain, Italy, and the Netherlands. After fighting for survival only a decade earlier, the BMW motorcycle had staged a miraculous comeback. However, lulled into complacency, this success was short-lived and a sales slump during 1978 and 1979 saw almost the entire management team replaced. The new team realised the need for innovation and rose to the challenge.

THE R100RS

If the R90S signalled that BMW was prepared to expand beyond their traditional horizons, the R100RS added a further dimension. Creating a vague association with the racing RS54, the R100RS didn't feature a new double overhead camshaft engine, but was the first series production motorcycle to be fitted with a full touring fairing. Wind tunnel-designed by Hans A. Muth, the nine-piece fairing featured an integrated cockpit and spoiler to reduce front wheel lift by 17.4 per cent. Air resistance was reduced by 5.4 per cent but the effectiveness of the fairing was particularly impressive. With low sporting-style handlebars, the R100RS was the most efficient high-speed touring motorcycle available.

Complementing the fairing was a 980cc engine (M65*), with new, 94mm pistons. Instead of the Dell'Orto 38mm carburettors of the R90S, there was a pair of Bing V94 constant-vacuum 40mm carburettors. Inlet valve diameter went up to 44mm, exhaust pipes up to 40mm, and the power to 70bhp. Because of the full fairing, most engine developments, many introduced for 1976, were aimed at reducing noise. There were now shorter and thicker cooling fins, O-rings to seal the cylinder bases, and a more effective crankcase ventilation system. The old-style rocker covers made way for new angular, heavier, black anodised ones, and there was a stronger clutch and revised starter ratio. The kickstart was no longer considered essential, but remained an optional extra. A smaller and lighter 240-watt alternator was also fitted to the R100RS (and R100S) to provide clearance at high rpm with more crankshaft whip, between the magnets and stator.

It wasn't only the engine that received tweaks for the R100RS. The chassis, with the stronger 1976 swingarm, featured an additional brace welded between the two front frame downtubes. The suspension was revised to provide a more progressive ride, and the RS received blue anodised front brake calipers. There was a choice of a single or dual seat, and wire-spoked or heavier cast-aluminium wheels. The rear 200mm drum brake on the cast wheel incorporated air scoops.

Although one of the most expensive motorcycles available, the R100RS immediately garnered a strong following. This wasn't surprising considering its capability. Not only did the fairing work superbly, but

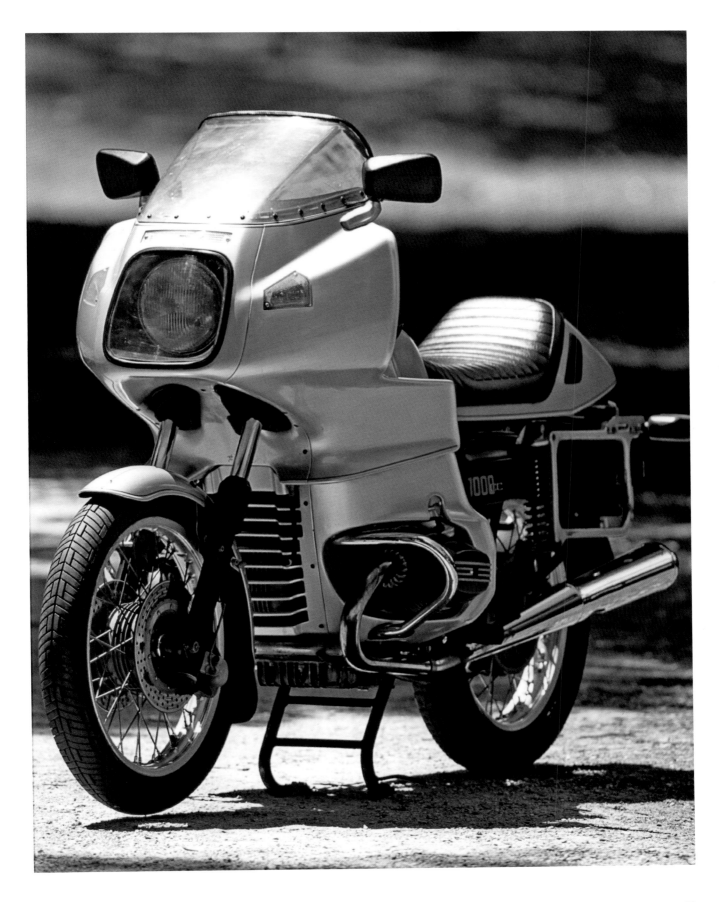

This 1979 R100S continued
the tradition of the classic
R90S, but featured cast-alloy
wheels and a rear disc brake.
BMW Group Archive

the R100RS was also fast (around 200km/h), reliable, good handling, and its 24-litre fuel tank provided a near 400km range. No other motorcycle could match it as a long-distance sport-tourer. For 1978, the wheels were cast aluminium only, with a rear disc brake and Brembo caliper, and there was a revised gearshift and linkage. The front brake calipers were no longer anodised blue.

The colour range expanded during 1978 from the original silver, with a fade-prone gold also available. There was also the first of multiple limited editions, the white Motorsport. These were followed by a handsome silver and Royal Blue for 1979. Engine developments this year included a single-row camchain with a spring-loaded and hydraulically damped tensioner, while the driveshaft was fitted with a ramped coupler-type shock absorber. Of all the developments aimed at improving the gearshift over the years, this was by far the most

successful. While the engine specifications for most markets continued unchanged for 1980, all that year's US R100s included an air suction emission system and a lower 8.2:1 compression ratio.

There were more changes for 1981 (shared with all R100s), the engine series now designated the A10 (with an internal designation of R246/247). Nikasil cylinders replaced cast-iron liners, saving weight and increasing longevity, and there was a new diaphragm clutch spring, a 4.5kg (10lb) lighter flywheel (sheet steel instead of cast), and a 40 per cent easier clutch action. The sump was shorter and deeper, increasing capacity, and there was a new air filter, the rectangular flat paper element now in a black plastic box with two removable plastic snorkels. Finally, there was breakerless electronic ignition, and the more-powerful, 280-watt alternator returned.

The short-lived R75/7 was replaced by the R80/7 during 1977; all /7s featuring the attractive R90S-style fuel tank.
Ian Falloon

To reduce noise levels while maintaining 70bhp, the exhaust system incorporated two balance pipes, while US versions received exhaust air-port injection to clean up emissions. Also new were Brembo front brake calipers, with the Magura master cylinder moved from underneath the fuel tank to the handlebar, accompanied by a new fork that incorporated some Teflon components, although fork travel remained the same. There was a stronger die-cast rear axle housing (intended for the forthcoming Monolever R80 G/S), and a stronger swingarm. The colours were Smoke Black or red, with an optional oil cooler (standard in some markets). With the standard oil cooler the centre section of the fairing was closed off. However, this increased heat build up and caused electrical problems. The year marked the end of further developments to the R100 series until its demise in 1984. All resources were now involved in the development of the new K series and although a 'Last Edition' white R100RS and blue and silver Series 500 became available in 1984, popular demand would see its return only two years later.

THE R100S & R100CS

Although the R100RS assumed the status of range leader in 1977, the earlier R90S style continued with the R100S. For 1977, the 70bhp, 980cc engine was reserved for the R100RS, while the R100S had a slightly lower rated (65bhp) engine. Still with Bing 40mm carburettors, the R100S had smaller diameter exhaust pipes (38mm). All other engine and chassis improvements were shared with the R100RS, and despite more weight and less power than the earlier R90S, the R100S provided outstanding performance.

This was ably demonstrated in the 1977 Australian Six-Hour production race. R90Ss finished third in 1975, and second in 1976, but for 1977 the local distributor hired four top riders to meet the challenge of the Kawasakis and Ducatis. Ken Blake teamed with veteran Joe Eastmure, while Helmut Dähne was flown in to pair with Tony Hatton. The pair of new R100Ss dominated, with Blake and Eastmure winning while Hatton and Dähne came third. Considering the race was for unmodified production motorcycles it was a spectacular performance.

Cast wheels and a rear disc brake made it to the R100S for 1978, with the R100RS 70bhp engine introduced for 1979. Then, for 1980, with sales stagnating compared with the R100RS, BMW introduced the almost-retro R100CS. Retaining the 70bhp engine, this was first displayed with wire-spoked wheels, but most production examples had cast wheels, with the Simplex single leading-shoe rear drum brake. Several versions were offered to stimulate sales, including a silver 'Outback' edition for Australia (with wire-spoked wheels). Despite its retro appeal, the R100CS was not particularly popular, and only around 4,000 were produced between 1980 and 1984. It is now considered one of the more collectable modern boxer twins.

THE R60/7, R75/7, R80/7, R100/7, R100/T & R100

There were three new /7 series models for 1977, and as with the preceding /6 series they were all visually similar. As before, the R60/6 featured smaller valves, Bing slide carburettors, and a milder camshaft, but now sported a single front disc brake instead of the previous drum. With the 24-litre R90S fuel tank and angular valve rocker covers, the styling was more modern, but it wasn't enough to disguise the fact that the R60/7 was still a 40hp, 215kg (474lb) motorcycle. Performance was barely adequate, and the under-stressed R60/7 was really a machine more suitable for diehard enthusiasts interested in long life rather than performance. As it was produced primarily for police forces requiring a budget-price BMW, the R60/7 was dropped for 1979, effectively replaced in this role by the R80/7 and later, the R80 Monolever.

While the R75/7 shared similar engine specifications with the R75/6, the R90/6 grew to become the R100/7. With a slightly lower compression ratio (9:1), smaller intake valves (42mm), and Bing 32mm carburettors, the R100/7 was 5hp shy of the R100S. The R75/7 still offered possibly the best balance between power, mid-range torque and smoothness, but more buyers preferred the 980cc R100/7. In an effort to widen the range appeal the R75/5 made way for the slightly larger R80/7 during 1977.

More displacement for the R80/7 (M85*) came through 84.8mm pistons, also bumping the compression up slightly to 9.2:1, and aiding in a power increase to 55bhp at 7,000rpm. A lower compression (8:1) 50bhp version was also available for markets that could only obtain low octane fuel. Shortly afterwards, for 1979, the R100T replaced the R100/7. In an effort to rationalise specification, the R100T featured the 65bhp engine with higher compression and 40mm carburettors, and cast aluminium wheels (but with a rear drum brake instead of the disc of the RS, S and RT). After only two years, the R100 replaced the R100T. Incorporating all the improvements of the 1981 Model Year, the R100 featured a lower compression (8.2:1) 980cc engine, but retained the 40mm carburettors. The power was rated at 67bhp at 7,000rpm.

THE R100RT & R80RT

Following the success of the R100RS, BMW decided to expand the luxury motorcycle concept to include a full-dress touring machine. Introduced for 1979, the R100RT was aimed squarely at the lucrative US market. It was not only the most lavishly equipped BMW ever, it was also the most expensive motorcycle available in America. Sharing its 70bhp 980cc engine and chassis with the R100RS, the R100RT added a full fairing with a tall screen to complement the high and wide handlebars. The screen was cleverly provided with adjustment for four different heights, and four rake angles. Lockable compartments were incorporated forward of the fuel tank, and there were air vents on either side. With Krauser saddlebags as standard equipment the touring specification was impressive, but the extra weight taxed the engine and suspension. No longer an exceptional handler, and certainly no dragstrip tearaway, the R100RT's sales

THE R45, R65 & R65LS

The demand for a cheaper, more compact, smaller capacity motorcycle led to the release of the R45 (M76*) and R65 (M84*) in 1978. Replacing the R60/7, but closely modelled on the bigger twins, these were either intended for specific insurance categories (such as the 27hp class in Germany), or as an entry-level model that would hopefully lead to the purchase of a larger twin. Although the crankcase castings were the same as for the larger versions, the R45/65 had a shorter-stroke crankshaft (61.5mm) that allowed the engine to be 56mm narrower. Also different was a single-row roller timing chain with oil-damped tensioner, and the ignition points cam was no longer incorporated with the camshaft. There was a lighter flywheel, and smaller clutch to encourage revs. The five-speed gearbox was shared with the larger twins, but there was a lower final drive ratio. Ultimately, the smaller R45 and R65 lacked power, especially when compared with cheaper Japanese middleweights, and even the R65 was afflicted with mid-range vibration and stumbles. The R45/65 frame was similar to the R80 and R100 models, but did not feature oval-section downtubes or additional gussets. With a 50mm shorter swingarm and new, shorter-travel centre-axle forks, the wheelbase was 65mm less. Also new was an 18in front wheel and special twin-piston brake caliper for the single front disc. A smaller angular-shaped fuel tank (22 litres) and lower seat height of 770mm contributed to a physically smaller machine, but the weight was only 10kg (22lb) less than an R100.

Over the next few years there were many minor developments to the smaller boxer series. After 1980, the engines were designated A20 (internal designation R248), and there was a lighter clutch, Nikasil cylinders, breakerless ignition and two connecting crossover pipes in the exhaust system. There was also a larger oil pan, additional cushioning in the driveshaft, and a 10mm longer swingarm. The R65 received larger valves (40mm and 36mm), and the power was increased to 50bhp (from 45bhp). To match the increased power there were optional dual front disc brakes, but these developments did little to endear the R45 and R65 to prospective buyers.

Below: As a styling exercise the R65LS was reasonably successful, but it wasn't enough to save the smaller boxer. *BMW*

Opposite: While not as popular as the larger twins, the R65, like this 1979 model, was an extremely competent and well-balanced motorcycle. *Cycle World*

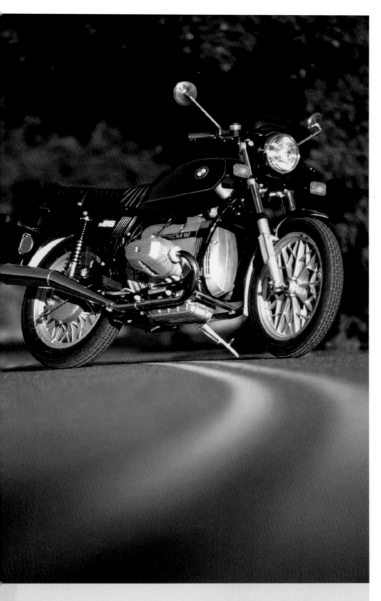

In an effort to widen the appeal of the series, the sporting R65LS was offered for 1982. Sharing its 50bhp engine with the R65, the R65LS was primarily a styling exercise that incorporated a cockpit with an integrated spoiler. Claimed to reduce front wheel lift by a third, the accentuated styling continued through to the seat with its integrated grab handles. The exhaust pipes were black chrome, and while the R65LS included dual front disc brakes, the most worthwhile feature was the new wheels. Jointly developed with Alusuisse, the front rim width was increased to 2.15in, yet was lighter than before. Undoubtedly a competent sporting middleweight, the R65LS was viewed by most BMW traditionalists as a cosmetic adulteration and was a poor seller. Unloved, and probably under-appreciated, the small twins were discontinued during 1985. When the next R65 appeared, its basis was the new R80.

were disappointing, especially in the USA. When the compression ratio was lowered on US versions for 1980, the performance deteriorated further.

BMW endeavoured to make amends for 1981. New Boge Nivomat load-levelling rear shock absorbers and revised fork damping improved the ride and handling, while other developments were shared with the R100RS. In 1982, the R100RT was joined by the R80RT. In an effort to overcome stagnating R100RT sales, the R80RT was almost an identical motorcycle, but with the R80/7 engine, a rear drum brake, and without standard luggage or Nivomat rear suspension. Significantly, it sold for a lot less than the R100RT, even though the performance was decidedly leisurely. The 50bhp engine struggled to power the 235kg (518lb) R80RT beyond 100mph (161km/h). Despite this, the R80RT proved popular, and when the revised boxers were offered in 1984, the R80RT survived. It wasn't until 1987 that the R100RT would make a return.

MONOLEVER TWINS THE R80 G/S & R80ST

The successful re-entry into the world of off-road competition during 1979 prompted the development of the dual-purpose R80 G/S. Indicating Gelände/Straße (off-road/street), initially it seemed incongruous that an off-road motorcycle could displace 800cc, incorporate shaft-drive, and weigh 186kg (410lb). Based on the street R80 and R65, the R80 G/S was certainly too large and heavy to be a serious off-road motorcycle, but BMW's engineers managed to create one of the best handling and most effective street BMWs ever. The R80 G/S successfully established a niche market, and created another classic motorcycle that would garner a following to match the R90S and R100RS.

The idea for the R80 G/S came from Rüdiger Gutsche, a suspension engineer and ISDT veteran. Gutsche had already produced a special one-off /5 series enduro machine back in 1975, and in 1979 caused a stir as a marshal in the ISDT when he rode a further-improved version. This machine influenced the design of the R80 G/S, and other members of the development team built similar machines for participation in the traditional Dolomite Rally in the Italian Alps. Using the engine of the R80/7, the R80 G/S incorporated the 1981 series improvements such as Nikasil cylinders, electronic ignition, and lighter flywheel for easier clutch action. The 800cc engine was placed in an R65-derived frame with a Monolever swingarm and single shock absorber. Claimed to provide 50 per cent more torsional rigidity, along with a 2kg (4lb) weight saving, the Monolever soon found its way on to the rest of the BMW motorcycle range.

Below: One of the most popular variations on the boxer theme was the R80 G/S. This featured the new Monolever swingarm and was a surprisingly competent street bike. *Ian Falloon*

Opposite top: To celebrate the victories in the Paris–Dakar Rally, this Paris–Dakar version of the R80 G/S was produced in 1985. *Australian Motorcycle News*

Opposite bottom: Although the R80 G/S was a resounding success, the street R80ST was a commercial failure, and lasted only two years. *Cycle World*

As it was intended as a dual-purpose motorcycle, the R80 G/S had a 21in front wheel, long-travel suspension (200mm from the front 35mm forks, and 170mm at the rear), and high plastic mudguards. Braking was by a single 260mm disc with Brembo caliper, and the ubiquitous Simplex drum. The power, weight and top speed of around 168km/h (104mph), required specific dual-purpose tyres developed by Metzeler. After a development period of 21 months, the R80 G/S debuted in the autumn of 1980.

There was no doubt the R80 G/S was a brilliant motorcycle, and unlike the R45 and R65, exceeded all initial expectations. With over 6,000 produced in 1981, 20 per cent of BMW's motorcycle sales were the R80 G/S that year. Production continued through until 1987, with an optional 32-litre Paris–Dakar fuel tank, red solo seat, and a luggage rack available from 1984. The tank carried a Gaston Rahier signature and included twin fuel petcocks.

So successful was the R80 G/S, particularly as a street bike, that BMW decided to capitalise on this in 1982 with the R80 ST. The R80 ST was essentially

Laszio Peres in the 1978 German off-road championship, on a prototype GS80. *BMW Group Archive*

PARIS–DAKAR SUCCESS

Off-road competition, particularly ISDT, was important for BMW throughout the 1930s, and after the Second World War. However, during the 1960s, without a suitable machine as a basis, BMW only supported these events half-heartedly. That all changed in 1973 when special 750cc machines were prepared for the ISDT in the USA. Based on the R75/5, the machines were outclassed, but they led to a special GS80 for 1979. With 95mm pistons and a 61.5mm R65 crankshaft, the GS80 displaced 872cc and produced 57bhp. There was also a 55bhp 750cc version entered in the 1979 German 750cc Cross-country Championship. The light duplex frame incorporated a monoshock swingarm and in the 1979 ISDT in Germany (Neunkirchen/Siegerland), Fritz Witzel took out the over 750cc award. The following year the team won the Silver Vase, but all this was a prelude to the most important off-road victories, those in the Paris–-Dakar rally.

Billed as the toughest rally in the world, the factory entered three machines in 1981. Prepared by HPN

Motorradtechnik, a small tuning firm in southern Bavaria, these had strengthened chassis and long-range fuel tanks. Hubert Auriol rode to an easy victory, repeating this in 1983. This year the engines displaced 870cc, and the suspension included 42mm Marzocchi forks and an Öhlins rear shock absorber. Three-time World Motocross Champion Gaston Rahier joined the team for the 1984 event, winning ahead of Auriol, repeating this on a special 1,000cc version in 1985. Following the death of Thierry Sabine, the rally promoter, during the 1986 rally, BMW disbanded its official works team. HPN continued to develop Paris–Dakar machines for privateers, and a 1,000cc HPN R80 G/S was available in limited quantities through BMW for privateers for 1987. Based on the R80 G/S, but with a Marzocchi fork and twin White Power shock absorbers, the HPN desert racer cost a princely DM29,000. It was still an eminently suitable desert racer, with Munich rider Eddy Hau winning the marathon category for privateers in the 1988 event on a standard HPN R80 G/S.

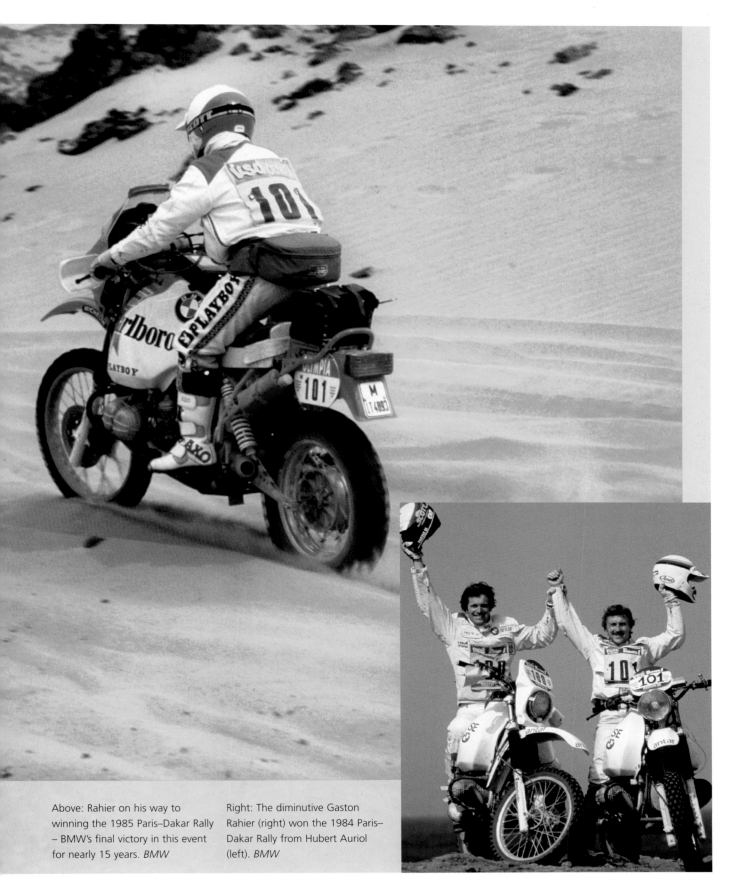

Above: Rahier on his way to winning the 1985 Paris–Dakar Rally – BMW's final victory in this event for nearly 15 years. *BMW*

Right: The diminutive Gaston Rahier (right) won the 1984 Paris–Dakar Rally from Hubert Auriol (left). *BMW*

Above: The 1995 R80 incorporated many chassis developments from the K-series, but the engine was largely unchanged from earlier models. *Ian Falloon*

Opposite: The Monolever R80RT remained in production for more than ten years, and virtually unchanged from this 1985 version. *Cycle World*

a parts bin special, and an amalgam of the R80 G/S, R65 and R100. The basic engine and chassis was that of the R80 G/S, but with a shorter shock absorber, wider rims (the front now a 19in), and an R65 fork. The kickstart was eliminated and for 1983, there was a revised gearshift providing further improvement to gear selection. Weighing only 198kg (436lb), and with short-travel suspension, BMW created arguably their most competent street bike of the early 1980s. Unfortunately, the market did not see it that way. The high-rise enduro-style exhaust system looked incongruous on a pure street machine, and the 19in wheel appeared to be too small for the R80 G/S frame. While the R80 G/S was in demand, the R80 ST lasted only until 1984. In the meantime, the reputation of the R80 G/S as an unsurpassed all-round motorcycle grew. When the Norwegian Helge Pedersen chose a

motorcycle for a ten-year around-the-world trip, it was an R80 G/S. Pedersen covered 350,000km (220,000 miles) on his epic journey.

THE R80, R80RT & R65

With the release of the K100, BMW initially decided to end production of the R100 and R80 series. There was already a three-cylinder K75 waiting to fill the mid-displacement class and to BMW's management team the venerable R series seemed an anachronism. The R100, seen at the end of its development life, was discontinued in favour of the K100, and it seemed unlikely that there would still be a market for the smaller twin with its moderate power. But BMW traditionalists saw it differently. To many, no matter how sophisticated and advanced it was, the K100 appeared to be little more than a motorcycle with a small car engine lying on its side. Therefore, in response to loyalist demand, the R80 made a surprising return in 1984. Later, the R100RS and R100RT were also resurrected in response to popular demand.

Although the engine of the R80 was almost identical to that of the previous 1981–84 version, the design of the rocker arm assembly was revised to lower the noise. The rocker arm spindle stanchions were now positively located in the cylinder head, with a plastic washer to eliminate end-play. The result was the side thrust from the rockers no longer pushed the supports apart. Further noise reduction was achieved through rubber buttons between the cylinder head fins. With a new exhaust system that incorporated a pre-silencer box interconnecting the left and right pipes upstream of the mufflers, the noise level was reduced by three decibels while the engine still developed 50bhp.

More changes were incorporated in the chassis. The 38.5mm centre-axle fork was a scaled-down K100-type, with an integral fork brace and a large-diameter hollow axle. Fork travel was less than on earlier boxers, at 175mm. The front brakes were either a single or double 285mm disc with forward-mounted Brembo brake calipers. The wheels were 2.50 x 18in front and rear, and were similar in design to those of the K100, also accepting tubeless tyres. The rear brake was a 200mm Simplex drum, but perhaps the biggest change was to the swingarm and final drive. This final drive, with a

bevel roller bearing, was similar to that of the K100, and able to accept a higher load than the previous needle bearing type. Although the alloy final drive casting looked more massive, it was actually lighter, and carried the lower ratio of the earlier R80/7 (10:32).

The single shock absorber-Monolever rear suspension represented the biggest departure from earlier boxers. Located in a laydown position, the top bolted to the trailing loop of the R80's strengthened main frame, with the bottom located on the final drive housing. There was no provision for damping adjustment and the shock absorber provided 121mm of travel. While the fuel tank was outwardly similar, many electrical components were shifted from the headlight shell to the frame backbone, resulting in a reduced fuel capacity of 22 litres. For 1991, the R80 was replaced by the R100 in the USA, with the 60bhp R100RS and RT engine, although it continued for other markets. From September 1990, all R series twins were available with SAS (secondary air system) as an option. This exhaust emission afterburning system was designed to reduce HC emissions by 30 per cent, and CO emissions by 40 per cent. Already fitted to US and Swiss models, the SAS used exhaust pressure pulses to move two

One of several R100RS final
editions was this Rennsport of
1992. *Ian Falloon*

Opposite: Even after the release
of the new R1100RT there
was still demand for the older

R100RT, as the fairing provided
such excellent rider protection.
Ian Falloon

diaphragm valves in the air filter housing, drawing
in fresh air. Two tubes directed this fresh air into the
cylinder head and exhaust system behind the exhaust
valve. Development of the R80 was minimal over its
lifespan. For 1990, all boxers received an improved
rear drum brake, the brake pad width was increased to
27.5mm (from 25mm), and there were new mounts for
the brake shoes. There was a floating front disc rotor
from 1991, and Marzocchi forks for 1992.

In addition to the R80, a Monolever R80RT,
replacing the twin-shock version, was also available.
With the same final drive ratio (11:37) the 50bhp

engine still struggled to push the R80RT's considerable
frontal area beyond 160km/h (100mph), but the type
acquired a following amongst those who enjoyed
touring at a more relaxed pace, and required agile
handling. For 1986, a smaller R65, ostensibly identical
to the R80 but with a 48bhp 82 x 61.5mm engine,
replaced the R45, R65, and R65LS. The slight
reduction in power (from 50bhp) allowed the new
engine to run on unleaded fuel, and there was a 27bhp
version for Germany. Production of the two-valve
boxer was envisaged to finish in July 1994, but was
given a reprieve until the end of 1995.

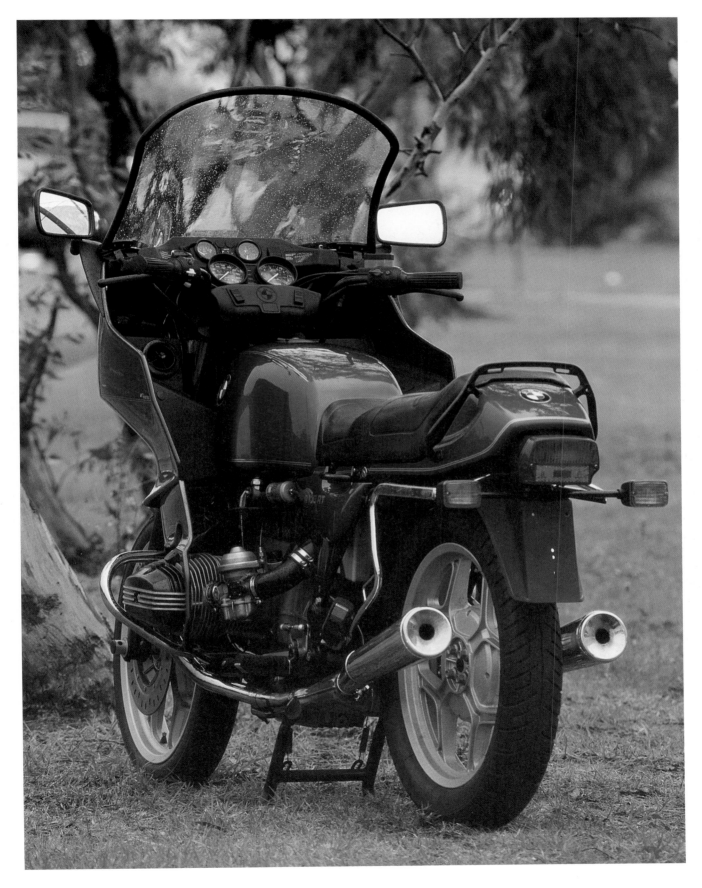

THE R100RS & R100RT

After a two-year hiatus, the R100RS made a surprising return at the 1986 Cologne Show. As with the R80, it was popular demand that saw a new R100RS, and it was originally intended to build only 1,000 examples, but the response was so overwhelming that regular production was instigated for 1988. While the new R100RS looked similar to the 1984 version, there were many differences as it was essentially a larger R80. Inside the engine were the same stronger rocker arm supports as on the R80, and the valve sizes were 42mm and 40mm. Carburation was by smaller, 32mm Bing carburettors, and the exhaust system included a pre-muffler like the R80. This lower state of tune saw the power down to 60bhp, at a moderate 6,500rpm. In a world of escalating Superbike horsepower levels BMW decided to recreate the mould of the R100RS, shifting it from Superbike (as it was in 1977), to that of a more realistic sport-tourer with useable mid-range horsepower. Some enthusiasts were riled that the R100RS was detuned, but it actually had little effect on performance as the new R100RS was as fast, if not faster, than the original. Also, on-the-road performance was superior, especially with the newer and more responsive R80 chassis.

The R80-style frame was similar in design to the pre-1984 version, but with a Monolever swingarm. The wheelbase was slightly less, and the fork rake steeper (27.8°) with 120mm of trail. The wheels, brakes (dual front disc), and suspension also came from the R80, providing the R100RS with lighter steering and more spirited handling than its predecessor. Interchangeable with the earlier R100RS was the fairing, still one of the most effective sport-touring fairings ever offered. There was no longer an optional sport solo seat, and although an oil cooler was standard, the front of the fairing incorporated the earlier open grille.

The R100RS was produced through until 1992, with few changes. There were also several limited edition final R100RS series offered to sustain its model life before the advent of the new R1100RS boxer in 1993, but somehow this didn't achieve the following of the earlier version. Most of the 6,000-odd new series R100RS ended up in Japan, where it was a cult model. Longer lived was the similar R100RT. Resurrected

in 1989, this shared its engine and chassis with the R100RS, but incorporated the larger touring fairing and handlebars of the R80RT. For 1992, it received a Marzocchi front fork and production lasted through until 1996. The final version was the two-tone grey R100RT Classic, initially one of four final 1,000cc 'farewell models' for 1995. Offering a high level of standard equipment, including a custom touring seat and 22-litre top box, the success of the farewell models prompted them to be offered for 1996. But this was their final gasp.

THE R100GS, R80GS & R65GS

While the R80, R100RS and R100RT offered little technological improvement over their predecessors, the R100GS (introduced for 1988) was considerably more than an older R80 G/S with a 1,000cc engine. Although the days of success in the prestigious Paris–Dakar Rally were over for BMW, they were still basking in the glory of their achievements, and this type of dual-purpose machine was still extremely popular in Europe. So good was the R100GS (and its almost identical brother, the R80GS), that it soon became the most popular boxer in the line-up. In order to move from the perception of a combined road/off-road motorcycle, the slash designation disappeared. Now the GS implied off-road sports, and it wasn't an idle claim. Virtually all-new, only the handlebar fittings and headlight were carried over from the previous G/S.

The 980cc and 797cc engines came from their respective road counterparts, although most versions of the R100GS featured 40mm Bing carburettors instead of 32mm ones. The power remained at 60bhp (58bhp with 32mm carburettors) and with the pre-silencer volume beneath the gearbox increasing to 3.8 litres (from 1.5 litres), the torque curve was improved with less noise. With 50bhp, the R80GS engine was identical to the R80's, but with more torque. A different feature from the R80 and R100RS was the layshaft starter (like the K series), weighing 2kg less due to the smaller electric motor but providing the same torque because of the intermediate transmission. The R100GS also included a five-tier oil cooler, which was rubber mounted on the right engine protection bar.

The chassis was more innovative. The frame was

Continuing on from the R80 G/S,
the R100GS was also available as
a Paris–Dakar version from 1990.
Ian Falloon

strengthened, with the oval tubes inside the reinforced tank tunnel, with a stronger rear subframe while the Paralever swingarm imparted a new level of handling prowess. This made the GS even more effective on the tarmac than the R100RS and R100RT. Complementing the Paralever swingarm were new 40mm Marzocchi forks providing increased (225mm) travel. Although non-adjustable, the Marzocchi fork incorporated Teflon sleeves, a fork brace, and hollow, 25mm (up from 17mm) axle. Also uprated were the brakes, the front disc increasing to 285mm with a larger Brembo caliper. The 200mm rear drum brake was also lighter, and operated by a cable instead of a rod. Almost as

significant as the Paralever were the cross-spoked wheels. The straight-pull spokes laced from the extreme edges of the rim, with the adjusting nipples in the hub, and permitted the use of a newer-generation Metzeler 'Sahara' tyre.

Although still a reasonably large (210kg) and tall (850mm seat height) motorcycle, BMW obviously realised the strength of the R100 and R80GS lay on the tarmac as there were two mounting positions offered for the front mudguard. There was also a softer spring strut for 1989, and the option of White Power sports suspension for 1990. There was also an improved footbrake lever for 1990, along with a Paris–Dakar

THE PARALEVER

Motorcycles, drive shafts, and Munich had been synonymous since 1896 when Hildebrand & Wolfmüller produced a motorcycle with two long con-rods connected to the rear axle doubling as a crankshaft. Then in 1904, the Belgian FN Four went a stage further by incorporating a fully enclosed driveshaft and bevel gears. This system of shaft drive was soon known as cardan-drive, after the Italian scholar Geronimo Cardano (1501–1576) for his design of cardan suspension for compasses. When Max Friz adopted the cardan shaft on the R32, it marked the beginning of BMW's commitment to this drive system, despite its drawbacks and limitations. As suspension travel increased during the 1950s, so did the effects of driveshaft movement on the motorcycle. Becoming more evident with increased power, the R100s in particular rose markedly under acceleration. This was not so much a problem on the road, but off-road riders were less enthusiastic about this characteristic as it used up suspension travel while accelerating. To cancel all forces, the swingarm length needed to be 1,700mm, an impractical figure as this was longer than the wheelbase. A longer swingarm on the Paris–Dakar racing machines helped, as did the Monolever of the R80 G/S, but a more effective solution was required.

During 1983, BMW suspension engineers René Hinsberg and Horst Brenner created the Paralever double-joint swingarm, based on von Falkenhausen's design of 1955 for Walter Zeller's 500cc racer. This design reduced the interference of torque reaction with suspension action and created the effect of a longer swingarm. Inside the single-sided swingarm was a second universal joint, with two additional bevel needle bearings, freeing the rear gearcase and hub assembly and allowing it to float on the rear axle. The gearcase motion was controlled by an alloy strut connecting the bottom of the case to the frame, just below the swingarm pivot. The swingarm, stay arm, gearcase and frame, formed a parallelogram, with pinion torque now feeding into the lower strut rather than the swingarm. The slight fore-and-aft movement of the gearcase was absorbed by the laid down single shock absorber. As the parallelogram arrangement increased the radius of the wheel elevation curve, it provided the same effect as a swingarm 1,400mm in length, and compensation for the acceleration and deceleration forces of 70 per cent, as the optimum wheelbase for a BMW was 1,700mm. This was considered acceptable because too much anti-squat may have appeared incongruous to long-time BMW riders.

Although the weight of the Paralever was 1.6kg (3.5lb) more than the earlier swingarm set-up, it transformed the handling of the boxer. Allowing the full 178mm use of rear wheel travel on the R100GS, the Paralever was so successful that it eventually found its way to the entire range of BMW shaft-drive motorcycles.

Left: The Paralever swingarm included a floating rear gearcase, a second universal joint, and an alloy strut connecting the bottom of the gearcase to the frame. *Ian Falloon*

Below: One of the most successful retro adaptations was the R100R of 1992. *Australian Motorcycle News*

version. This included additional instrumentation (tachometer and clock), rectangular K75S headlight, and a fairing connected to the enormous 36-litre fuel tank.

While the Paris–Dakar version stretched the off-road association to the hilt, most buyers still thought of the R100GS as an adventure-tourer; a motorcycle ideal for mountain passes and pavements less suited to large touring motorcycles. So, for 1991, the R80 and R100GS became even more street orientated. A new frame-mounted half fairing, resembling that of the previous Paris–Dakar version, provided improved rider protection over the earlier headlight shell/number plate, and included an adjustable windshield. This could tilt back and forth by 75mm. As on the Paris–Dakar, the fairing supports were outside the bodywork, there was a K75S headlight, and inside the fairing was full instrumentation (including a larger tachometer than the Paris–-Dakar). The front

mudguard was low-mounted, and there was a tougher seat with different seat foam. The handlebar switches now came from the K series, with separate buttons on either side for turn signals. Unlike the K series though, they weren't self cancelling.

For 1991, the R80 and R100GS (and Paris–Dakar) also received a floating front disc rotor, and an adjustable Bilstein rear shock absorber with ten positions for rebound damping. Steering head bearing adjustment was changed to the finer thread of the K75 for more precise bearing-play adjustment. The engine was the same as before, but for a 30° exhaust valve seat contact angle to improve seat life on unleaded fuel.

Alongside the R100 and R80GS was a 27bhp R65GS primarily for the German market. Rather than utilising the Paralever swingarm, the R65GS Monolever chassis was identical to the earlier R80 G/S. The engine was from the R65, but building a decade-old model was not really a recipe for success despite its entry level price. By the time production finished in 1992, only 1,727 had been produced. Not since the days of the R50S of 1960–62 had a BMW motorcycle been so unpopular. The R100 and R80GS on the other hand were outstandingly successful, with over 45,000 manufactured. In 1988 and 1989 in Germany, the R100GS was the biggest selling model of any brand.

The R80 and R100GS were available unchanged through until the end of 1994, and for 1995 the 'farewell model' R100GS PD Classic was the only version available. This featured a wider, high-mounted front mudguard, and the older-style round rocker covers of the R100R. As with the other final Classic R100s, production of the R100 GS PD Classic was also extended to the end of 1995.

THE R100R & R80R

By 1992, it was no secret that BMW was developing an all-new generation of boxer twins. As the release of the new model was still a year away, the R100R was created to sustain interest in the boxers. Whereas the R80 and its street derivatives were similar to designs of the early 1980s, the R100R followed the earlier R80ST, and was an attempt to incorporate some of the R100GS developments in a traditional street package. There was no doubt that the R100R was a functionally superior machine to the R80, but for many, the styling was non-cohesive and unsuccessful.

Derived from the successful R100GS rather than the older R80, the R100R was essentially a classic-style roadster. Many components also came from the K series. While the engine was the same 60bhp unit as the R100GS, with 40mm Bing carburettors (32mm for the USA), the classic look was enhanced by a return to the rounder valve covers, introduced on the R68 back in 1952 and last seen in 1976 on the /6 series. Rather than mounting the oil cooler on the engine protection bar like the GS, this was now positioned in front of the engine, and the single round stainless steel muffler was similar to the K series. From the GS came the instruments and 24-litre fuel tank, while the round headlight was from the K75. With an abundance of chrome, and the option of an additional chrome kit, the R100R was a little gaudy for the traditionalist.

The Paralever chassis also came from the GS, but with different wheels, brakes and suspension. For the

first time on a BMW, the suspension was from Japan, Showa supplying the non-adjustable 41mm fork and rear shock absorber. At 135mm, the front fork travel was less than on other boxers, while the rear gas-charged shock provided adjustable rebound damping and 140mm of travel. The front brake was the single 285mm floating disc of the GS, but with a four-piston K series caliper and the option of a second disc. In keeping with the classic theme, the R100R had wire-spoked wheels, a 2.5 x 18in front, and 2.5 x 17in rear. Like the GS, these cross-spoked wheels allowed the fitting of tubeless tyres.

There may have been a few dubious details (like the plastic instrument surround), but the R100R definitely hit the desired mark. It was reasonably light at 218kg (480lb), and with its Paralever swingarm and tighter suspension was the best handling boxer yet. Unlike the ill-fated R80ST, the R100R was seen as a successful adaptation of the GS to the street, particularly in Germany where it became BMW's best selling model since the R45 in 1980. For 1993, there was also a similar R80R, primarily for the German market, replacing the R80. Ostensibly identical to the R100R, but without an oil cooler, the R80R was also available in 27bhp and 34bhp versions for those licence and insurance categories in Germany.

Although the release of the new R259 boxer was creating all the headlines during 1994, the older boxer continued to be extremely popular. The R100R accounted for 22.4 per cent of motorcycle production during 1992, and for 1994, was joined by the R100R Mystic. Designed to present a more classic look than even the R100R, this featured Mystic Red metallic paint, chrome instrument surrounds, lower handlebars, and a more conservatively styled and sporting seat and tail section. As a result, the Mystic was a more successful interpretation of the classic boxer look than the basic R100R. Both versions received twin front disc brakes for 1994, with the SAS emission control system as standard.

'Farewell models' of both the R100R and Mystic were also available for 1995. These were identical to the earlier versions, but for slightly different decals and colours for the seat and various fittings. Production was extended through for the 1996 Model Year and that was the end for the 1,000cc air-cooled boxer. The 800cc engine lasted one more year, in the R80 GS Basic, primarily for the German market. Essentially an

A further development of the
R100R was the more conservative
Mystic of 1994. *Ian Falloon*

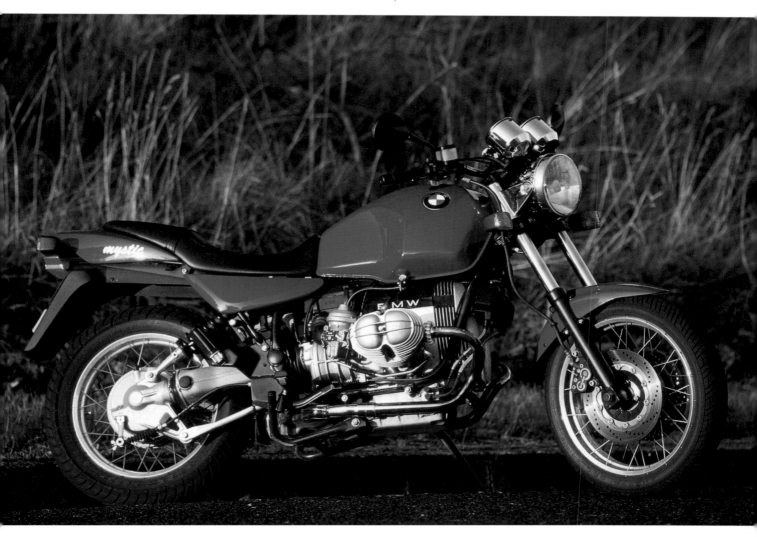

earlier R80 GS with a small fuel tank and headlight cowl, the colours were white, with a blue frame, and it featured a Paralever swingarm and the older-style rocker covers.

The final air-cooled boxer, an R80 GS Basic, left the Spandau factory on 19 December 1996. This was the end of an era, but by 1997, the incredible success of the new A60 boxer engine virtually ensured the demise of the two-valve A10 unit. Further competition came from the F650 Funduro single that provided similar power to the smaller air-cooled boxers, in a lighter and more compact package. In the wake of both these newer designs, and struggling to meet increasing noise and emission requirements, the end was inevitable for

the A10 engine. With production lasting 28 years, it was not only the longest lived of all BMW motorcycle engines, but had amassed a huge following of loyal supporters. These engines were astoundingly reliable and refused to die, and a good number of the more than 430,000 produced are still in active service today. Many BMW enthusiasts bemoaned the end of the days of the simple fix-it-yourself motorcycle, but even the most ardent enthusiast could not fail but to be impressed by the new four-valve A60 engine and its innovative chassis. There was no denying the A10 was a great engine, and it powered some wonderful motorcycles, but it wasn't the answer as BMW looked towards the new millennium.

For 1995, the K1100RS was
available as a special model in
Marrakech Red. *BMW*

6 THE K-SERIES

Even when the ground-breaking R100RS was released in 1976, it was evident that the venerable air-cooled boxer engine could not sustain BMW forever. At 980cc and 70bhp, the boxer was at the limit of reliability, but already the market demanded more power. Honda's CB750 of 1969 had rewritten the rules for motorcycles, and like most motorcycle manufacturers, BMW considered a variety of designs between 1970 and 1976. One of these was a 1,000cc air-cooled boxer with overhead camshafts, the K1 of 1976, but the resurrection of the boxer twin would wait. At the end of the 1970s, four cylinders were considered the optimum for higher horsepower with acceptable reliability. BMW needed a different solution to the ubiquitous air-cooled transverse four, but they could no longer follow the flat-four layout they preferred because Honda had 'stolen' that idea with the Gold Wing in 1975.

During 1977, one of BMW's younger design engineers, 28-year-old Josef Fritzenwenger, proposed a longitudinal four-cylinder engine, with horizontal cylinders. Although a longitudinal four-cylinder engine wasn't a new idea, the Belgian FN of 1904 had also featured this design, but with upright cylinders, Fritzenwenger's solution with the engine on its side was unique. Patented under the name of 'The Compact Drive System', initial plans called for the development of two engines; a 1,000cc three-cylinder, and 1,300cc four-cylinder. These two projects, known internally as the K3 and K4, featured engines quite similar in design to those used in BMW's cars, with a single overhead camshaft and rocker valve actuation. The cylinders were inclined to the right, resulting in an extremely large and heavy engine on which it was impossible to install an exhaust system on the same side as the driveshaft.

A reconsideration of the concept led to a pair of smaller engines, a 1,000cc four, and a 750cc triple. With both models able to share the cost of production and development the two-tier concept appealed to BMW Motorrad's new management, Dr Eberhardt C. Sarfert, Dr Wolfgang Aurich, and Karl Gerlinger, who were appointed on 1 January 1979. On 20 February the same year, these directors gave the go ahead for development to proceed. It was a huge step to take. The elegant simplicity of two air-cooled cylinders with pushrod operated overhead valves and twin

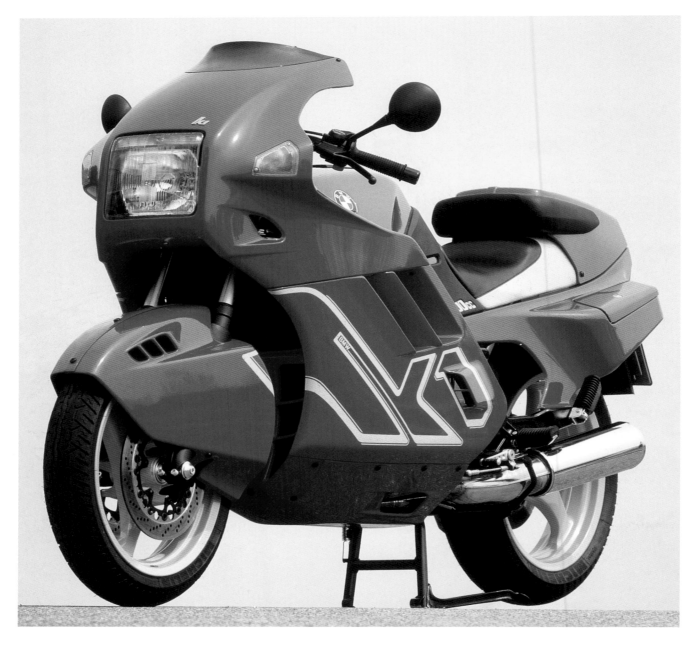

carburettors, made way for a liquid-cooled overhead camshaft three and four, with electronic fuel injection.

THE K100, K100RS, K100RT AND K100LT

Under the direction of Martin Probst, the new head of BMW's motorcycle engine development, work began on the four-cylinder engine, known internally as the K589. Probst came directly from working with Paul Rosche on BMW's highly successful Formula 2 four-cylinder racing engines, while Stefan Pachernegg coordinated the design. The first modification was to incline the cylinder heads to the left, and incorporate double overhead camshafts. The engine became known as the A30, and the motorcycle, the K100 (K for Kraftrad, or wheel power).

Almost dimensionally cubical, the horizontal layout provided a low centre of gravity, and exceptional access to the valve gear and crankshaft. The 987cc engine was also remarkably narrow at 504mm, but to keep the engine length to a minimum the bore was 67mm (with a longer, 70mm stroke), with only 74mm spacing between the Scanimet (nickel and carbide)-coated cylinders. As ultimate horsepower wasn't a consideration there were only two valves per cylinder (34mm and 28mm), set at a shallow included angle of 38°, with twin overhead camshafts driven by a single roller chain. The target was only 90bhp, with a broad powerband, and this was comfortably achieved.

To quell the inherent vibration of an inline four-cylinder engine, and the characteristic BMW sideways pitch, the output shaft was positioned underneath the crankshaft, meshing directly and rotating (along with the 460-watt alternator) in the opposite direction at

Opposite: The K-series not only represented a significant departure from the traditional boxer, but the K1 of 1989 was almost surreal. *BMW*

Below: The K100 development team. From the left: Stefan Pachernegg, Josef Fritzenwenger,

Günther Schier, Martin Probst, Richard Heydenreich, and Klaus-Volker Gevert. *BMW*

a ratio of 1:1. This secondary shaft carried a torsion damper and incorporated spring-loaded staggered teeth to suppress noise and minimise gear lash. The 180mm dry clutch fed directly from the rear of this secondary shaft, rather than the crankshaft as in the boxer twins. A peculiar characteristic of the K100 was the cloud of smoke which was produced when started following prolonged sitting on the sidestand. Oil seeping past the piston rings would collect in the combustion chamber on the left side of the engine, drawn in by a vacuum if the cylinder was at the compression stroke.

Both the ignition and fuel injection were Bosch, and simplified versions of systems from BMW cars. The LE-Jetronic fuel injection system measured the volume and temperature of the air intake, engine speed and temperature, and throttle valve position. There were individual 34mm throttle valves for each cylinder and the injector-opening period was computed in

STEFAN PACHERNEGG

Born in Graz, Austria in 1943, Stefan Pachernegg, was a member of the Austrian ISDT team between 1966 and 1973, winning two gold medals, and one silver. After working at Bombardier Rotax between 1974 and 1975, he became director of development at Steyr-Daimler-Puch AG Avello in Spain from 1975 to 1979, moving to the company's works in Graz in 1980. He went to BMW as managing director in charge of motorcycle development in 1981, where he initially coordinated the K589 project and initiated the R259 boxer design.

association with the Hall-effect digital trigger ignition. The ignition advance curve was dual stage, one for open throttle applications, and another for partial throttle. The engine layout, along with noise and emission requirements, dictated liquid-cooling, with the water pump driven from the front of the output shaft. The biggest problem with the A30 engine and transmission layout was the length, and the 'Compact Drive' system enabled the wheelbase to be restricted to 1,516mm. From the three-shaft five-speed gearbox (in its separate alloy housing), the driveshaft was secured directly with a wire snap ring to splines on the gearbox output shaft. The Monolever swingarm pivoted on taper roller bearings from the gearbox housing rather then the frame, and the driveshaft incorporated an integral rubber shock damper, with the rear drive by bevel gears. The driveshaft and swingarm were of necessity as short as possible, and contributed a noticeable torque reaction.

There were more departures from BMW tradition in the frame and suspension. The engine and drivetrain were attached at five points to the tubular steel space frame as a stressed member. The frame was constructed of almost straight tubes (30 x 1.5mm and 20 x 2mm). Weighing 11.3kg (24.9lb), it was an exceptionally rigid structure, but the engine could not be rubber mounted. The centre-axle front forks were considerably more substantial than earlier BMW examples, with 41.4mm tubes, a rigid 25mm axle, and less travel than before (185mm). At the rear was a single gas-filled Boge shock absorber, providing 110mm of travel, and there were new wheels and brakes. The triple 285mm discs were slotted, each with a Brembo 38mm twin piston caliper, while the 2.50 x 18in and 2.75 x 17in cast alloy wheels were designed for tubeless tyres. Completing the modern specification was a new instrument panel with an electronic speedometer which took its readings from a sensor on the driveshaft. The sculpted 22-litre fuel tank was made of aluminium.

When the K100 was released in 1983, there were initially two models: the basic K100 and the faired K100RS. For the first time on a BMW motorcycle, the automobile connection was emphasised in the shape of the radiator grille of the K100. On the K100RS, the frame-mounted fairing continued the form of the R100RS, but wind tunnel testing resulted in a smaller structure, incorporating the mirrors with turn signals, and an adjustable aerofoil to deflect air over the rider's

helmet. As the fairing increased the top speed from 215 to 220km/h (134–137mph), the K100RS had a slightly higher final drive ratio.

Although they were still not mainstream motorcycles, the K100 and K100RS were immediately successful. The K100RS in particular was arguably the finest sport touring motorcycle produced up to that time, and received an enthusiastic reception. Because of its wider appeal, and despite a six-week metal workers' strike, production of motorcycles rose to 34,001 during 1984. To accommodate the increase in production, new manufacturing machinery and robots were installed at the Spandau works in Berlin.

There were a few improvements made to the K100 for 1985. To combat vibration the front three gearbox mounting points were changed from rubber-bushed to solid mount, and the footpeg mounts were shortened, and mounted solidly. This was intended to shift the resonant points to make the vibration tolerable. The 1985 version also featured an improved rear disc brake without slots. The author was one of those converted to the K100RS during that year. While the unique character of the twins was absent, and there was still an annoying high-frequency vibration through the footpegs at certain touring speeds, the K100RS, with its optional factory luggage, provided unsurpassed two-up touring in all conditions. Hard riding could provoke fading of the rear shock absorber, but the K100RS was an amazingly competent motorcycle, despite its considerable dry weight of 249kg (549lb). With its tall seat height of 825mm, the K100RS was more suited to larger frame riders. Once the pronounced front-end dive under braking was mastered through deft control of the rear brake, and torque reaction controlled through smooth riding, the K100RS was an exceptional handler. It provided the author with many thousands of highly enjoyable touring miles and is rated as one of the most satisfying, if not the most satisfying, motorcycles he has owned.

Over the next few years, there were only a few developments to the K100, many of which were inherited from the K75. For 1986, there was a redesigned seat, with grab handles incorporated in the rear of the seat base, a new footpeg design, and a mechanical fuel-level sensor. Instead of the previous two low fuel level warning lights, there was now only one. Also, there were now fuel tank knee guards for the K100, and lower fairing air deflectors on the

Opposite: Joining the K-series line-up for 1987 was the most opulent touring BMW ever, the K100LT. All K-series were distinguished by the double-overhead camshaft cylinder head on the left, and the LT came with optional ABS from 1988. *BMW*

K100RS. By 1987, sales of the standard K100 were considerably slower than the sporting and touring variants and it received a facelift. There was now no streamlining, while a lower seat with a 760mm seat height, a smaller K75 fuel tank, and higher handlebars were all fitted. Both the engine and wheels were black with silver highlighting, and the rear brake master cylinder was moved out of sight to under the right side panel. There was also improved fuel tank venting, and from 1990, it came with a digital clock.

There were also developments to the K100RS. A Pearl White motorsport version was available for 1987, featuring blacked-out engine and wheels, and the stiffer, more sporting suspension of the K75S. Using the same outer components, stiffer spring and damping rates provided much less travel (135mm). The fork internals were similar to the K75S, with damping rods in the left leg and a dummy rod serving as a spring guide in the right. Each fork leg carried two full-length springs to provide a two-stage progressive spring rate. The closely spaced coils of the spring were at the bottom, touching the damper piston and ensuring low spring movement. The single gas-charged shock absorber also came from the K75S.

For 1984, a full touring K100RT joined the K-series line-up. With fundamentally the same engine and chassis as the K100, this came with higher handlebars and a larger fairing than the K100RS. The multi-piece fairing rested on vibration dampers and was fastened by a multi-arm support to the handlebar centrepiece. There was also a redesigned two-tiered seat, a wide range of options (including a Nivomat shock absorber), and although the weight of 253kg (558lb) made it the largest ever BMW, when compared with full-dress touring motorcycles from Japan, the K100RT was svelte. Developments for 1985 mirrored those of the other K100s, but included a redesigned windshield and deflectors to flow more air over the engine instead around of the rider's legs.

There was an even more opulent K100LT for 1987. Aimed more at the US market than Europe, this included a Nivomat self-levelling rear shock absorber, factory-installed alarm system, 30Ah battery, engine guards, dual accessory electrical sockets, and a radio installation kit built into the fairing (with speakers, antenna, and wiring, and an optional stereo). With the K100LT, BMW finally began to make some inroads into the full-dress tourer market in the USA,

and its success eventually led to larger, and even more luxurious versions. For 1988, it received three accessory power outlets, a larger rear top box capable of holding two crash helmets, and an additional high-mounted instrument panel with coolant temperature gauge and cigarette lighter. There were new wind wings on the windshield.

The final significant development to the K100 was the introduction of ABS on the K100RS Special and K100LT of 1988. These were the first production motorcycles to feature anti-lock brakes as factory equipment, the electronic BMW/FAG-Kugelfischer system being the result of several years' development. The development of ABS for motorcycles followed that for cars, in 1978, with the early adaptation of the automobile system for an R100RS. This was followed by an English hydro-mechanical system on an R90S but results were unfavourable until the incorporation of the ALD anti-lock devise of FAG Kugelfischer in 1983. With this version of ABS, the wheels incorporated 100-tooth pulse generating rings behind each disc. From these rings, inductive sensors sent wheel movement data to an ECU in the tail section under the seat. The ECU compared pre-programmed wheel movement values and when lockup was imminent, a signal was sent to a solenoid/master cylinder pressure modulator mounted above the left footpeg bracket. This reduced braking pressure to the front and rear wheel, and provided a level of safety hitherto unknown to motorcycles. It proved to be a very popular option on the K-series, and by 1992, 50,000 examples, 89 per cent of all the K100-series, were sold with ABS.

There were some other developments for 1988. After five years of trying to overcome smoking start-ups after resting on the side stand, new Citroën-patented pistons and rings solved this problem. Previous attempts through pinning the piston rings, new ring material, and a new cylinder finishing process had failed, but milled cuts and a pinned second ring ensured an air passage through the rings. This prevented a cool-down vacuum. Additionally, the pistons were 15gm (0.5oz) lighter and the K100 engine slightly smoother than before. The final two-valve K-series models were the K100LT and Limited Edition of 1991, with Pearl Green metallic paint, engine spoiler and sports suspension. From May 1991, a retrofitting catalytic converter kit was also available for two-valve models.

THE K75C, K75, K75S AND K75RT

As K100 development progressed, work also began on the A40 (known internally as the K569) three-cylinder 750cc project. From the outset, the 750 was envisaged to complement the larger K100. Providing increased smoothness, with less weight, the K750 was a result of the 'building-brick' principle. This expediency was to reduce development costs, and speed the developmental process. Although essentially three cylinders of the K100, the K75 was to be in a slightly higher state of tune, developing 75bhp (100bhp/litre) at 8,500rpm. Retaining the bore and stroke of the K100, the K75 piston was no longer flat, but designed as a stump cone with valve pockets, which provided an increased compression ratio of 11:1 (as opposed to 10.2:1 for the K100). Contributing to the increased power were shorter intake manifolds and a three-into-one exhaust system incorporating three shorter exhaust pipes. The

valve timing was unchanged while the engine weighed 66kg (145lb), about 10kg (22lb) less than that of the K100 unit.

The three-cylinder crankpins were spaced at 120°, and while this provided perfect balance of the free mass forces, there was a first-order imbalance, similar to that of the boxer twins. Much time was spent overcoming this problem, resulting in two forged balance weights positioned on the output shaft that still rotated at a ratio of 1:1 in the opposite direction to the crankshaft. The rubber damper on the K100 driveshaft to output shaft/clutch connection disintegrated during tests, so the K75 obviously required a larger, more rigid output shaft, without a damper. The damper was shifted to the clutch with a modified smaller and lighter R80-type replacing the K100 clutch. It wasn't until the summer of 1983 that these vibration problems were solved, with the first dynamometer 300-hour endurance tests taking place in October. The Bosch LE injection system was similar to that of the K100, but the VZ-51 L digital ignition was simplified to provide only a single-stage advance curve, which ran somewhere between the two of the K100.

When road testing began in the winter of 1983–84, the three-cylinder engine was placed in a K100 chassis, with re-angled front downtubes to compensate for the shorter engine. Günther Schier, head of Running Gear Development, considered a new shorter frame, but testing confirmed the long K100 frame provided excellent handling, even though the weight distribution was different. With the K75 sharing the basic chassis of the K100, it was then left to designer Klaus-Volker Gevert to provide the K75 with an individual quality. The first designs of 1981 were for the K75S, eventually with a more discreet sporting fairing than the K100RS, the basic K75C design coming a little later. The K75C, like the K100, was planned initially without a fairing, but during 1982 a handlebar-mounted cockpit fairing

was incorporated. The frame-mounted K75S fairing was not designed to provide maximum protection, but to emphasise the more sporting nature of the smaller K-series motorcycle. The wind tunnel-developed nine-piece fairing provided less drag than that of the K100RS (0.45CdA instead of 0.50CdA), as well as a reduction in front and rear wheel lift. For 1986, US models also received a lower cowling which fitted closely underneath the engine, and as this won a prize in the Stuttgart Design Centre, it soon appeared on all versions. With a smaller radiator and fuel tank, the K75 also imparted a feeling of considerably less bulk than its larger brother.

It seemed a simple procedure to create a 750cc triple out of the K100, but vibration was more problematic than expected. The first of the new K-series was this K75C of 1986. *Cycle World*

Released for 1986, the K75C shared its 18in wheel, twin discs, and front fork (but with new dampers and an integral fork brace) with the K100, while at the rear was a 2.75 x 18in wheel with an integral, rod-operated 200mm drum brake. The rear shock absorber also had a lighter spring to compensate for the lighter weight. For the US market there was a K75T (Touring) model available, with a clear touring windshield and contoured seat. The sporting K75S retained the K100 17in wheel and rear disc brake, but the most significant development was the shorter travel and stiffer front fork (also shared with the 1988 K100RS, and described earlier). As a result, the K75S was a considerably more lithe handling machine than the K100. Not only was

the dry weight less at 229kg (505lb), but with reduced weight on the front wheel the steering was lighter. With its smoother engine, the K75 offered a surprising, and cheaper, alternative to the K100, while the K75S was arguably the best-handling BMW motorcycle yet.

One of the problems faced by the K75C and K75S at that time was that the 750cc category was targeted by the Japanese with lightweight high-performance racing-style motorcycles. The Suzuki GSX-R750 and Yamaha FZ750 epitomised this trend, and while the K75 appealed to conservative buyers, it was still more expensive, heavier and less powerful than the Japanese 750s. However, like the K100, the K75 managed to garner a following independent of this fashion-led Japanese incursion, and 20,000 examples were produced in the first three years.

There was an unfaired K75 for 1987, and for 1988, the K75S received 30mm wider handlebars,

The K75S was one of the most underrated BMW motorcycles, and was largely unchanged from 1986 until this 1994 version. *Australian Motorcycle News*

and blacked-out engine and wheels. The seat height of the K75C and K75 was lowered to 760mm and they benefited from a new seat which was without side covers, while the fuel tank gained a wraparound kneepad. The K75 for 1990 also received the sporting K75S suspension, along with the 17in rear wheel and disc brake. New for 1990 was the K75RT, with a similar fairing to the K100RT. This was produced predominately as a police motorcycle, and all K75s this year were available with ABS as an option. The K75S now came with three-spoke K1-style alloy wheels, and with an option of purple paint. The production of the one millionth BMW motorcycle occurred on 18 March 1991. This was a K75RT, donated to the German Red Cross, Berlin, as a first aid accident vehicle.

While the larger K100 was updated and improved during the 1990s, plans to do the same with the K75 were shelved following the release of the new boxer. Consequently, the K75 engine remained almost identical in specification through until its demise, and the K75 never received the superior Paralever

swingarm, but there were a few small developments to the series over the years. For 1992, all K75s were available with a catalytic converter, which was also available as a retrofit option. The K75RT had an optional electrically adjustable windshield for 1993, and all K75s were fitted with a Showa front fork this year. Then, for 1994, the 700-watt three-phase alternator, developed for the new R259 boxer, along with the smaller and lighter 19Ah battery, appeared on the K75.

There were no changes for 1995 as the K75 entered its tenth, and penultimate year, although there was a white (with red seat) final edition K75S. For the final K75 series of 1996, there were two special 'Ultima' editions, the K75 Ultima and K75RT Ultima. With the three-spoke K75S wheels and a few additional features, the K75 bowed out after 11 years with barely a whimper. Production had numbered nearly 68,000, but of all the K-series machines, the K75 was perhaps the least appreciated.

Opposite: From 1988 there
was an optional lower seat
for the base K75, and from
1990, there was sportier, K75S
suspension and a 17in rear
wheel. *Cycle World*

Below: The K75RT was
visually similar to the R100RT,
and from 1993 had an
electrically adjustable windshield.
Australian Motorcycle News

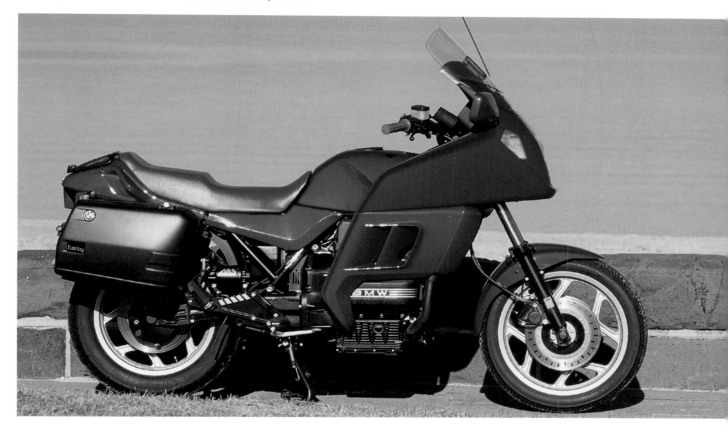

THE K1

By the end of the 1980s, the Japanese had rewritten
the rules for sporting motorcycles. High horsepower
engines, excellent handling, and full-coverage fairings
were standard fare, but all the Japanese offerings
featured chain drive. BMW decided the time was ripe
for a shaft drive Superbike, and considerably more
performance-focused than the K100. Titled the K1, in
the manner of BMW's performance cars (M1, M3, M5,
Z1 etc.), this was intended to emulate the classic R90S
that had provided unsurpassed performance in its day.
Not only would the K1 stand out, but BMW hoped its
performance would be class-leading.

When it was first displayed at the Cologne Show
at the end of 1988, the K1 certainly shattered the
perception of BMW producing conservatively styled
touring and sport-touring motorcycles. The styling
was dramatically different, and underneath the all-
enveloping bodywork was a significantly developed
K100. The styling history of the K1 followed a path

of aerodynamic development that began with Henne's
record-breaking 500 Kompressor of 1937. Following
the release of the K100 in 1983 stylist Karl-Heinz
Abe created a sports machine called 'Racer', for the
Time Motion exhibition of 1984. This 1:2 scale model
inspired the creation of the prototype K1, which was
presented to the management on 22 June 1986, when
the project was given the go-ahead.

As BMW was committed to the voluntary 100bhp
limit for motorcycles sold in Germany, Abe and
Klaus Volker Gevert worked at incorporating the
aerodynamic advantages of the earlier styling exercise.
With its large enveloping, two-piece front mudguard
almost mating to the leading edges of the seven-piece
fairing through to its large tail with miniature pannier,
the CdA factor was a remarkable 0.34, with the
rider in a prone position. This drag coefficient was
by far the lowest of any production motorcycle. The
large tail section incorporated two integrated six-litre
storage compartments, and there was a specific 42-litre
baggage system available. The bright colours of red or

blue with yellow graphics and highlighting also made the K1 stand out.

There was much more to the K1 than its aerodynamic bodywork. Inside the engine (designated A31), the cylinder head incorporated four valves per cylinder, with two 26.5mm inlet and two 23mm exhaust valves and a central spark plug. This was not exactly ground-breaking technology, and many thought it was surprising that the original K100 hadn't been four-valve, especially considering Martin Probst's racing car background. On the K1, the twin overhead camshafts acted directly on bucket tappets without adjustment shims, with buckets of different thickness used to adjust valve lash. This resulted in a reduction in the mass of reciprocating parts, but required camshaft removal for valve adjustment although the intervals for this were necessarily long, at 30,000km (19,000 miles).

While retaining the undersquare dimensions of 67 x 70mm, there were slightly lighter higher compression pistons (11:1), lighter con-rods, a 1.3kg (2.9lb) lighter crankshaft, and a digital Motronic injection and ignition system. Similar to the systems on BMW cars, there was now no butterfly-type airflow meter,

with airflow being calculated from throttle position and revs. Other sensors determined air and coolant temperature, and atmospheric volume, with an ECU determining ignition timing and injection pulses from a pre-programmed EPROM. While this low resistance digital Motronic injection system contributed around 4–5bhp, unlike the LE Jetronic, it no longer compensated for changes in engine tune. A shorter, cylindrical stainless-steel muffler connected to an expansion chamber underneath the gearbox, and the power was 100bhp at 8,000rpm. There was a slightly higher fifth gear, stiffer clutch springs, and a taller final drive ratio.

Under the direction of Lothar Scheungraber, the chassis of the K1 was developed to provide considerably more sporting performance. Weighing 13.5kg (29.8lb), the frame front downtubes were increased in diameter to 32mm, with 13mm larger rear seat tubes, with the steering head angle reduced to 27°, and with 90mm of trail, the K1 was lighter steering than the K100, despite the wider front tyre. For the first time ever on a BMW motorcycle, the front wheel was a smaller diameter than the rear, the 3.50 x 17in front and 4.50 x 17in rear wheels being wider than before. Manufactured by FPS in Italy, the yellow, three-spoke wheels allowed for the fitment of low-profile radial tyres.

Complementing the wheels and tyres were upgraded suspension and brakes, the K1 using the Paralever swingarm from the GS models, with a single gas-charged Bilstein shock absorber providing 135mm of wheel travel. As the swingarm incorporated an

Opposite: Following an aerodynamic path begun with the 1937 record-breaking Kompressor, the unique K1 bodywork provided the lowest drag coefficient of any production motorcycle. *BMW*

Below: Underneath the radical bodywork was a completely revamped engine and chassis, with a Paralever swingarm for the first time on a K-series. *BMW*

additional U-joint, it was longer than the K100 (450mm), contributing to the long, 1,565mm (62in) wheelbase. The front 41.7mm forks were by Marzocchi, with 135mm of travel, and there was a state-of-the-art Brembo braking system. Larger, twin spirally perforated 305mm front brake discs were gripped by four-piston calipers, with 32mm and 34mm pistons to distribute the pad wear evenly. The floating brake discs were thicker at 5mm and revised lever ratios, with a 20mm master cylinder piston, reduced braking effort. ABS was optional, but standard for some markets like the USA.

The K1 was designed for high-speed use, and the riding position accentuated this. A 780mm seat height, lower and wider handlebars, and higher and wider footpegs created an uncompromising sporting riding

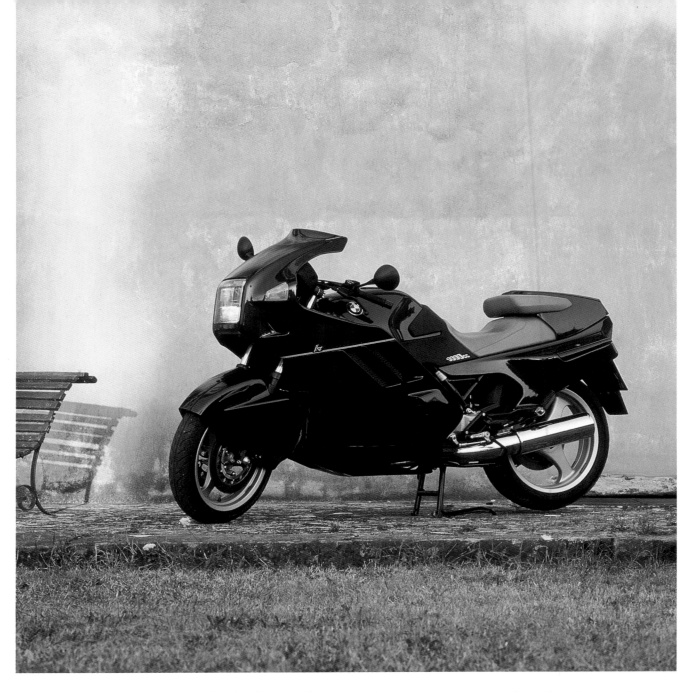

position. However, even once the lurid colours and unique styling were accepted, the K1 failed in its quest to offer leading Superbike performance. Certainly the faster throttle response, lighter steering, and tighter suspension and brakes made the K1 closer to the Japanese Superbikes than previous K-series, but the dry weight of 234kg (516lb) was intimidating for a sporting motorcycle. The engine, while providing a superb broad powerband with excellent fuel economy, just wasn't powerful enough to overcome this weight obstacle. While the Paralever provided a vast improvement in overcoming the inherent deficiencies of shaft drive for a sporting motorcycle, it still couldn't disguise the considerable unsprung weight. There was no denying the K1 was the best handling and strongest

performing BMW motorcycle to date, but somehow the true nature of the machine was lost in a confusion of purpose.

The first deliveries of the K1 were in May 1989, and it was popular initially, winning many industry awards. Yet, after producing nearly 4,000 during 1989, sales stalled. For 1991, there was a more subdued colour of Classic Black metallic, with silver wheels, and lightened fork compression damping was introduced through increasing the holes in the damper rod from 2.1mm to 2.4mm. This overcame the harshness of the earlier fork when absorbing large jolts at high speed. As extreme engine heat was a problem, there were new baffles to direct more heat out of the fairing slots, but this wasn't enough to save the K1. By the end of 1993, the K1 was

Opposite: In an effort to resurrect
stalled sales, the K1 received
subdued colours for 1991. *BMW*

Below: The four-valve K100RS
soon followed the K1 during
1989, retaining the familiar

K100RS fairing but incorporating
the more powerful K1 engine
and chassis developments. *BMW*

dead, but today it remains an important representative
of BMW's technological development of the late 1980s.
As less than 7,000 were produced, the K1 is becoming
increasingly sought after as a future classic.

THE K100RS (FOUR-VALVE)

It was inevitable the four-valve engine and Paralever
chassis would eventually find its way to the K100,
and this happened less than a year after the release of
the K1. Whereas the K1 struggled in its quest to be a
Superbike, the four-valve K100RS made no pretensions
as to its intended function. It also represented a
significant improvement over the previous K100RS,
already the definitive sport-touring motorcycle, but

one that was virtually unchanged from 1983. Not only
did the 100bhp engine with Bosch Motronic MA 2.1
electronic fuel injection come from the K1, but it also
shared the reinforced chassis with Paralever swingarm,
cartridge-style Marzocchi front fork, three-spoke FPS
wheels, and four-piston Brembo brakes. Unlike the
K1, the new K100RS featured rubber front engine
mounts to cut vibration, and the handlebar was wider
(although not as wide as on the K1) for increased
leverage. The rear shock absorber, with less travel
(120mm) came from the K75S, and the front fork
received softer damping and springing than on the K1.
Although the K100RS now shared the higher, K1 fifth
gear, it retained the lower final drive ratio. There were
no changes to the K100RS for 1992 except the rear
shock absorber, which was now Showa, and gained
infinite rebound damping adjustment.

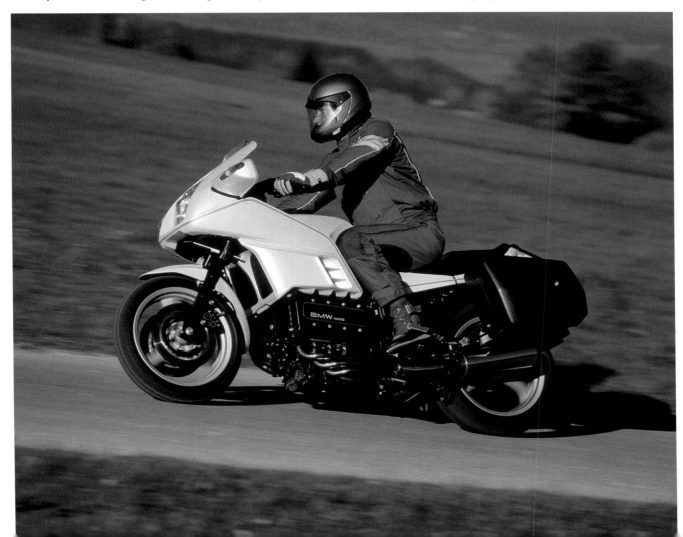

As the four-valve K100RS shared the excellent fairing of the earlier two-valve version, it functioned similarly. To widen its appeal there was also an optional engine cowling and a lower seat. With improved power, handling, brakes, and minimal driveshaft effect, the K100RS four-valve was just the sport-touring motorcycle traditional BMW enthusiasts were looking for. The K100RS provided the heart of the radical K1 in a more familiar environment, and it proved to be considerably more popular than the K1. From May 1991, a three-way regulated catalytic converter with oxygen probe (reducing hydrocarbons, carbon monoxide, and nitrous oxide) was also offered as an option on four-valve K-series motorcycles with the Motronic injection system. Despite a slight decrease in torque, requiring lower final drive gearing, environmentally friendly BMW buyers accepted the catalytic converter with enthusiasm. By 1992, 41 per cent of all K1 and K100RSs were so equipped.

THE K1100LT AND K1100RS

By 1990, the K100LT was the only K-series motorcycle retaining the two-valve, four-cylinder A30 engine and it was still virtually the same as it was eight years earlier. As had happened with the K100RS, it appeared to be certain that the K100LT would also adopt the four-valve cylinder head and chassis improvements of the K1. The success of Honda's GL1500 Gold Wing proved there was no substitute for displacement with a heavy full-dress tourer, so for 1991 the 987cc engine was boosted to 1,092cc. The displacement increase came through a bore enlarged to 70.5mm, creating the largest capacity BMW motorcycle to date. To reduce vibration the new engine (designated A34) used lighter pistons and 6mm longer connecting rods. With a Bosch Motronic MA 2.2 injection system the power was the same 100bhp as the four-valve K100, but at a lower, 7,500rpm. Most improved was the torque, up to 107Nm at 5,500rpm which was significantly higher than the two-valve K100 (86Nm at 6,000rpm), and the four-valve K100 (100Nm at 6,750rpm).

The chassis specifications were similar to the K1 and the four-valve K100RS, with a Paralever swingarm, dual front discs with four-piston calipers, and three-spoke wheels. These were not the more modern wider type of the K1, but retained the 18in front and 17in rear of the K100LT (although the rear rim width went up to 3.00in). The rear shock absorber was the Showa unit, shared with the 1992 K100RS. The fairing was moved 30mm forward and incorporated frame-mounted instruments, while the windshield was electrically adjustable. The luggage also provided a larger carrying capacity, and the footrest support plate

was remotely mounted to reduce vibration. However, the K1100LT still vibrated, and the rather soggy suspension didn't invite spirited riding.

One year after the release of the K1100LT, the K1100RS replaced the K100RS. The high-torque engine came from the successful touring model, along with the new 700-watt alternator and 19Ah battery of the new generation boxer. There were thicker exhaust headers for increased durability, and the K1100RS featured a modified K100RS chassis. Reinforcement was added to the frame through tiebars connecting the steering head to the rear subframe, and the Marzocchi fork and Showa shock absorber were modified. The fairing received the most development, the trend towards full-coverage bodywork resulting in a new lower section and engine cowl. This incorporated the distinctive BMW 'kidney' grille, along with side air scoops similar to those on a Ferrari Testarossa car. Completing the updates was a four-way adjustable front brake lever and newly designed handgrips. All these developments made the K1100RS the most sporting K-series motorcycle yet. It still had its foibles

Opposite: For the tenth anniversary of the K-series in 1994, there was this special edition K1100LT. *BMW*

Below: The K100RS grew to 1,100cc for 1992, and received a new fairing with distinctive side air scoops. *Cycle World*

though, weight and vibration, but as a high-speed long-distance tourer the K1100RS had no peer. Compared with the cheaper Honda ST1100 which was clawing away at its market share, the K1100RS provided superior handling, luggage, and overall capability.

Developments for both the K1100RS and K1100LT for 1994 included several features from the new R259 boxer. This included not only the new alternator, but the Motronic MA 2.2 electronic injection and ignition system, and the option of second-generation ABS II. The K1100LT received the higher final drive of the K1100RS, and there was a 10-year K-series anniversary K1100LT Special Edition. For 1996, the K1100LT received ABS II as standard equipment, and it continued largely unchanged for another two years, but by that time, it really was an anachronism.

As ABS was proving an exceptionally popular

option, the development of the second-generation ABS II began early in 1990. Again undertaken in cooperation with FAG Kugelfischer, this retained the 100-tooth gear and sensor on each wheel, but incorporated a single, two-channel pressure modulator instead of two separate modulators as on the earlier system with three computers monitoring the signals. The new ABS components were lighter, weighing 6.9kg (15.2lb) instead of 11.1kg (24.5lb).

There was a special red edition of the K1100RS for 1995, and a black and silver version for 1996, but it was still out-powered by the new and larger Japanese sport-tourers, and vibrated too much. The K1100RS also failed to win the hearts of traditional BMW buyers. They wanted a new boxer, and the success of the R1100RS hastened the demise of the K1100RS.

Opposite: Not only did the
K1200RS feature the BMW
Telelever front suspension, but
the aluminium frame was a
radical departure from the earlier
K-series. *BMW*

THE K1200RS

As development resources were fully engaged on the
R259 boxer during the early 1990s, it was not until
1993 that the much overdue development of the
K-series could begin. Rather than continue along the
path initiated by the K1, the development team headed
by Jürgen Bachmann decided on a change in direction.
Although financial constraints and development time
still tied the design to the longitudinal horizontal four-
cylinder layout, the new K-series would provide real
Superbike performance in a state-of-the-art chassis.

The heavy engine and transmission layout was
never going to power a lithe Superbike, so the design
parameters were aimed towards a powerful sport-tourer
in the best BMW tradition. The first task was to cure
the vibration that had plagued the K-series since its
inception. Lancaster-type double speed counter-rotating
balancers, such as on the Honda Super Blackbird, were
investigated, but there was insufficient room inside the
existing crankcases for the two shafts and the proposed
front Telelever lower arm. Isolating the rider from the
chassis by rubber-mounting the handlebars, footpegs,
and seat was then considered, but this resulted in
imprecise handling. The third solution called for a
conventional engine rubber-mounting approach.

Deciding to support the engine in rubber mounts
required a new design approach for the frame, so
BMW turned to the Italian frame specialist Bimota,
in Rimini. Bimota designed a monocoque aluminium
backbone-style frame that connected the swingarm to
the front suspension mounts. Two 'Silentbloc' bushings,
with two lateral steel braces, held the engine in the
front, and two rubber/steel mounts were inserted in
the frame above the transmission case at the rear. By
mid-1994, Bimota's prototype was accepted, and after
three versions, the eventual frame used welded cast
aluminium components. Four aluminium castings, with
honeycomb reinforcing ribs, were welded together to
create a hollow backbone frame. Aluminium shanks
attached to the rear of this backbone and provided
pivots for the rear suspension and mounts for the
bolted-on rear subframe. Built by Verlicchi, this frame
provided excellent handling, successfully isolated
engine vibration, and was easy to manufacture. The
only disadvantage was the weight, more than 27kg
(60lb), and 7kg (15lb) heavier than a frame design with
a stressed engine.

With the vibration problem solved, the engine
could now be developed to produce more power. The
voluntary limit of 100bhp in Germany, initiated back
in 1978, was now irrelevant and engine development
chief Wolfgang Dürheimer coordinated a programme to
create the most powerful BMW motorcycle ever. As the
70.5mm bore of the K1100 already left the cylinders
with marginal bore spacing, an overbore was out of
the question. Stroking was the only way to achieve
more displacement, and this required new crankcases,
crankshaft, and stronger balance shaft bearings, with
a stroke of 75mm providing 1,171cc. This engine was
known as the A35.

Although the bore remained the same at 70.5mm,
the A35 engine included higher compression (11.5:1),
lighter pistons and gudgeon pins, and forged-steel
con-rods. The four-valve cylinder head now included
26.5mm inlet and 23mm exhaust valves with thinner
stems (reduced from 6mm to 5mm), and with longer
duration K1 camshafts, and 38mm throttle bodies,
the power was increased significantly, to 130bhp
at 8,750rpm. This also saw the maximum revs rise
to 9,000rpm, where the piston speed was 22.5m/
sec (4,400ft/min). A figure reminiscent of racing
engines only two decades earlier, this pushed the
crankcase design to the limit so it wasn't surprising
the electronic rev limiter cut out at 9,400rpm (which
was still up on the 9,000rpm of the K1100RS).
There was also an alternative, 98bhp version
available, for those who demanded lower insurance
premiums. This was essentially identical but for fuel
and ignition mapping, and smaller and longer intake
manifolds.

Contributing to the power increase was a redesigned
intake and injection system. Taking advantage of
developments in air-box design, the volume of the air-
box increased from 1.0 to 7.0 litres, and was fed by
a ram air intake from the front of the fairing. There
was also a third-generation Bosch Motronic MA 2.4
engine management system. This had an automatic
choke, and it allowed for external diagnostic checking
for faults. The alternator was uprated to 720 watts and
the exhaust system featured larger diameter manifolds.
Because of the horsepower increase, a less restrictive
dual catalytic converter set-up was employed rather
than a single larger one. Also uprated was the cooling
system, with a dual radiator instead of the previous
single unit.

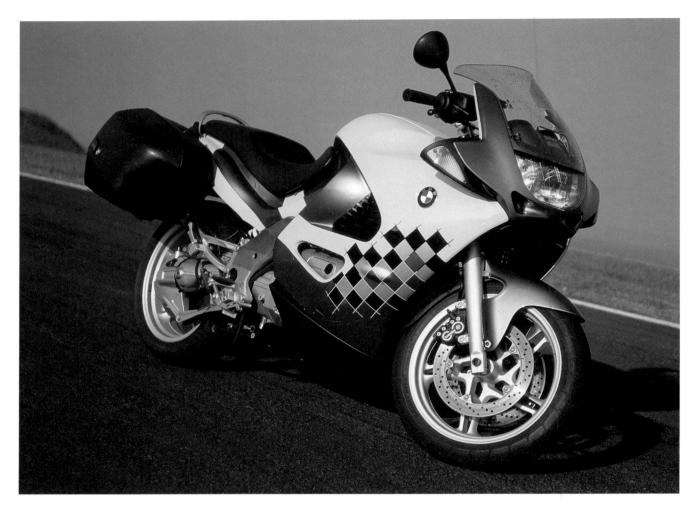

The gearbox and clutch were also new for the K1200RS. The smaller diameter clutch (165mm) was hydraulically actuated and connected to a new, six-speed Getrag gearbox. The three-shaft dog-type gearbox was installed in a more compact housing, as it didn't have to support the swingarm pivot, and incorporated an improved torsional damper.

Complementing the more powerful engine was enhanced, sporting orientated suspension. The telescopic forks of the earlier K-series made way for a BMW Telelever system pioneered on the R259 boxer (see Chapter 7). This substituted an A-arm, fork brace, and a ball-joint for the usual telescopic fork lower triple clamp, and differed in detail to the boxer set-up. Marzocchi provided the 35mm forks, while the longitudinal A-arm that braced the lower fork bridge was rectangular in section. Rather than being attached to the engine, this was pivoted on the frame, just above the engine. The ball-joint for the upper fork bridge was contained in the front of the backbone frame and there was a single gas-charged shock absorber. This provided a relatively short, 115mm of wheel travel. The geometry of the A-arm was altered from that of the

R1100RS to provide an anti-dive ratio of 90 per cent (rather than 70 per cent). With 100 per cent providing no dive at all, this greater figure was considered more appropriate for the sporting nature of the K1200RS. A hydraulic steering damper connected the A-arm to the lower Telelever, and the engine was raised 30mm higher than on the K1100RS to allow for an increase in the maximum lean angle from 46° to 50°.

The Paralever swingarm was modified to be mounted on the aluminium frame, and featured revised shock absorber mounting points. As the single shock absorber was mounted at a pronounced angle, it provided a rising rate action, with 150mm of wheel travel. The new chassis provided a slightly shorter wheelbase (1,555mm/61in) than the K1100RS, and more conservative steering geometry (27.25° rake and 124mm of trail). The brakes and wheels were also upgraded for the K1200RS, with the front, 305mm floating discs not now mounted on separate carriers, but directly on the wheel spokes. The five-spoke wheels too were lighter, and wider, with a 5.00 x 17in on the rear. This allowed the fitting of the largest tyre yet on a BMW motorcycle, a 170/60ZR17.

Opposite: With its new bodywork and this distinctive colour scheme, there was no mistaking the K1200RS for its predecessor. *Australian Motorcycle News*

Above: The 2000 Model K1200RS was more subdued in styling, but many found the riding position too sporting in its orientation. *Ian Falloon*

There was also new enveloping bodywork for the K1200RS. David Robb's first major motorcycle design project, he and his 15-strong team set out to create a sporting design that retained an association with the previous K-series. With its slightly more sporting riding position, the seat, and footpegs were adjustable, the K1200RS had a lower fairing, with two-position windscreen, and more modern twin headlight set-up. There were two reflectors in a single housing, with the high beam reflector in front of the low beam. The hand protectors, with their integral turn signals, were intended to retain K-series links, but no longer incorporated rear view mirrors. The large rounded plastic fuel tank and cover seemed excessively wide but the proof of the excellence of the K1200RS was in the riding. Despite the considerable weight of 285kg (628lb),

the K1200RS was possibly the first BMW motorcycle without any peculiar quirks that always set a BMW motorcycle apart. With surprisingly light steering, exceptional stability, no vibration, and a tight driveline, the K1200RS could be ridden incredibly fast with ease.

As the sporting riding position wasn't universally accepted, during 1998 a comfort handlebar and seat were available as an option. This moved the handlebar 40mm closer to the rider, and increased the seat height for both rider and passenger. There was also the option of a wider, 5.50 x 17in, rear wheel, allowing a 180/55ZR17 tyre. By the end of 2000, production numbered more than 21,000, but it was time for a facelift.

Customer demand required improved comfort and weather protection, along the lines of the previous K100RS and K1100RS, along with a less aggressively sporting riding position. For 2001, wind tunnel development resulted in a more slender upper fairing, and a wider and taller windshield. The windshield area was increased by 20 pr cent, and was still two-way manually adjustable. As on the K1200LT, the

R1150RT and the R1100S, the two water radiators were now integrated in a BMW kidney grille in the fairing, with the air scoop feeding air into the intake system opening up at the front right above the radiators. The instrument cover and inner cockpit cover were redesigned, and there were larger rear-view mirrors. The previously optional comfort handlebar was now standard, with both the rider's and passenger footpegs lower. The seat remained with a two-position variable height adjustment, and the rear spring preload featured a hydraulic adjustment. While rider comfort was improved, the biggest development was the incorporation of the new generation Integral ABS. Along with larger, EVO 320mm front disc brakes and new calipers, the K1200RS used a semi-integral ABS with the footbrake only activating the rear disc, and the hand lever acting on all discs. Also new was the option of cruise control. There were no changes for 2002, but the 2003 K1200RS came standard with the previously optional wider rear wheel, direction indicators featuring white glass covers, and there was an option of sports suspension that included stiffer springs and damping.

Although undeniably fast and competent, the K1200RS was still an extremely large and heavy motorcycle in the world of sportsbikes. As its focus shifted towards sports-touring the K1200RS faced increased competition from the Honda ST1300 and the Yamaha FLR1300. Therefore, the next incarnation of the K-series RS was expected to displace nearly 1,300cc, and incorporate some subtle styling alterations to further improve rider protection as the design criteria moved even further away from that of pure sports.

THE K1200LT

Largely undeveloped since its inception back in 1991, the K1100LT was, by 1998, the only remaining Compact Drive System K-series motorcycle. Arguably outclassed by the six-cylinder Honda Gold Wing even when it was released, sales of the K1100LT in the full-dress luxury touring market in the USA were largely insignificant compared with the Gold Wing. The K1100LT was essentially a development of the sport-touring K100RS, and not sufficiently focused and competent to tackle the Gold Wing head on. Like BMW, all the Japanese manufacturers had attempted to break Honda's stranglehold in this lucrative market, but none had been successful. Even as the Gold Wing aged, it remained the standard by which large touring motorcycles were judged, until the advent of the remarkable K1200LT.

Following on from David Robb's K1200RS and R1200C Cruiser, both of which had distinctive new personalities and were aimed at a specific rider

DAVID ROBB

In 1993, the 37-year-old American-born David Robb was appointed motorcycle chief designer. After graduating from the Pasadena Art Center College in 1979, Robb went to work briefly at Chrysler, and then Audi. In 1984, he moved to BMW, where he was instrumental in implementing computer-aided design for cars. At this time, Robb also developed an interest in motorcycles, and his personal transport of a Kawasaki-engined Bimota KB2 didn't go unnoticed. When Robb went to the motorcycle division of BMW, he not only brought his computer expertise, but also a new approach to design. Rather than maintain the traditional BMW philosophy of continual, and sometimes ad hoc, refinement, Robb advocated an emphasis on creating a unified design that achieved its desired purpose from the outset. He also wanted to create new models that were distinctively different from others in the range, moving away from the previous homogeneous line-up where the entire family appeared closely related. This was to broaden the overall appeal and create greater distinctions between the various models.

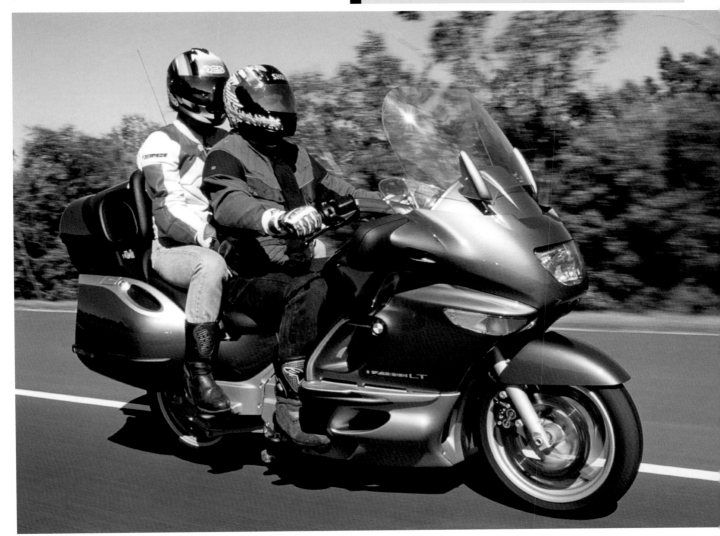

Opposite: With its integrated luggage, the K1200LT provided unsurpassed touring in style and comfort. This is the 2003 edition, with Integral ABS and EVO front brakes. *BMW*

demographic, the K1200LT was intentionally designed to sit at the extreme end of the spectrum for touring motorcycles. This was unusual, as all previous street BMW motorcycles (and to some extent also the GS versions) were essentially fine graduations on the sport-touring theme. Some were more biased to sport, and others to touring, but sport-touring was the BMW genre and it resulted in some models within the line-up competing directly with others. Thus, the R1100RT boxer, introduced in 1995, was seen as an alternative to the K1100LT, which it was and not a motorcycle with a different focus. This changed with the K1200LT, a serious effort to create a true competitor to the Gold Wing, and one that offered a significantly different interpretation of a touring motorcycle to the R1100RT. There was also a conscious automotive association, with the K1200LT emulating the luxury 7-series executive saloon by providing exceptional comfort, storage space, and luxury.

Although the basic architecture of the K1200LT was closely related to the K1200RS, unlike the earlier LT that was essentially a K100 or K1100RS with extra equipment, the new LT design was unique. The 1,171cc four-cylinder engine was similar to that of the K1200RS, but with a lower compression ratio (10.8:1), longer and smaller intake manifolds, 34mm throttle bodies, and milder camshaft timing. This produced a smoother idle and more consistent off-idle running, essential for low-speed manoeuvrability for such a large motorcycle. The intake system also benefited from a four-chamber Helmholtz resonator that not only improved airflow, but also reduced intake noise. A new stainless-steel exhaust system, with a catalytic converter in the pre-muffler, and a modified Motronic MA 2.4 engine management system, saw the power down from the K1200RS, at 98bhp at 6,750rpm, with the torque 115Nm at only 4,750rpm. Also important for this type of motorcycle was the flat torque curve, with 100Nm available between 2,800rpm and 6,800rpm. As there were many optional electrical accessories, the alternator was uprated to 840 watts.

The clutch and gearbox was different from that on the K1200RS. The hydraulically operated single-plate dry clutch reverted to the larger, 180mm of the previous LT, and the gearbox only featured five speeds, with the fifth gear an overdrive. Like the GL1500 Gold Wing, the K1200LT received an electric reversing assister, operated by the electric starter motor.

Activated only while the engine was running, the switch which reversed the starter motor direction was located above the gearshift lever.

With the intention of producing a large full-dress tourer that provided safe and predictable handling, the chassis was also a development of the K1200RS. The previous K1100LT wasn't known for exceptional handling, as the additional weight taxed the suspension. It was a brave rider who dared push a fully laden K1100LT beyond the threshold of weaves and wobbles, and although the new K1200LT was to weigh a substantial 378kg (833lb), it required sure-footed handling. As engine smoothness was also a priority, the cast-aluminium frame, with rubber-mounted engine, was similar to that of the K1200RS. The steel rear subframe included supports for the integrated luggage.

An advantage of the Telelever was that it was possible to provide front suspension characteristics suitable for a specific purpose. The anti-dive ratio could be altered through the geometry of the A-arm, as could the amount of spring travel while maintaining damping control. This feature was particularly appropriate on a large luxury touring motorcycle that required soft and supple suspension with positive wheel control. The front shock absorber provided 102mm of spring travel, and while the huge, tiller-style, handlebars were rubber mounted as on the R1100RS, they had separate bearings to neutralise the Telelever sway forces.

Although the K1200RS had a long wheelbase, the K1200LT was stretched out even further to provide more space for the rider and passenger. Achieved through an 80mm longer Paralever swingarm, the rear shock absorber spring travel was 130mm, with hydraulic spring preload adjustment. The front 17in wheel and 305mm brakes came from the K1200RS, as did the rear 17in wheel, but the rear disc was increased to 285mm, with a four-piston caliper. ABS II was standard.

Intended to convey an aura of luxury, comfort, and convenience, the integrated bodywork was quite unlike earlier BMW motorcycles, and was a new concept in motorcycle design. The fairing, fuel tank, seats, side luggage, top-box, and even the exhaust system were integral parts of the complete motorcycle body. The cockpit was almost automotive-like, the wide fairing offering unparalleled wind and weather protection, with the built-in, non-removable luggage compartments flowing out of the slowing side panels. Tipping-over protection was sensibly provided through impact strips at the rear and a bumper on the sides of the fairing, with the tipping forces feeding directly to the frame in the style of older crash bars.

Comfort levels were predictably high, with BMW engineers thinking of nearly everything. A thumb switch on the handlebar adjusted the windshield height, and there were even two sizes of windshield available. Transparent deflectors on the sides of the windshield protected the rider's hands, with additional wind deflectors beneath the rear-view mirrors. Easy adjustment of the rider's seat was provided through a lever under the seat, while a gas damper kept the seat open. The seat could be set at 770mm or 800mm, with the passenger backrest adjustable by 25mm through moving the top-box. A sophisticated locking system on the two, 35-litre side-storage compartments allowed them to open at the pull of a lever, with a gear inside the compartment cover activating a consistent seal so there was no need to lock them while riding.

Unlike the K1100LT, it was clear the K1200LT's luxury features were intentionally integrated into the design from the outset. No longer was the radio an afterthought installed in the fairing glove box. Now, the sound system included hand-operated controls, with separate switches at the rear for the passenger, four speakers, and the option of a six-CD changer. Other options extended to heated seats, a trip computer, cruise control, intercom, and a mobile phone. The most extraordinary option was a dealer-fitted refrigerator installed in the top-box. There were additional chrome kits available, and for the 2000 Model Year the top-box incorporated an additional brake light.

To many, the K1200LT may have seemed incongruous in the predominantly sport-touring line-up, but it provided BMW with credibility in the full-dress tourer market for the first time. It may have been extraordinarily heavy, but weight wasn't considered a handicap in this sector. BMW set out to build a better motorcycle than the GL1500 Gold Wing, and they succeeded. The K1200LT was lighter, had superior suspension, a considerably more efficient engine management system, and a higher level of equipment. Despite giving away 300cc, the engine was much more economical, and performance was comparable. The press enthused over the LT, and in the market where

The third generation of ABS, the BMW Integral ABS system, was first offered on the K1200LT from 2001. *BMW*

it was intended, the USA, it immediately jumped the R1200C cruiser to become the best-selling BMW motorcycle in 1999. In the USA, it was available in three equipment levels, the Standard, Icon, and Custom, and by the end of 2000 production numbered around 15,000 units.

The big news for the 2001 Model Year was the introduction of the third-generation ABS on the K1200LT. Known as BMW Integral ABS, and developed in conjunction with FTE Automotive in the Bavarian town of Ebern, this system was initially only available on the K1200LT, but was to be installed progressively on new models in the future. Even lighter than ABS II, weighing only 4.36kg (9.6lb) including sensor rings and wheel sensors, Integral ABS provided

many more functions than the earlier system. An electro-hydraulic brake servo for each wheel built up brake pressure more quickly and equal brake distribution was provided to both the front and rear wheel brakes through either the foot pedal or hand lever. The system provided faster ABS response, and the larger (320mm) front discs produced 20 per cent more stopping power. All the control components were located in one compact housing, the so-called pressure modulator. Also new for the K1200LT for 2001 was optional GPS navigation, the first time this was available for a motorcycle, the map screen being located on top of the dummy fuel tank with control from the handlebars. Like the K1200RS, cruise control was available for 2002.

New for 2003 was the K1200GT,
a grand tourer based on the
sporting K1200RS. *Ian Falloon*

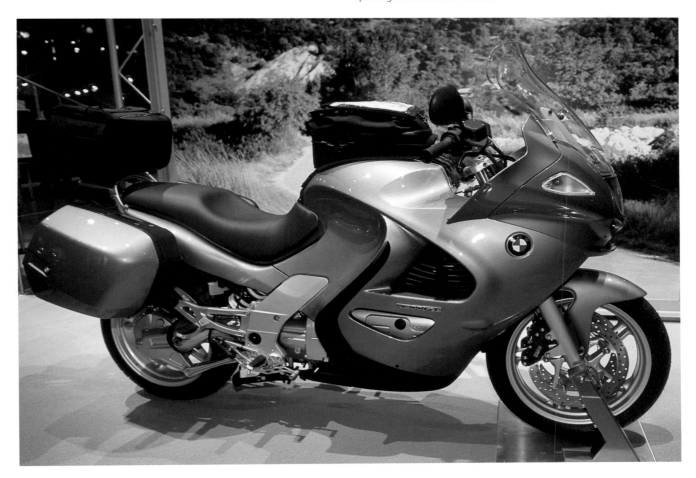

THE K1200GT

Supplementing the full-touring K1200LT, but providing a more touring emphasis than the K1200RS, was the K1200GT (Gran Turismo or Grand Touring) for 2003. Another example of the new BMW design philosophy of focusing on specific categories, the K1200GT was intended to plug the wide gap between the luxurious LT and the almost-Superbike sporting RS. This was the motorcycle for fans of high horsepower four-cylinder engines, but who required touring comfort. In many ways the K1200GT continued where the K100RT left off back in 1989. While the subsequent K100LT, K1100LT, and K1200LT expanded the luxury quotient, becoming increasingly opulent in the process, all this equipment sacrificed ultimate performance. The K1200GT still offered the essential touring equipment, but at 300kg (660lb) was not excessively heavy for this type of motorcycle, and was only marginally heavier than the R1150RT boxer.

The engine and drivetrain of the K1200GT was identical to the K1200RS, all K-models for 2003 receiving a modified oxygen sensor, catalyst coating, and engine management, to further reduce emissions. New for the K1200GT was the fairing, now wider at the bottom, and the electrically adjustable taller windshield. Complementing the taller fairing were higher handlebars, which provided a more upright riding position, and a new two-way height-adjustable seat. Standard equipment on the GT included partially integrated ABS, and a luggage rack and cases to match the bodywork. As with the K1200RS, the range of options extended to a heated, lower seat, and cruise control system.

Optional on the R1100RS was
an integrated full fairing that hid
most of the engine. This 1997
version included a standard
catalytic converter. *Australian
Motorcycle News*

7 THE NEW BOXER

Although the K-series of 1983 was designed to supplant, and eventually replace the boxer twins, this did not actually happen. Public demand for the R-series boxer was such that production not only continued alongside the K-series, but the boxer's share of BMW motorcycle production remained consistently between 40 and 50 per cent throughout the 1980s. It was obvious that the boxer was not about to die, and as early as 1984, plans were considered for a modern boxer. This 800cc boxer was initially envisaged to supplement the K-series, and was positioned in the mid-range market. By the time development was approved, market considerations dictated 1,000cc, and the basic layout of a longitudinal twin with the cylinders protruding into the airstream was a required design parameter. It was important to BMW that the boxer tradition was maintained, but the new engine needed to be more powerful, and narrower, to provide increased ground clearance with the higher lean angles possible with modern tyres.

Under the guidance of Stefan Pachernegg, a 'Boxer Workshop' was instigated. Increasing noise and emission regulations demanded four-valve cylinder heads, after testing with both three-valve and five-valve layouts showed them to be unsatisfactory. A conventional double overhead camshaft layout was also unsuitable because of the requirement to limit engine width. This led to the consideration of several valve train designs during 1985, and in April 1986 the first design model was presented to the management of BMW Motorrad. At this stage the valve layout was still undecided, and it was not until Georg Emmersberger produced a hybrid layout during 1986 that a solution was found. Emmersberger's design featured an intermediate shaft beneath the crankshaft, driving two roller chains to a single camshaft in each cylinder head. To minimise engine width, the camshafts were below the four valves, and were actuated by rockers through short pushrods. By April 1987, the prototype engine with Emmersberger's valve layout was complete, and the development was authorised under the designation R259. The project manager was Richard Kramhöller, and what was eventually a 1,100cc engine, became known as the A60 as 1,000cc and A61 as 1,100cc. From the outset, it was also agreed that the engine structure would be load-bearing, and even before the engine's valve train system

One of the most successful
series in the history of BMW
motorcycles has been the RT, and
undoubtedly one of the finest of
these is the R1150RT. *Ian Falloon*

The R259 project did not only include a new boxer engine, but the chassis with its Telelever front suspension was equally innovative. *BMW*

was finalised, work was progressing on a new front suspension system.

Seven development 1,000cc engines were prepared, the first running in February 1988. Although it immediately produced an impressive 84bhp, there were problems with valve control over 7,000rpm, the rockers not following the camshaft. The first step in solving this problem was to mount the camshaft, with the rockers, in a separate sub assembly within the cylinder head. Successive rocker designs culminated in chill-cast tappets operated by the camshaft, with steel ball heads on the other end of the short aluminium pushrods. This prototype engine was tested in May 1988, and presented to the management in October. The project received the go-ahead for further technical development, but not for the styling. This was to

involve the car stylists from sister companies BMW AG and BMW Technik.

It was not only the engine design that was innovative – even more so was the chassis, and, in particular, the suspension. BMW had a long tradition of following a path in motorcycle suspension design different from other manufacturers. From the first production hydraulic telescopic forks of 1935 to the Earles fork of 1955, they had shown they were not afraid to break with tradition. The Earles fork, with its excessive unsprung weight and high steering inertia, was no longer considered suitable, but BMW considered the telescopic fork overworked. It had to perform four functions; guiding the wheel, springing and damping, steering, and support under braking. For the new boxer, BMW decided to develop a new front suspension set-up, one combining the telescopic fork with support arms resting on the frame and serving as a separate, independent suspension.

First patented in Britain in the early 1970s by Laurence King and John Pizzey, with the support arms linked to the bottom of the telescopic fork, it was not until 1981 that the system was considered by BMW. The British engineer Hugh Nicol, sent BMW details of his Nicol Link Suspension System which combined the telescopic fork with a longitudinal arm linking the fork bridge to the frame. At around the same time, Phil Todd and Nigel Hill produced the Motodd Laverda with an identical suspension layout to Nicol's. When this received positive test reports in 1984 BMW's engineers decided to reconsider the design, concluding that it provided the ideal solution for front-wheel control. With the self-supporting engine block, it was possible to mount the control arm on the engine, directly transmitting the brake forces and providing an anti-dive effect without additional components. Further development led to a longitudinal A-arm connecting the telescopic fork and the engine, with ball-joints between the arm and the lower fork bridge, upper fork bridge and the steering head tube. A single shock absorber connected the A-arm to the frame.

THE R1100RS

The first model to feature the new A61 engine and A-arm fork was the flagship model, the sport-touring R1100RS. The initial designs for the R1100RS were produced during 1989, alongside the development of the engine and suspension. At this stage, the 1,000cc engine was still fuelled by carburettors, and incorporated an oil bath alternator running from the crankshaft on the front of the engine. This was subsequently moved on top of the engine, driven by a V-belt. Testing revealed noise and vibration problems, poor performance and crankcase cracking, and the engine therefore required considerable redesign. Dr Burkhard Göschel, the new Head of Motorcycle Development, decided to increase the capacity to 1,100cc, and concentrate exclusively on development with Motronic injection. The power remained at 90bhp, but with increased torque and with a maximum lean angle of 49° provided by the narrower engine this ensured the R1100RS would prove to be a competent sporting motorcycle.

By the second half of 1990, three developmental motorcycles were successfully completing endurance tests, and by early 1991 there were new crankshafts and a modified valve control system. The engines were now proving reliable, but the front suspension required further development. Lothar Scheungraber headed the running gear development team, and longer and thinner front sliding tubes, a shorter and less-rigid control arm, and less brake dive compensation, all contributed to the fine tuning of the front suspension. In 1992, this became known as the BMW Telelever suspension. The drive development team of Christoph Schausberger also modified the rear Paralever, with the suspension strut positioned in the middle of the round-section swingarm.

The R1100RS styling initially presented many problems for the team headed by Klaus-Volker Gevert and Markus Poschner. The fairing and fuel tank were required to provide ample protection, streamlining, ergonomics, and sufficient fuel capacity. However, the large alternator and front subframe made it difficult to incorporate a conventional fuel tank. The final solution involved testing in the BMW wind tunnel in South Africa, with the plastic, 23-litre fuel tank enveloping the sides of the motorcycle.

When it appeared in its final form at the Cologne Show at the end of 1992, the R259 represented a continuation of Max Friz's nearly 70-year-old boxer concept, while incorporating many new developments. Instead of the long-serving one-piece tunnel housing the crankcase that presented a number of manufacturing difficulties, there was now a pressure die-cast vertically split two-piece crankcase. This incorporated the oil sump and was necessarily strong as it formed a load-bearing member of the chassis. The four-valve cylinder head featured two 36mm inlet, and two 31mm exhaust valves, with a single, centrally positioned spark plug, and the cylinder bores were coated with Gilnisil, a nickel-silicon layer by the Italian manufacturer Giladoni.

Despite their larger diameter, the 99mm pistons provided a 10.7:1 compression ratio, and weighed a third less than those of the older boxer. While the con-rods were made of sintered and forged steel, these were more consistent in weight and featured the crack technology used on BMW cars. The big-end of the con-rod was intentionally fractured rather than sawn, and the advantages were the larger common surface when

The team responsible for the R259 project. From the left: Wolfgang Dürheimer, Klaus-Volker Gevert, Markus Poschner, Burkhard Göschel, Jürgen Kurzhals, Christoph Schausberger, Richard Kramhöller and Lothar Scheungraber. *BMW*

bolted together. The one-piece crankshaft provided a marginally shorter stroke than the earlier boxer (70.5mm), also using only two bearings. A centre bearing would have necessitated additional cylinder offset, but the rear bearing was a double journal type that didn't require thrust washers to set the end-play during assembly. With a displacement of 1,085cc, the R259 was the largest BMW boxer engine yet.

One of the biggest developments was the incorporation of two oil circulation systems, one for lubrication, and one for cooling. Two Eaton pumps were housed in a separate unit on the front of the intermediate shaft, the cooling pump at the front and the lubrication pump at the rear. The cooling oil pump was a volume type, designed to circulate as much oil as possible. With oil travelling to the cylinder heads,

and around the exhaust valves from the oil cooler to the sump, the engine became known as the 'Oil-head' in the USA (as opposed to the older 'Air-head'). There was also a sophisticated crankcase ventilation system, including an oil separator.

The intake system for the R1100RS reflected all the recent advances in technology with this development being coordinated by Jürgen Kurzhals. The air was drawn into a large air-box through carefully designed intakes and a snorkel beneath the fuel tank. One of the advantages of electronic fuel injection, especially for twin-cylinder motorcycles, is that large-diameter venturis can work acceptably over the entire rev range. The exhaust headers were 38mm in diameter, and with a Bosch Motronic MA 2.2 system, the R259 engine produced 90bhp at a moderate 7,250rpm.

With its high camshafts and short pushrods, the A61 engine provided nearly all the advantages of a double-overhead camshaft design, but in a narrower layout. *BMW*

Torque was an impressive 95Nm at 5,500rpm. As with the earlier Motronic MA 2.1, several sensors determined the engine's current operating conditions and compared this data with that of an EPROM in the CPU. A catalytic converter was also available, this incorporating an oxygen sensor upstream (rather than downstream like the K1100). Although the drivetrain, including single-plate dry clutch, K-series three-shaft five-speed gearbox, and Paralever double U-jointed driveshaft was similar to other BMW motorcycles, the electrical system was upgraded considerably. A three-phase 700-watt alternator ensured reliable starting, and allowed for a smaller and lighter 19Ah battery.

The engine may have continued the boxer tradition, but there was nothing traditional about the chassis of the R259. Not only was there a new front suspension design, the BMW Telelever, but there was no conventional frame as such. The engine unit supported both the front aluminium and rear steel subframes, along with the front Telelever and Paralever rear swingarm. The production form of the BMW Telelever

consisted of a 35mm fork, with 620mm tubes for increased overlap. The tubes were oval section with Teflon-coated bushings, but did not contain springs or dampers. The fork was thus only for wheel location and steering, with most of the braking forces absorbed by the A-arm, with springing and damping by the central, non-adjustable Showa shock absorber. The Telelever provided 120mm of front wheel travel, and allowed for excellent weight distribution, with 52.7 per cent of weight on the front wheel. The steering head angle was a steep, 24.1°, with only 104mm of trail. At the rear, the Paralever swingarm was 520mm long, the Showa shock absorber providing infinite damping and 135mm of travel. The wheels and brakes were identical to those of the K1 and K1100RS, twin 305 x 5mm floating cross-drilled discs on the front with four-piston Brembo calipers (32mm and 34mm pistons), and a single, 285 x 5mm disc with a dual, 38mm piston Brembo caliper on the rear. The second-generation ABS II was an option.

Although it was no lightweight, at 239kg (527lb),

the R1100RS was an eminent successor to the much-loved R100RS. The styling, while undoubtedly aerodynamically excellent was not to everyone's taste however. Not classically beautiful in the mould of the R90S or R100RS, to some observers it appeared like a large grasshopper, especially from the front. Another unloved feature was the rubber-mounted handlebar that followed the Telelever movement and provided a feeling of vagueness. Although the gearbox was often considered to be unrefined, there was still no denying the overall excellence and competence of the R1100RS. BMW had gambled considerably with the R259, and they had got it right. Here was a BMW motorcycle that appealed to both the traditional enthusiast and the modern rider, and the new boxer

The R1100RS was a sport-touring motorcycle par excellence, providing adequate power with superb handling. *Australian Motorcycle News*

soon overtook the K1100RS as the premier BMW sports-tourer. Despite its intensive development, the first year was not without teething problems. There were cases of oil leaks caused through poor crankcase ventilation, and some gearbox problems also. These were rectified the following year, with O-rings between the gears and their shafts, and tighter tolerances on the input shaft.

Standard for 1994 (in Germany and some selected markets) was the previously optional ergonomic kit that included an adjustable windscreen and handlebars, a variable seat height, and rider information display. The front Showa shock absorber now included more compression damping and a stiffer front spring. Many suspension and engine components were available in black. The ergonomic kit was standard worldwide for 1995, as was a catalytic converter for 1996. This year the front mudguard extended rearward with a component from the new R1100RT, and the inside of the fairing was no longer black, but the same colour as the full fairing.

From 1997, the front shock absorber received

RETURN OF THE SINGLE: THE F650

Looking for an entry-level machine to complement the R259, BMW decided to follow a different path to that pursued back in 1978 with the R45 and R65. The smaller twins were almost as expensive to produce as their larger brothers and profitability was marginal. A smaller displacement version of the R259 was thus discounted, and in the interests of developing a motorcycle as quickly as possible BMW considered a joint project with another manufacturer.

During 1990, BMW noticed with interest, the development of the Aprilia Pegaso 650, and project E169 was approved in June 1991. The design for a light, enduro-style motorcycle began immediately. Following the approval of Bavarian-based British designer Martin Longmore's styling proposal, a full-scale model was completed by January 1992. The first road-going prototype was completed by June that year, and this led to the signing of the three-way joint-venture contract with Aprilia and Rotax. Aprilia, already a major motorcycle manufacturer, producing over 50,000 motorcycles per annum, would assemble the new model at their plant at Noale in Northern Italy. The Austrian engine manufacturer Rotax, would supply engines similar to that used on the Pegaso. Development proceeded extremely quickly, with the first production versions rolling out of Noale in September 1993.

Various changes were made to the existing liquid-cooled Rotax Pegaso engine. The crankshaft bearings were plain instead of roller, and there was a four-valve, rather than five-valve, cylinder head. The valve sizes were 36mm and 31mm, and the double overhead camshaft set-up with bucket tappets was similar to the K1. A roller chain on the left drove the camshafts. Carburation was by two Mikuni 33mm CV carburettors, and there were two spark plugs per cylinder.

The bore and stroke were 100 x 83mm, giving a displacement of 652cc, and there was an engine-speed gear-driven balance shaft in front of the crankshaft. The power of the A80 engine was 48bhp at 6,500rpm, with a lower power, 34bhp version available for the two-tier European licence regulations. Lubrication was dry sump, with the oil tank in the upper part of the frame, and in a departure from usual BMW practice, the five-speed gearbox was incorporated in the crankcases. Perhaps the most significant departure though was the final drive, which was an O-ring chain. The E169 was the first BMW motorcycle not to feature shaft final drive.

Unlike the Aprilia Pegaso, BMW chose to include a steel rather than an aluminium frame. Single-loop, this consisted of sheet and square-section steel, with the engine serving as a semi-stressed member. The steering geometry of a 28° steering head angle and 116mm of trail, indicated an emphasis on road rather than off-road use. The swingarm was a twin-sided deltabox type, with a rising-rate linkage to a single Showa shock absorber and 165mm of rear wheel travel. Also from Showa came the 41mm telescopic fork (with 170mm of travel), the 300mm front and 240mm rear disc brakes were Brembo, and the 19in front and 17in rear wheels wire spoked. Weighing in at 189kg (417lb), the F650 was marketed as a 'Funduro' and soon set new standards for middleweight, dual-purpose machines. Its off-road capability may have been marginal, but as in the tradition of the classic R80 G/S, the F650 was one of the most competent handling tarmac motorcycles available. Not surprisingly, it was an immediate success, and by July 1994, 10,000 had been produced.

There were minimal developments to the F650 over the next few years, but standard for 1995 was a catalytic converter, and there was a centrestand (previously optional) for 1996. With the demise of the traditional air-cooled boxer during 1996, the F650 range was expanded for 1997. Not

Opposite: The A80 engine for the F650 was built by Bombardier-Rotax to BMW requirements. There was a four-valve cylinder head and twin Mikuni carburettors. *BMW*

Right: Although not a true off-road motorcycle, the F650 Funduro was an excellent back road machine. *Australian Motorcycle News*

Right: After a facelift for 1997, the final F650 left the Noale production line at the end of 1999. *Australian Motorcycle News*

only did the Funduro receive a facelift, the F650ST 'Strada' joined it as a pure road bike, primarily for city use. There was now a taller fairing and windshield, a clock, and lower seat for the Funduro, while the F650ST featured an 18in front wheel, a smaller fairing, and an even lower seat (785mm). This could be lowered further to 735mm with an optional suspension kit. The ST also had more street-orientated steering geometry, and a shorter wheelbase.

A special version of the F650 was launched early in 1999,

followed by a similar F650ST. These were provided with additional equipment, the ST receiving heated handlebars, higher windscreen, a rear top-box, and a catalytic converter. Production of the F650 and F650ST by Aprilia at Noale concluded at the end of 1999 following the termination of the assembly contract. With more than 64,000 units manufactured, production of the F650 and F650ST had exceeded all expectations, and a new assembly plant was then built at Berlin-Spandau.

adjustable rebound damping through a slotted screw, with hydraulic adjustment of the rear shock spring preload, and for 1998 there was a special 75th Anniversary edition. The final R1100RS of 2002 received larger front discs (320mm) and EVO brake calipers. By the time it was replaced by the R1150RS, the R1100RS was the longest-serving boxer in the line-up, but it never proved to be as popular as the GS and RT variants.

THE R1100GS & R850GS

The second new-generation boxer was the R1100GS, introduced for 1994. Given the popularity of the GS-series this was no surprise. From 1980 until mid-1993, sales of G/S and GS models numbered 62,000, making this series one of BMW's most successful. The R1100GS was designed to continue the tradition of the spirit of adventure that began with the first R80 G/S, although it was considerably larger (both in size and displacement), and more complicated. As with earlier GSs, the R1100GS was derived from its street relation, in this case the R1100RS, but unlike earlier versions, the engine was developed to improve off-road performance. Tuned to produce less power, but more torque, the A61 engine received different camshafts, modified exhaust manifolds with stainless steel mufflers, recalibrated Motronic injection, and a slight reduction in the compression ratio (to 10.3:1). This translated into 80bhp at 6,750rpm, with torque up slightly to 97Nm at 5,250rpm. A lower final drive ratio ensured more sprightly top gear roll-on performance than the R1100RS.

While retaining the three-piece frame layout of the R1100RS, there were a number of developments to provide dual-purpose performance. The front suspension travel was increased to 190mm, requiring a longer stroke shock absorber, and the A-arm and front subframe were modified, resulting in a steeper steering head angle (26°), a longer wheelbase (1,509mm/59.5in), and 115mm (4.5in) of trail. The different geometry of the A-arm also resulted in a stronger 90 per cent anti-dive ratio. The rear shock absorber incorporated a hydraulic spring preload adjuster, the longer travel unit providing 200mm of wheel travel.

Another important difference to the R1100RS was the handlebar mounts, and the extremely wide (820mm) handlebar now mounted rigidly on the fork bridge, and connected to the Telelever fixed-position tubes through two ball-joints. This isolated the handlebar from the tilt and swivel motion of the Telelever, that was evident on the R1100RS.

The wheels were the familiar cross-spoke style, a 2.5 x 19in on the front and a wide, 4.0 x 17in on the rear. Also familiar were the Brembo brakes, although there was a smaller, 276mm, disc on the rear. ABS II was also available as an option, but due to the desirability of being able to lock the wheel in gravel this could be deactivated manually. Completing the level of equipment was a 25-litre plastic fuel tank, small cockpit fairing with adjustable windscreen, and no less than four mudguards. At 243kg (535lb), the R1100GS was certainly no off-road motorcycle for the faint-hearted. The size, too, was intimidating for a smaller rider, and if the styling of the R1100RS hadn't met with universal acclaim, that of the R1100GS was almost contentious. There was certainly no mistaking the R1100GS for any other motorcycle. With its upper 'beak-like' front mudguard, channelling air into the oil cooler under the headlight, the R1100GS may not have been beautiful, but it was undeniably purposeful. Here was a motorcycle that successfully continued the GS tradition. Also more suited to the tarmac than the dirt, the R1100GS, with its wide handlebars, unlimited ground clearance, and supple suspension was arguably a more effective street bike than most repli-racers. Weird looks or not, the R1100GS was a hit from the outset, and proved more popular than the R1100RS. Of the 80 A61 engines produced every day at Spandau in early 1994, 60 were destined for the R1100GS. There were only detail changes to the R1100GS over the next few years. The lower front mudguard was moved forward by 192mm (7.5in) for 1995, a three-way catalytic converter was standard from 1996, and there was a special BMW 75th Anniversary version for 1998. This year also saw the debut of the similar R850GS, with the A62 engine of the R850R. While the R1100GS was undoubtedly effective in its intended function, continual problems with the chassis cracking at the gearbox frame mount led to several interim modifications until the R1150GS appeared during 1999. After the introduction of the six-speed R1150GS,

Below: From the beginning, the R1100GS was a success, providing outstanding all-round performance, particularly on the tarmac. *Australian Motorcycle News*

Right: Despite its size and weight, a strong rider could still manage to make the R1100GS work off-road. *Australian Motorcycle News*

the R850GS continued unchanged to use up the supply of earlier components.

THE R1100R & R850R

As the air-cooled boxer range limped into its final years of production, with minor variations on the existing theme, the range of new boxers was expanded. After 18 months, the new R259 boxer was proving outstandingly successful, and motorcycle production escalated during 1993 and 1994 to nearly 45,000, buoyed by the F650. The success of a new generation of naked bikes, such as Ducati's Monster and BMW's own R100R, prompted the release of the naked R1100R for 1995. There was also a similar, but smaller displacement version, the R850R, although this wasn't as popular.

Continuing a long BMW tradition of mix and match, the R1100R took the milder tuned, higher torque, engine of the R1100GS, placing it in the more sporting R1100RS chassis with R1100GS front and rear subframes. Without a fairing, this was termed a 'grass roots' motorcycle, and again, BMW had created

The R1100R Telelever combined features of both the RS and GS to provide unique characteristics. The wire-spoked wheels and screen were options. *Australian Motorcycle News*

a winner. The only difference between the powerplants of the R1100GS and R1100R was the location of the oil cooler, with the R1100R receiving two smaller oil coolers, mounted on either side above the cylinder head. The high-rise stainless steel exhaust system also came from the R1100GS.

New for the R850R was the 848cc A62 engine. While the lower end was the same as on the larger engine, there were 87.5mm pistons and smaller valves (32mm inlet and 27mm exhaust). The power was still a respectable 70bhp at 7,000rpm, and there was an electronically governed 34bhp version for graduated European driving licence regulations. Except for a lower final drive ratio on the R850R, both the R1100R and R850R shared the same running

gear. By combining features of both the R1100RS and R1100GS, BMW engineers managed to create a unique motorcycle. The front and rear subframes were from the R1100GS, as was the separately mounted handlebar, but this was a narrower, two-piece aluminium unit. As the R did not require such long travel suspension, the Telelever A-arm was from the RS, along with the front and rear shock absorbers. This combination of components resulted in slower steering geometry to both the R1100RS and R1100GS. The steering head angle was 27 degrees, with 127mm of trail, while the wheelbase of 1,487mm was midway between the two parent models.

As there was no fairing to provide any front down force, a non-adjustable hydraulic steering damper was

With its upright riding position
and high handlebars, the
R1100R was a surprisingly
sporting motorcycle. *Australian
Motorcycle News*

fitted between the slider bridge and the A-arm. Two
types of wheel were also available for the R: the 17in
and 18in cast-alloy wheels of the RS were standard
and traditional cross-spoked wheels (18in front) were
available as an option. The front Brembo brakes were
from the RS, while the rear brake came from the GS,
and ABS II was an option with either set of wheels.

New styling set the R apart from its two parent
models, the round headlight establishing a theme that
was accentuated by the 21-litre steel fuel tank. The
low and wide seat was adjustable for height, down
to a low 760mm, so even the shortest-legged rider
could feel comfortable. The standard equipment was
relatively basic though, with no tachometer or clock,
although these were available on the long list of

options. The only real disadvantage of the R was that
at 235kg (517lb) it was no lightweight. The lower-
powered R850R was even more disadvantaged by the
considerable weight, and proved so unpopular in some
export markets that it was soon discontinued.

The rather hefty weight aside, the R1100R was an
impressive motorcycle. If the R1100RS and R1100GS
had not managed to convert the diehard traditionalist
to the benefits of the modern boxer, the R1100R
certainly did. Although disconcertingly wide to those
used to older style narrow motorcycles, one ride on
the high torque, easy-handling R1100R was enough to
convince anyone that this was the best handling BMW
boxer yet, and possibly the perfect all-round street
motorcycle. Even the most cynical detractor had to

Opposite: The fourth variation of the new boxer was the R1100RT, and this proved an immediate success. *Australian Motorcycle News*

Below: The cockpit of the R1100RT was perfect for comfortable long-distance sport touring. *Australian Motorcycle News*

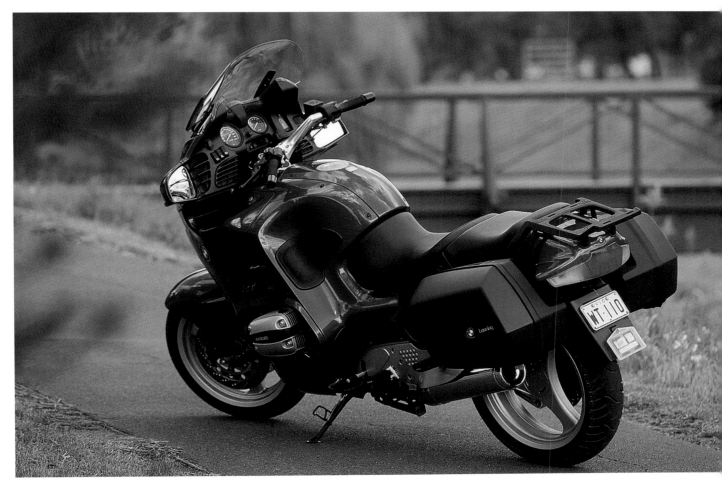

admit that electronic fuel injection was not only here to stay, but was vastly superior to any carburettor. The styling was still unusual, but the R1100R set a new standard for naked motorcycles.

Changes were minimal until the R1100R was replaced by the R1150R for 2001. For 1996, there was a standard catalytic converter, and the R1100R received a redesigned cockpit for 1997 that included a clock and a tachometer. There was a larger diameter chrome-plated headlight, now with an aluminium support. A special BMW 75th Anniversary edition was available for 1998, and all R models again received a moderate facelift. This year there was more chrome, and several powder-coated silver components. Throughout its six-year lifespan, the R remained very popular, with nearly 54,000 R850R and R1100R models produced. To use up the stock of R1100R and

R850R components after the introduction of the new R1150R, a R1100R/R850R classic 'Special Model' was produced. This ivory retro-style model featured wire-spoked wheels and chrome-plated cylinder head covers. While the R1100R Special Model ended production during 2001, the R850R version continued for 2002.

THE R1100RT

The continual expansion of the new boxer line-up saw the fourth incarnation, the R1100RT for 1996. Like the R100RS-series, the R100RT, after a shaky start back in 1978, garnered a strong following over its 18-year production run. With its similar brother, the R80RT, sales numbered over 57,000 by the time the final R100RT Classic rolled out of the Spandau factory. Yet, even though the old air-cooled models had proved popular, the new versions totally eclipsed them. Total sales of more than 53,000 for the R1100RT between 1996 and 2001 almost matched the air-cooled RT figures, and were vastly greater than the 28,000 odd for the R100RT alone.

There was a good reason why the new R1100RT was so popular. Carrying on from the R1100R by incorporating components from the R1100RS and R1100GS, the R1100RT provided a level of touring comfort and seamless power that made it almost comparable to BMW's own K1100LT, rather than the sometimes lumpy R100RT. Using the 90bhp R1100RS engine, but with a lower final drive ratio to compensate for the larger fairing, the R1100RT, like the R1100R, used the front subframe of the R1100GS, with the Telelever A-arm, rear subframe, and shock absorbers of the R1100RS. As on the GS, the rear shock absorber also included the remote hydraulic spring preload adjuster. The wide two-piece handlebars were separately mounted, and isolated from the Telelever tilt as on the R1100GS and R1100R. As the R1100RT used a combination of suspension components, the steering geometry was similar to the R1100R, with a steering head angle of 27.2°, 122mm of trail, and a 1,485mm wheelbase.

The 17in and 18in wheels and 305mm front brakes were also shared with the R1100RS, while the rear disc was the smaller (276mm) unit of the R1100GS. Antilock brakes were standard, and the level of protection offered by the thermoplastic and rubber full fairing was extremely high. Emanating from the styling direction of David Robb, the small integrated rectangular headlight and large rounded panels may have taken some getting used to, but the plump fairing was aerodynamically excellent and worked well. A drag coefficient of 0.494 CdA with a flat windscreen and panniers was testament to this.

There was a new two-piece front mudguard designed to improve stability and reduce front wheel lift, while the windshield was electrically adjustable for rake by 22°, and height by 155mm (6in). Completing the touring specification was a large, 26-litre fuel tank, rather ineffective vents to supply warm air from the oil cooler to the rider's hands, and a three-way height-adjustable seat. As expected from BMW, a company with so much experience in producing touring and sport-touring motorcycles, the level of standard and optional equipment was comprehensive. Standard was a luggage rack, and 33-litre panniers, while the options

included a cassette radio and a rear top-box.

Weighing in at 282kg (622lb), compared to the earlier R100RT, the R1100RT exuded an almost intimidating presence. Not only significantly heavier, the R1100RT was huge compared with the earlier incarnation. Yet, on the road, the R1100RT defied the sceptics and was a remarkable long distance touring motorcycle, and one that was surprisingly agile away from the autobahn or highway. Apart from a 75th Anniversary special edition in 1998, there were few changes to the R1100RT before it was replaced by the R1150RT in 2001. For the 2000 Model Year there was a choice of two optional windshields, one higher, and one higher and wider, and as it was so popular it was a natural candidate for the updated 1,130cc engine and new Integral ABS during 2001.

THE R1200C & R850C

To many enthusiasts, one of the more unlikely renditions of the new boxer appeared in September 1997, the R1200C cruiser. However, as motorcycle industry observers were well aware, a cruiser was inevitable, as this was the fastest growing market segment in the early 1990s. In the world's largest motorcycle market, the USA, cruiser sales were outstripping sportsbikes three to one, and by 1997 numbered 150,000 units. To expand, BMW also needed a foothold in this lucrative area, and early in 1994 the new director of BMW Motorrad, Dr Walter Hasselkus, and the board of directors sanctioned the development of a cruiser.

The traditional cruiser was a high-torque, large-capacity V-twin, and most other motorcycle manufacturers pursued this route. Not one for following others, BMW maintained their independent path, and it was quite a task to create an American-style cruiser out of the high-performance R1100RS and R1100RT. The first step was to enlarge the engine, with a 2mm bore increase to 101mm, and a longer stroke of 73mm. The displacement jumped to 1,170cc. Known as the A63, the compression ratio went down to 10:1, and as peak power was no longer a consideration, there were smaller valves (34mm and 29mm), and milder camshafts providing less valve lift. The throttle bodies were reduced by 15mm, to 35mm, and while the peak power was only 61bhp at 5,000rpm, the torque was 98Nm at a low 3,000rpm.

More significantly, the torque curve was flat in the important 2,500–4,500rpm range. Flywheel weight was increased, and the only real shortcoming of the larger engine was increased vibration. From the K1200RS came the smaller diameter (165mm) hydraulically actuated clutch, and the more compact transmission housing. The gearbox was also based on the design of the K1200RS, but with only five speeds. Also from the K1200RS came the third-generation Motronic MA 2.4 engine management system which provided an automatic choke and diagnostic facility, and a catalytic converter was fitted as standard.

The design of the chassis was quite different to the four previous versions of the new boxer. Whereas these were all a product of mix-and-match, the cruiser style demanded something unique. BMW was already committed to the Telelever front suspension, and while the frame and A-arm could be comfortably hidden by large fuel tanks and fairings on the other four-valve boxers, on the cruiser these would need to be integrated into the styling. Thus, there was a new aluminium front subframe, incorporating the dual oil coolers, and the longer longitudinal A-arm was of welded aluminium (instead of steel on the other boxers), and which was highly polished to accentuate the cruiser image.

The Telelever fork retained the usual, 35mm telescopic tubes, the long handlebars were separately mounted as on the GS, and the single front shock absorber provided 144mm of wheel travel. To suit the

Opposite: Like all BMWs, there was a wide range of options available for the R1200C, including screen and saddlebags. *Ian Falloon*

Above: The R1200C Independent for 2001 included a solo seat and cast aluminium wheels. *BMW*

expectations of a cruiser the steering geometry was much more extreme than on the other boxers, with a steering head angle of 29.5°, with only 86mm of trail. The wheelbase was a gigantic 1,650mm (65in).

Some of the wheelbase length was obtained through the 90mm longer swingarm. Rather than the usual Paralever set-up, this reverted to the earlier Monolever style, but with two universal joints like the Paralever, which was considered aesthetically difficult to incorporate in the cruiser image, but also, it did not allow enough room for the twin exhausts that were envisaged. Unlike earlier Monolevers, the single

shock absorber was mounted centrally on the cast arm, behind the front pivot. The swingarm did not pivot on the gearbox housing (allowing the use of the more compact K1200RS unit), but on the tubular steel rear subframe. The engine was still a stressed member, supporting the pivots of the A-arm, and front and rear subframes. Because there was no Paralever, rear wheel travel was limited to 100mm, and this, in combination with the longer swingarm, largely compensated for the negative effects of the shaft drive acting on the suspension. The original spring and rear shock absorber were very hard and from November 1998, a more comfortable unit was substituted.

Specific wire-spoked wheels were designed for the cruiser. Retaining the cross-spoke design that allowed the fitting of tubeless tyres, the front was a narrow, 2.50 x 18in and the rear a wider 4.00 x 15in wheel. The rims were chrome plated, while the front brakes came from the R1100GS and the rear brake from the

R1100RS. As was now usual, ABS was also available as an option.

Charged with the cruiser's styling, David Robb went for a lot of chrome and polishing. From the A-arm to the rocker covers and air intake shrouds, the R1200C was certainly distinctive, and the quality of materials and execution was extremely high. There were new handlebar switches, moisture-resistant leather handlebar grips and seat, and a 17-litre steel fuel tank. The rather extreme cruiser riding position, with its huge buckhorn handlebars, was non-adjustable, but a flatter, drag-style bar was an option. For 1999, there was an optional 20mm thicker comfort seat. Not everyone took to the R1200C's extravagant styling, but its supporters far outweighed its detractors. During 1998, it was the best-selling BMW motorcycle, and this success continued. By the summer of 2001, production numbered more than 30,000. A similar R850C was offered during 1998, identical to the R1200C apart from the smaller displacement A62 engine. However, like the R850R, this proved unpopular and was discontinued for 2002. The cruiser buyer wasn't budget conscious, and there was no substitute for capacity with this type of motorcycle.

Avantgarde versions of the R1200C and R850C supplemented the Classic cruiser for 2000. In contrast to the heavily chromed appearance of the R1200C, the Avantgarde featured a black enamel finish for the engine and drivetrain, and graphitane (graphite and magnesium) for a host of previously chromed components ranging from the fork tubes, the A-arm and front and rear frames. Also setting the Avantgarde apart was a set of lower touring handlebars. In an effort to widen the appeal of the cruiser further, BMW followed the lead of other cruiser manufacturers by offering a third incarnation, the Independent (or Phoenix in the USA), for 2001. This had a solo seat, oval mirrors, new wheels, an additional headlight, and a small speedster-type handlebar fairing, to impart a 'bad boy' image. The aluminium wheels were two-piece, with three-spoke inner hubs replacing the usual cross-spoke wheels, and were fastened together by titanium bolts.

There was the option of higher or lower handlebars, and even more chrome than on the Classic model. Chrome extended to the alternator cover, the air intakes for the oil coolers, and the brake and clutch reservoir covers. For 2003, the cast aluminium wheels were an option for the R1200C, and the Independent was available with a small passenger seat.

THE R1100S

Even as the sport-touring R1100RS was in the final stages of development, a more sporting boxer was envisaged. In 1993, a pure sports R1 engine with desmodromic valves was developed, but it was discontinued after a short test period. This 996cc boxer engine (98 x 66mm) featured a high-mounted crankshaft and two high water-cooled cylinders, with all the engine accessories underneath the engine. Each cylinder featured twin overhead camshafts, driven by four chains, with four desmodromically actuated valves set in a very shallow combustion chamber. There were vertical intakes above the cylinders incorporating a Bosch injector and throttle position sensor, while the exhausts exited straight downwards. Installed in an aluminium twin-spar chassis with a Telelever front suspension system, the projected 140bhp boxer was not produced. Water-cooled cylinders seemed incongruous to the boxer concept as envisaged by Max Friz. He put the air-cooled cylinders out in the air stream for maximum cooling, and while this layout still provided perfect primary and secondary balance, there were the disadvantages of engine width, particularly in a modern sportsbike. As BMW remained committed to the boxer layout for traditional reasons it seemed more logical to base the sporting boxer on the existing A60 engine.

One of David Robb's first projects upon joining the BMW motorcycle division was to produce a sporting concept boxer prototype. This was displayed at the Cologne Show at the end of 1994, and spawned a rebirth of the 'S', not seen on a boxer since the demise of the R100S in 1979. The 'S' designation for BMWs was traditionally reserved for higher performing sports versions, and was initiated with the R50S and R69S of the 1960s, culminating in the classic R90S and R100S.

In the manner of the earlier classic R90S, the R1100S would be the most powerful incarnation of the boxer yet, with sharper handling and styling to match. Although not as radical as Robb's prototype, the 'S' was to be a refined sportster rather than an out-and-out street racer. BMW's designers were well aware that the large shaft-drive boxer could not match the powerful and light four-cylinder Japanese race replicas, but set about creating a more focused performance boxer that would excel as a high speed, long-distance machine. The R1100S was also representative of a new design philosophy which was evident with the K1200LT luxury tourer. This saw the creation of more extreme motorcycles, positioned outside the traditional BMW sport-touring mould.

Central to the R1100S was a hot-rodded 1,085cc A61 engine. Forged pistons with a 2mm higher dome provided an increase in the compression ratio, to 11.3:1, and allowed the redline to climb to 8,400rpm (from 7,900rpm). A reshaped inlet tract, less restrictive plate-type air filter, and a two-into-one-into-two stainless-steel exhaust system with integrated catalytic converter, saw the power rise to 98bhp at 7,500rpm.

Featuring the highest horsepower version of the boxer engine and top-quality chassis components, the R1100S emulated earlier sporting boxers. *Cycle World*

The R1100S twin muffler set-up was almost Ducati 916-like, but the Paralever was traditional BMW. *Cycle World*

DAKAR RALLIES AND THE F650GS

After a 12-year hiatus, BMW was back in the Paris–Granada–Dakar Rally with an official entry of four F650-based machines in 1998. There was little joy this year however, and only one machine finished the event (in 35th place), but BMW was back in 1999. Gottfried Michels and team manager Richard Schalber prepared four F650RR rally machines, with perimeter-style chrome-molybdenum frames and a titanium rear subframe. With twin Mikuni flat-slide carburettors the power of the 700cc single was boosted to a claimed 75bhp. The 28-year-old French rider, Richard Sainct, switched from KTM, and narrowly won the Granada–Dakar Rally. His BMW was heavier, but faster than the equivalent KTM, continuing a tradition in this rally established by BMW with the R80 G/S in the 1980s. Sainct was back on a BMW for the 2000 Paris–Dakar–Cairo Rally, and this year the BMWs totally dominated the event. Not only did Sainct win by a massive margin of 32 minutes, but F650-mounted Spaniard Oscar Gallardo finished second. Frenchman Jean Brucy was fourth, also on an F650, completing a BMW whitewash in this prestigious and gruelling event. This was the final year for works BMW singles, except for the entry for Andrea Mayer who finished 30th in 2001, the first woman home.

The success in the Paris–Dakar Rally coincided with the decision to move production of the F650 to Berlin-Spandau. A new assembly line was created, and for the 2000 Model Year, there was a revised F650GS, along with a special Dakar version. As before, all the components were outsourced, the only parts actually manufactured in Berlin were the camshafts, and these were then shipped to Bombardier-Rotax in Gunskirchen, Austria for installation in the engines. Along with the camshafts, BMW redesigned the cylinder head, incorporating features from the Motorsports M3 car, with the throttle butterfly very close to the injectors of the new BMW (BMS) electronic engine management system. There was a higher, 11.5:1 compression ratio, and with a large stainless steel dual muffler exhaust system, the power was increased slightly over the F650, to 50bhp at 6,500rpm. Along with the digital engine management set-up, the F650GS was also the first single-cylinder motorcycle to feature a standard catalytic converter.

Also new was the rectangular steel bridge-type frame with a bolted-on steel lower section and rear subframe. The 41mm Showa fork (with fork brace) and rear shock absorber were

carried over from the F650, as were the 19in and 17in wheels, and Brembo brakes. A new type of ABS developed with Bosch was also available as an option. Weighing only 2.1kg (4.6lb), this more compact system was better suited for lighter motorcycles, and could be manually deactivated if required. Intended more for off-road use, the Dakar F650 came with a 21in front wheel, increased suspension travel (210mm front and rear), a higher (870mm) seat, and an F650RR windshield.

The styling of the F650GS was strongly influenced by the new R1150GS and F650RR. Underneath the re-styled plastic dummy tank hid the large air-box, and pressure-cast aluminium oil reservoir and coolant tank, with the 17.3-litre fuel tank located under the seat. Fuel filling was through an aircraft-type filler on the right. A wider range of options was also available for the F650GS, extending from a seat lowering kit, to heated handlebar grips, and an integrated luggage system. As it weighed a considerable 193kg (425.6lb), the F650GS was still more suited to the tarmac than the dirt, and even the 192kg (423lb) Dakar was a handful in difficult off-road situations. This did not detract from their popularity, with production of the F650GS and Dakar exceeding 30,000 units by the summer of 2001. The Dakar version accounted for more than 6,000 units and double shifts were required to meet demand. This year, the F650GS was the best-selling BMW motorcycle worldwide. For 2002, the Dakar was also available with optional ABS. The single cylinder engine included a dual ignition and new BMS-CII engine management system for 2004. Power and torque were unchanged, but fuel economy improved. F650GS styling updates included a new front fender, fairing, headlight, windshield and instruments.

From the year 2000 the F650 was built in Berlin, and an F650GS was created to celebrate the F650 victories in the Dakar rallies of 1999 and 2000. *Australian Motorcycle News*

The exhaust system, which included much larger (45mm) headers and two Ducati 916-style mufflers under the seat, was said to be responsible for 70 per cent of the claimed power. Forged con-rods provided security at the higher revs, and the oil capacity was increased by 350cc to improve cooling. This was achieved through modified crankcases which soon found their way to other four-valve boxers. There was the new Bosch Motronic MA 2.4 injection system, a lighter (by 0.97kg) 600-watt alternator and 14Ah battery, while magnesium valve covers shaved a few additional grammes off the weight of the engine. This more powerful engine was then mated to the smaller clutch and six-speed gearbox of the K1200RS, and installed in a new four-piece frame. The front section included a lightened Telelever, the steel A-arm bolting to a die-cast aluminium frame. A welded aluminium main frame supported the swingarm pivot and top rear shock absorber mount, and there was a tubular steel rear subframe to support the seat and luggage rack.

For the 'S', the Telelever was developed further. The fork sliders were now machined rather than cast, imparting almost an upside-down fork look, but also contributing to the loss of about a kilogram of unsprung weight from the Telelever set-up. The front suspension unit was a single-sleeve gas-pressure damper, providing 110mm of spring travel. Rebound damping was adjustable by an innovative wheel between the fuel tank and upper fork bridge, enabling easy adjustment while on the move. There was the usual Paralever rear swingarm, the single shock absorber featuring a 40-position hydraulically adjustable spring preload. The new frame and suspension provided different steering geometry to the other five four-valve boxers, with a rake of 25°, 100mm of trail, and a wheelbase of 1,478mm (58in).

Another carryover from the K1200RS was the beautiful, finely cast five-spoke wheels and front brakes with discs mounting directly on the wheel spokes. Not only were the wheels an aesthetic triumph, they were also technically superior to those on the R1100RS. A significant reduction in unsprung weight was achieved with the front wheel weight down to 5.59kg (from 6.05kg) and rear wheel weight down from 6.47kg to 6.13kg.

The front master cylinder diameter was reduced to 16mm (from 20mm on the R1100RS) to decrease braking effort, and the rear disc was the smaller, 276mm unit of the R1100R and R1100GS. There was even a carbon-fibre front mudguard, another first for BMW. A result of all this attention to weight saving saw the R1100S tipping the scales at 229kg (505lb), still no lightweight, but not too shabby when put into the context of the earlier 220kg (485lb) R100S that was a lot less powerful, but which was still a formidable performer.

Designer David Robb intentionally set out to provide an environment where the rider felt part of the motorcycle, and not perched on top as with many sports bikes. An 18-litre, almost sculpted, aluminium fuel tank lay underneath the flowing plastic bodywork that virtually enveloped the rider. The four-piece fairing was developed in the wind tunnel and incorporated turn signals and hand protectors, and featured an attractive, and distinctive, automotive-type of ellipsoidal dual headlight incorporating an asymmetrical large, low beam (H7) and a smaller high beam (H1). The clip-on handlebars bolted directly to the vertical tube beneath the fork bridge and accentuated a sport-touring riding position, rather than aggressive sport. On the road, the R1100S was undoubtedly the sharpest steering and most sure-footed boxer yet.

Once underway there was no evidence of the weight and here was a boxer that could use all of its 50° lean angle (up from 49° on the R1100RS). If required, there were also options, including higher-comfort handlebars and a taller windscreen, ABS, a wider, 5.50 x 17in rear wheel, steering damper, true rear-set footpegs, black engine covers, and a chin spoiler. For those requiring a sportier orientation, the sports package comprised a handlebar damper and longer shock absorbers which raised the motorcycle by 18mm at the front and 20mm at the rear. The maximum angle of lean increased to 52°, and just to show how efficient they were, BMW included a longer side-stand in the kit. And as always, there was the option of BMW's hard luggage, which was still the best available. The R1100S was surely the finest sport-touring motorcycle obtainable, especially if the required emphasis was on sport rather than touring. Many buyers thought so, and production had amounted to more than 20,000 by Summer 2001.

THE R1150GS
The R1100GS received what was termed 'mid-life freshening' during 1999. Despite a tarnished

Opposite: Carrying on from
the successful R1100GS was
the considerably revised
R1150GS for 1999. *Australian
Motorcycle News*

durability image, sales of the four-valve GS models over their six-year lifespan numbered over 45,000. It made sense to incorporate some of the developments of both the R1200C and R1100S in a replacement version. To provide an even flatter torque curve, the engine displacement was increased to 1,130cc with the 101mm cylinders of the R1200C cruiser (without polished fins), but with higher compression (10.3:1) pistons. From the R1100S came the cylinder heads, lighter magnesium valve covers, and crankshaft, but there was a new camshaft designed to further optimise the torque curve. Like the R1100S, a larger diameter exhaust system (45mm) was responsible for much of the increase in power to 85bhp at 6,740rpm. The exhaust system was also restyled to emulate older boxers, the twin chrome-plated stainless-steel header pipes arcing under the cylinders. They were then joined by a cross pipe, a double tube feeding into the pre-muffler, and a redesigned muffler. Other features shared with the newer models were the Motronic MA 2.4 engine management system, and a standard, fully controlled three-way catalytic converter. Cooling was also uprated through the larger oil cooler of the R1100RT, and like the R1100S, a lighter, 600-watt alternator and small, 14Ah battery were standard (although the 700-watt and 19Ah battery were standard if heated handlebars were specified).

Also from the R1100S came the smaller diameter (165mm) hydraulic clutch and six-speed transmission. Although the lower five ratios were identical, the R1150GS featured a higher sixth gear, designed as an overdrive for more comfortable touring. The six-speed gearbox was certainly an improvement over the sometimes-recalcitrant five-speed unit, but it still wasn't perfect and would be replaced by a revised transmission for 2003.

A significant improvement over the R1100GS was the revised three-piece frame set-up, a development of the existing R1100RS and R1100GS type, rather than the R1100S's twin-spar top frame. Although the engine and transmission housing were still load-bearing components connected directly to the front and rear subframes, the rear set-up was revised considerably. The longer gearbox housing was strengthened, and an outboard aluminium casting, which supported the rear subframe, reinforced the swingarm pivot. Not only did these two outboard plates provide additional rigidity and footpeg supports, but they were designed to finally overcome the problems of rear frame failure in arduous conditions. Because the six-speed transmission case was longer than that of the previous five-speed unit, the Paralever swingarm was shortened from 520mm to 506mm to maintain the same wheelbase as before.

The front Telelever was also modified, incorporating the lighter-assembled A-arm of the R1100S rather than the previous cast type, and machined fork sliders. These also imparted an upside-down fork look, and while this was only an illusion, it did provide the R1150GS with a more conventional front-end appearance. However, both the A-arm and single shock absorber were still strongly evident, with both the front and rear shock absorbers carried over from the previous R1100GS. Also shared with the earlier model were the cross-spoked wheels (with a modified hub at the rear), and Brembo brakes. The front brake pads were now sintered metal rather than organic.

David Robb set out to create a distinctly different machine from the R1100GS, and while the dimensions were similar, the two designs could not be mistaken. While retaining two front mudguards, the lower front guard was now inconspicuous black, matched by a redesigned back wheel cover. Although still beak-like, the front upper mudguard served as an oil-cooler air scoop and wind deflector. It was also now integrated into the 22.1-litre fuel tank. Quite different to the previous rectangular headlight were the two asymmetrical ellipsoidal headlights, similar to those of the R1100S. These also featured a large H7 bulb for low beam and a smaller, free-form H1 bulb for high beam. Completing the new look was a three-position windshield that could be removed if required. The separated handlebars incorporated the new generation switches, and vibration-isolating rubber handgrips, and were even wider than before at 903mm. These provided incredible leverage, belying the considerable 249kg (549lb) weight. Although the seat could be adjusted to two positions (840mm or 860mm), the R1150GS was still an intimidating machine for a shorter rider. This was even more pronounced if taken off road, where the GS was a remarkably good performer but it took a strong person to control if it fell over. Less of a problem on the tarmac, and just like the earlier GSs, the R1150GS could surprise many a sportsbike on a twisty road. The R1150GS continued the success of earlier GSs, with more than 32,000 produced by the summer of 2001. For 2003, the

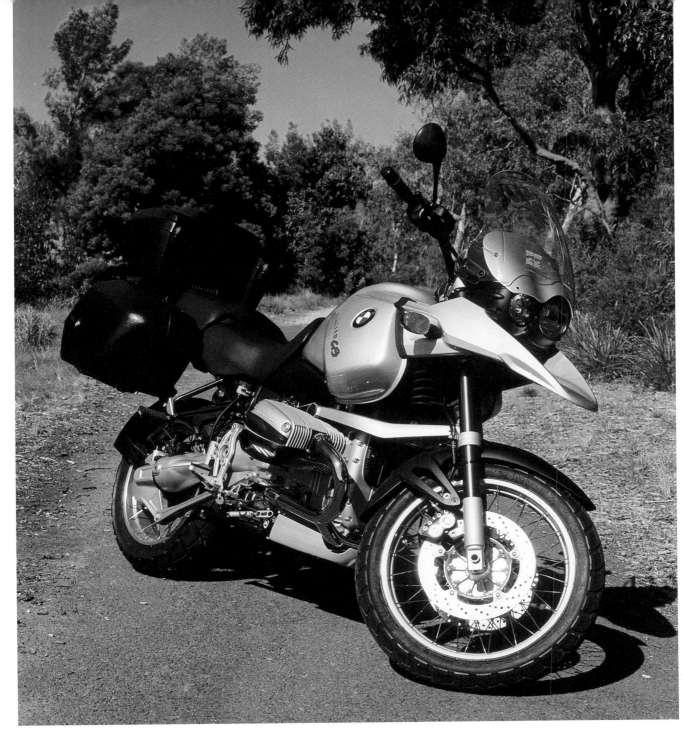

R1150GS received the updated six-speed gearbox of the R1200CL, and optional, partial Integral ABS that could be deactivated if required.

Coinciding with the release of the R1150GS, two works GS/RRs were prepared to run alongside the F650RRs in the 2000 Paris–Dakar–Cairo Rally. As with the rally-winning GSs of the 1980s, these were prepared by HPN. One displaced 900cc, and weighed 190kg, while the other was a full 1,100cc. Running on carburettors rather than fuel injection (due to the dubious fuel in Africa), and with enough power to top nearly 200km/h (125mph), conventional White

Power upside-down telescopic forks were fitted at the front instead of Telelevers. At the rear was a special Paralever swingarm with a PDS shock. British rider John Deacon rode the '1100', crashing out, while *Cycle World* staffer, Jimmy Lewis, took the R900RR into third position in the gruelling rally, his boxer running the entire race without an engine strip down.

Lewis was back on the works R900RR for the UAE Desert Challenge, the Dubai Rally, which is a prelude to the 2001 Paris–Dakar Rally. Although largely unchanged, a more aerodynamic fairing, lower fuel tanks for improved weight distribution, and new

Created as the ultimate city transport, the C1, with its integral roll cage, was designed to provide motorcycle manoeuvrability with automotive safety. In Germany it could be operated without a motorcycle helmet. *BMW*

Opposite top: Almost everything was new on the R1150R, while the chassis was similar to that of the R1150GS. *BMW*

Opposite bottom: The R1150R was a successful development of the R1100R, with more purposeful styling. *BMW*

THE C1

A design study initiated in 1989 called for a vehicle suitable to overcome the severe traffic congestion in the central zones of large cities. This led to BMW producing the prototype C1, providing safety comparable to a car, but with motorcycle mobility. A joint development by BMW Technik and BMW Motorrad, the C1 design study was first presented at the Cologne Show at the end of 1992. With its integral roll cage, safety-cell, and seatbelt, BMW envisaged the C1 to be ridden without a helmet and on a car driving licence. The C1 remained a fantasy until the end of 1997 when BMW announced it would implement development as the German authorities had agreed to its use without a helmet. As a further incentive, drivers who obtained a car licence in Germany before April 1980 could operate the C1 without a motorcycle licence, and there were exemptions from road tax.

The C1 finally materialised for the 2000 Model Year, with a liquid-cooled double-overhead camshaft four-valve single-cylinder four-stroke engine producing 15bhp. For 2001, there was also the 176cc C1 200, producing 18bhp. Compared with many city-type vehicles, the C1 boasted a very high specification. There was Telelever front suspension, Brembo disc brakes front and rear, and optional Bosch ABS. The C1 was also very manoeuvrable with its small, 13in and 12in wheels, and was easy to ride having a centrifugal clutch, continuously variable transmission and belt final drive. The weight was 185kg (408lb), and the C1 200 was capable of around 120km/h (75mph). The engine could not be started without the rider strapped into the safety cell, but in the UK, most of the C1's appeal was negated through the requirement to wear a crash helmet.

suspension made the R900RR a rally winner. Lewis provided the boxer with its first race victory since the days of Gaston Rahier and Hubert Auriol. Expecting to repeat this in the Paris–Dakar Rally, the event turned out to be slower and more tortuous than expected. Spaniard Juan Roma was well placed until he crashed, and John Deacon managed sixth place, winning the twins class. Jimmy Lewis crashed, breaking a collarbone, but somehow managed to finish the rally in seventh.

THE R1150R & R850R

In response to the backlash against repli-racers, nicknamed 'yoghurt-cups' in Germany because of their extreme multi-coloured plastic bodywork, David Robb restyled the naked R1150R to emphasise its elemental nature. The 1,130cc 85bhp engine came directly from the R1150GS, including the Motronic MA 2.4 electronic engine management and magnesium valve covers with R1100S cylinder heads and crankshaft being used. Also from the R1150GS came the six-speed gearbox, with the lower sixth gear ratio of the R1100S. The stainless-steel exhaust, with catalytic converter, was also similar to the R1150GS. Compared with the previous R1100R, the final-drive ratio was higher, to provide more relaxed high speed cruising, and the twin oil-coolers were now integrated into ducts at the side of the fuel tank.

The chassis of the R1150R was continued from the R1100R in that it was also an amalgam of components from the R1100RS and R1150GS. The basic frame layout was that of the R1150GS, with the Paralever swingarm supported by two additional aluminium plates that also served as footpeg mounts. To retain the same wheelbase and steering geometry as the successful R1100R, the front steel A-arm was based on the street R1100RS, but built out of steel tubing to enhance aesthetics. The Telelever fork tubes were not machined to imitate conventional upside-down forks and the Paralever swingarm was shortened by 14mm to compensate for the longer transmission housing. Although the spring travel on both the front and rear shock absorbers remained unchanged, the units were a new type. The front shock incorporated a single sleeve damper, and through an adjustment bolt on the A-arm, infinite adjustment of rebound damping was available. The rear shock absorber also provided hydraulic spring preload adjustment, while both shocks featured linear compression damping (rather than progressive as on

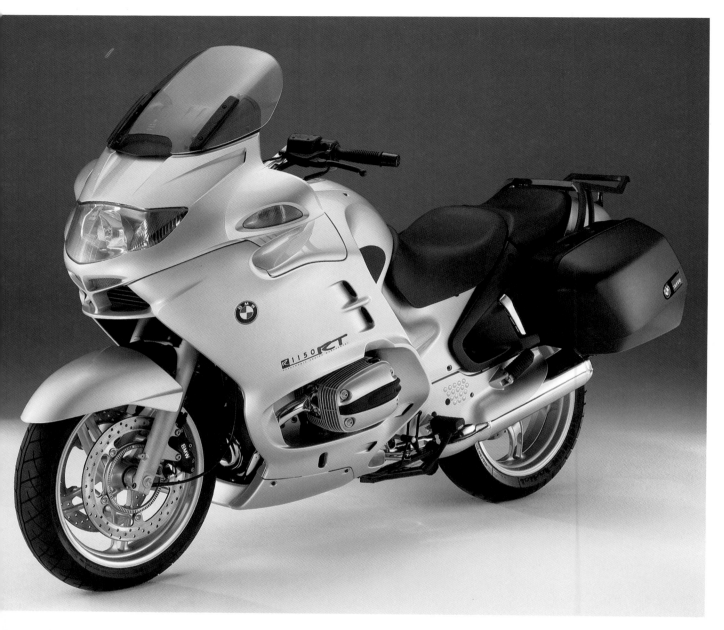

the R1100R). Reflecting the trend towards wider, more sporting tyres, only cast, 17in aluminium wheels were offered on the R1150R. These were the five-spoke type from the R1100S, the rear wheel growing to 5.00 x 17in, allowing for a 170/60ZR17 rear tyre.

Complementing the new wheels were larger EVO front brakes. With the disc rotor size up to 320mm, and upgraded Brembo-Tokico four-piston calipers, not only was brake power increased, but the lever pressure was claimed to be 15 per cent less than before. Unsprung weight was reduced by 10 per cent, and the new, sintered brake pad life was extended by 50 per cent. It was also possible to change the brake pads in situ, without dismantling the caliper as was required previously. The rear brake was identical to that of the

R1100R, and ABS was available as an option. This was the new Integral ABS system as first specified on the K1200LT, but was a 'partial' variant with the foot pedal operating only the rear caliper, while the linked front lever worked all three discs. This partially integrated system was designed for more sporting applications The reduction in unsprung weight from the wheels and brakes negated the necessity for the R1100R's steering damper.

Compared with the R1100R, the styling of the R1150R was fresher, and quite different. Apart from the round headlight and the instrument layout, everything else was new. This included the radical front mudguard (although the rear part came from the R1100RS), and the larger, 20.4-litre fuel tank. The seat

Opposite: With a more powerful engine, and updated wheels and brakes, the R1150RT was an even more accomplished touring motorcycle than its predecessor. *BMW*

Below: The R1150RS looked very similar to the first R1100RS of nearly a decade earlier, but benefited from developments to the engine, transmission, wheels, and brakes. *BMW*

Bottom: With aggressive "Streetfighter" styling, the R1150R Rockster was aimed at a younger, more extrovert rider. BMW Group Press

height was 800mm, but a lower, 770mm seat was an option. The entire riding position was lower, further enhanced by the wider and lower handlebar. The only impediment to unsurpassed sportsbike performance was the weight of 238kg (525lb). However, the R1150R continued to provide excellent all-round performance, and remained one of the most appealing naked bikes available.

There were only minimal developments made over the next few years. The new, six-speed gearbox was fitted from 2003, along with braided steel brake lines. The R850R also made a return this year; identical to the R1150R but for the 70bhp or 34bhp 848cc engine. The six-speed transmission featured a lower sixth gear.

The R1150R also spawned a concept Roadster Boxer, designed by David Robb's Motorcycle Design Team, which was displayed at the Munich Intermot towards the end of 2002. Reflecting a trend towards

The single-sided swingarm with belt final drive was a unique feature of the F650CS. *BMW*

THE F650CS

Continuing a tradition which proved they were not afraid to redefine existing concepts, BMW released the astounding F650CS (City Sport) in 2002, replacing the mundane F650ST. Unlike the F650ST that was very similar to the F650 Funduro, the F650CS was a distinctive creation. Intended primarily for city riding, the F650CS also incorporated unique solutions to the problems of storage on this type of motorcycle. The BMW-developed Rotax engine and five-speed gearbox were from the F650GS, but because of air-box and exhaust modifications, the power of 50bhp was at a higher 6,800rpm, with a slight increase in torque to 62Nm at 5,500rpm (up from 60Nm at 6,000rpm). There was a new exhaust system, with the catalytic converter and oxygen sensor integrated into the silencer. There was no need for a pre-silencer which allowed the designers more freedom in styling the muffler so as to coordinate it better with the rest of the motorcycle.

There was also a larger cross-section rectangular steel frame, which reverted to include the engine oil reservoir, as on the first F650. The two upper arms of the bridge-type frame were connected to one another at their lower end, holding 2.5 litres of oil. This was done to provide an integrated storage compartment in the central fairing and dummy tank above the air-box, as the 15-litre fuel tank remained under the seat as on the F650GS. Featuring a translucent fastening rail on both sides, this compartment could house a special waterproof, 12-litre soft bag, plastic hard case, helmet, or audio system with two integrated, weatherproof loudspeakers.

Another new feature was the aluminium single-sided swingarm with toothed-belt final drive, continuing a path of innovative wheel guidance systems. The toothed-belt-drive was particularly suitable for street motorcycles, as it required no lubrication, and boasted superior durability. The toothed drive belt was 26mm wide, with an 11mm partition. Like the F650GS, the F650CS had a central rear shock absorber, with a rising rate linkage, but with less (120mm) spring

Accessory soft bags, and the provision for storage in the dummy fuel tank, provided the F650CS with a new dimension in practicality. *BMW*

travel. To provide better street operation, the Showa fork also provided shorter spring travel of 125mm. Completing the chassis components were new, 17in three-spoke cast-aluminium wheels with a 'curved' design from the hub to the rim to accommodate the brake and toothed-belt sprocket. From the F650GS came the 300mm single front disc with twin-piston floating caliper, while the rear brake was a single, 240mm with a single-piston floating caliper. ABS was optional, and was selected by more than half of all purchasers.

Completing this radical design concept was styling that included a greyish-blue tinted, clear-view windshield, a translucent windshield support, and dual ellipsoid headlights. A standard rear luggage rack incorporated aluminium grab handles and accommodated an accessory soft bag that could

connect to another over the passenger seat, creating 62 litres of storage. And if all that wasn't enough, the range of options allowed customers to choose from three base colours, two fairing inset colours, and two seat colours, for ultimate personalisation. Further options extended to a lower (750mm) seat, GRP engine spoiler, and an on-board computer.

Although low and narrow, making it a perfect city motorcycle, out of the city environment the F650CS was limited by its moderate power and 189kg (417lb) weight. Stability was ensured through the long, 1,493mm (58.7in) wheelbase, but there was no denying the practicality of the well-thought-out luggage and low-maintenance belt drive. The riding position, accentuated by a low seat and wide handlebars, emulated that of a dirtbike in that the rider sat 'in' the bike rather than 'on' it. But in the city, where it was intended to be used, the F650CS provided all the advantages of both a motorcycle and a scooter. Scooter manoeuvrability, with motorcycle performance. The F650CS continued until 2004, updates including a dual ignition engine and a new BMS-CII engine management system.

Opposite: The R1150GS
Adventure provided the
ultimate platform for any
serious motorcycling in remote
areas. *BMW*

more sporting and aggressive naked bikes and aimed at the younger rider, this incorporated some components from the R1100S, like the Telelever fork legs and wider rear wheel, plus R1150GS headlights. This concept roadster went into production in March 2003 as the R1150R Rockster. With aggressive 'Streetfighter' styling, the Rockster was aimed at a younger, more extrovert rider. One of the Rockster's technological innovations were new dual spark cylinder heads, providing more efficient combustion and lower emissions, these eventually being phased in across the boxer range during 2003. Most Rockster components were shared with the R1150R, but the headlights came from the R1150GS, with the Telelever and wider rear wheel from the R1100S. For the 2003 model year, the R850R also made a return, now with a six-speed transmission and R1150R styling.

THE R1150RT

Alongside the R1150R for 2001 was an updated R1150RT. As the R1100RT was one of the most popular models in the range, it was logical to incorporate updates to this model ahead of the long-lived, but less popular R1100RS. For the R1150RT the engine was also increased in size, to 1,130cc, using the R1150GS cylinders, but with higher compression, 11.3:1 pistons. Also using the Motronic MA 2.4 engine management system, the power increased to 95bhp at 7,250rpm, with torque up to 100Nm at 5,500rpm. More than 90Nm was available between 3,000rpm and 6,500rpm, providing a wide powerband. The power was transmitted through the smaller hydraulic clutch and six-speed gearbox of the other '1150' models, with sixth gear an overdrive, like on the R1150GS.

The chassis and suspension geometry were similar to the R1100RT. The steering head angle was an almost identical 27.1°, with the same 122mm of trail. The shock absorbers were also unchanged, providing identical travel, and the rear spring load featured an hydraulic adjuster. The longer, six-speed gearbox housing required a modified Paralever support, and a reduction in swingarm length from 520mm to 506mm to maintain the 1,485mm wheelbase. As with the R1150R, there were new supports for the rear shock absorber and redesigned footrest plates. One of the most significant developments was to incorporate the lighter and more modern-looking 17in wheels

of the R1100S and R1150R. While the front wheel dimensions were unchanged, the rear wheel was a much more suitable 5.00 x 17in, allowing for the use of the latest generation of tyres.

On the front wheel was the new EVO brake, with the rear wheel featuring the same brake as on the R1100RT. Standard on the R1150RT was the Integral ABS braking system, but unlike the R1150R, this was the fully integrated version as fitted to the K1200LT, and more suitable for a tourer: the handbrake and footbrake levers both acted simultaneously on the front and rear wheel brakes. There was no longer any pulsing through the brake lever as on the earlier ABS II, but the system came under some criticism as it was tailored more for inexperienced riders rather than the seasoned traditional BMW pilot.

Completing the upgrades was a facelift, the new styling effectively silencing critics of the rotund R1100RT. Two fog lamps were integrated at the sides of the two tandem headlights, with the headlight adjustable for height by a hand wheel in the cockpit. The upper part of the fairing was redesigned, along with the front mudguard, but the windshield had the same dimensions as before. This was also adjustable electrically through 22°, and 155mm via a switch on the left handlebar controls. The fairing included a warm airflow duct, air flowing from behind the oil-cooler to the cockpit. Holding 25.2 litres, the plastic fuel tank provided an ample cruising range. Other improvements extended to the seat, the two-piece, three-way height-adjustable seat offering improved comfort, particularly for the rider. The result of these developments widened the appeal of the RT even further. Offering almost as many luxury features and options as the full touring K1200LT, the R1150RT provided almost sport-touring capability when it was compared to its 100kg (220lb) heavier brother. Here was a touring motorcycle that worked perfectly anywhere, no matter what the road or the weather, and 11,000 buyers thought the R1150RT was the perfect touring motorcycle in its first full year of production.

THE R1150RS

Although the least popular model in the new boxer line-up, the R1100RS always maintained a loyal following from those interested in carving miles and apexes. Less bulky than the RT, but not as extreme as the 'S', the 'RS' still filled a niche so it was inevitable that it too would share in the developments of the other 1,100cc boxers. For 2002, the R1150RS replaced the long-serving R1100RS. The 95bhp engine was identical to that of the R1150RT, as was the six-speed gearbox with overdrive sixth gear, and the catalytic converter. The clutch used was also the smaller hydraulic unit.

The chassis and steering geometry were unchanged, with identical shock absorber travel, although the Telelever telescopic tubes were from the R1150RT. The rear shock absorber and shorter swingarm were also from the R1150RT, but the rear swingarm pivot points were altered to suit the different characteristics required for the 'RS'. The footrests came from the R1150R. The 17in five-spoke wheels were new, now being shared with all the street models except the cruiser. The front EVO brake was also a new design. Unlike the R1150RT, the Integral ABS was an option, and it was the more sporting orientated partial set-up that was also featured on the R1150R.

Visually the R1150RS was akin to the R1100RS. The fairing and rectangular headlight were similar, but the windshield was 80mm higher and 60mm wider, increasing the area by 30 per cent. As in the past, the windshield was easily adjustable for inclination. The previously optional full fairing, which continued underneath the cylinders and enclosing the engine, was now standard. Other new features were the handlebar controls, and the front white direction indicator lights, while the wide range of options extending from luggage to chrome-plated cylinder protection covers remained as before. Carried over from the R1100RS were the rubber-mounted handlebars which still conveyed a feeling of imprecision. Considering that all the other new boxers had separately mounted handlebars, this seemed incongruous, and detracted from its ultimate sporting ability. Another feature of the R1150RS was the 285mm rear disc brake, as used on the R1100RS, while most other R-series models used a 276mm disc. Compared to the updates on the 'GS,' 'R,' and 'RT,' the R1150RS was less intensive, and possibly an interim design. Even before its release, rumours abounded of a new motor, and a further restyling.

THE R1150GS ADVENTURE

Expanding the GS line-up was the R1150GS Adventure for 2002. Designed as the ultimate go-anywhere motorcycle, this was either the perfect desert motorcycle, or one for the ultimate Walter Mitty outback dreamer. Whatever the intended use,

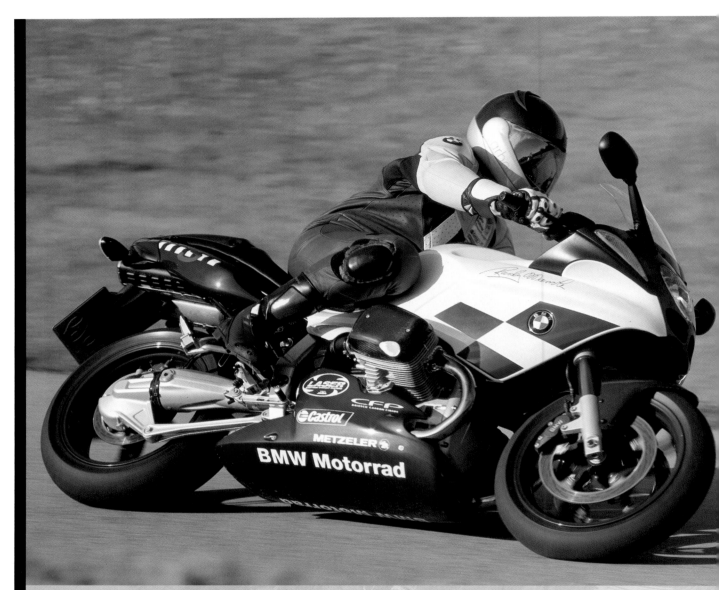

THE BOXER CUP AND BOXER CUP REPLICA

Following a tradition of celebrity boxer support races for the Daytona 200 during the mid-1990s, the French and Belgian BMW distributors inaugurated the Boxer Cup in 1999. As support races for the Motorcycle World Championship, by 2001, the Boxer Cup series for R1100S motorcycles grew to include seven events. Few modifications were allowed, and the machines were essentially stock, but for racing exhaust systems and the sports package of a wider rear wheel and longer suspension. The enormous prize money (225,000 Euros), attracted many former professional racers, including Randy Mamola, Kevin Schwantz and Luca Cadalora, as did the chance of winning a BMW M Coupé, or R1150GS Adventure. The third prize of a C1 may not have been quite as actively contested.

From a field of 32 riders, former Belgian World Superbike star Stéphane Mertens won the series in 2001. Expanded to eight races for 2002, and receiving FIM and UEM cup status, tight racing saw seven different winners in the first seven races. Ultimately, Mertens took out his second International Boxer Cup, ahead of Thomas Hinterreiter and Andy Hoffman. For 2003, there were nine rounds, the first at the Daytona 200, followed by one at the British Superbike Championship round at Oulton Park, five with MotoGP, and two with the Masters of Endurance and World Endurance Championship.

The success of the International Boxer Cup series led to the release of the R1100S Boxer Cup Replica for 2003. Featuring paintwork modelled on that of the racing machines, complete with Randy Mamola signature, the

Opposite: Although still essentially an R1100S, the Boxer Cup Replica was lighter and featured more sporting suspension. *BMW*

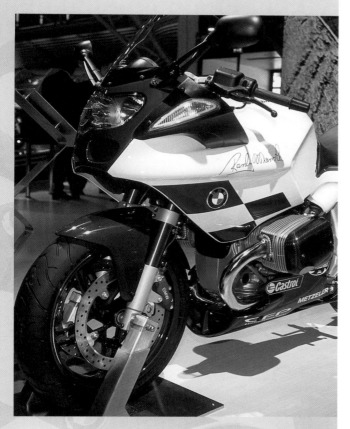

Above; Setting the Boxer Cup Replica apart from the R1100S Boxer Cup was the Randy Mamola signature and carbon-fibre reinforced valve covers. *Ian Falloon*

engine and the drivetrain was standard R1100S, but with a few performance enhancing modifications. The Replica included the sports suspension package and wider rear wheel, along with carbon-fibre reinforced plastic valve covers, engine spoiler, and seat cowling. Shared with the R1100S were the larger front brake discs, EVO brake calipers, and optional partial Integrated ABS. In addition to the Boxer Cup Replica, there was a plainer Boxer Cup, without the special decals, spoiler, seat cowl or carbon valve covers. This retained the sports suspension and wider wheel. Neither the Boxer Cup, nor Replica, featured a centrestand. Even though the claimed weight for both Boxer Cup editions was the same 229kg (505lb) as the R1100S, the Boxer Cup was undoubtedly lighter, and the sharpest handling BMW yet. The Boxer Cup Replica continued into 2004, now with a new tri-color paint scheme and white-faced instruments.

with its optional huge, 30-litre fuel tank, and 105-litre aluminium baggage system, the Adventure raised the ante for the size of off-road motorcycles. If the R1150GS seemed intimidating to smaller riders, the 253kg (558lb) Adventure was even more so.

The 1,130cc engine was shared with the R1150GS, but as the Adventure was designed for use in any part of the world, an optional coding plug for the Motronic MA 2.4 activated an alterative ignition map to allow the engine to run on regular, 91-octane fuel. The sixth-gear ratio was also shortened (as on the R1100S), and there was an optional lower first gear to improve manoeuvrability in difficult terrain.

There were a number of developments to the chassis to provide increased suitability in tough, remote terrain. The front spring travel was increased 20mm to 210mm, while a new White Power rear shock absorber provided 220mm of travel. The damping also increased proportionally to spring deflection. There were no changes to the cross-spoked wheels, but the front brakes now included the EVO calipers, but with braided steel brake lines. The brake disc diameter remained at the earlier 305mm, and the optional ABS was the older ABS II system that could be switched off for off-road use.

A special seat, designed for hours in the saddle, was new for the Adventure. The rider could either sit forward for slow, rough going, or back for extended touring. There was a larger windshield, longer and wider front mudguard, handlebar protectors, and a huge aluminium bash plate under the engine. Options extended to engine protection bars, steel protection covers for the headlights, and knobby off-road tyres. Introduced as a mid-2002 model, for 2003 the Adventure incorporated a few developments. The six-speed transmission was updated, and there was now a Showa rear shock absorber and the optional ABS was the partial Integral ABS as featured on the more sporting boxers. Although set for imminent replacement, during 2004 he R1150GS Adventure took centre stage in Ewan McGregor and Charley Boorman's epic *Long Way Round* circumnavigation of the world.

THE R1200CL

Although it appeared that every sector of the touring market was well covered with the both the R1150RT and K1200LT, 2003 saw the release of a further variant, the R1200CL (Cruiser Luxury). Based on the R1200C cruiser, this was intended as an American-style cruiser that could also swallow up miles in comfort, steering a different path to its touring brethren.

There was more to the R1200CL though, than simply bolting on touring equipment to the existing R1200C.

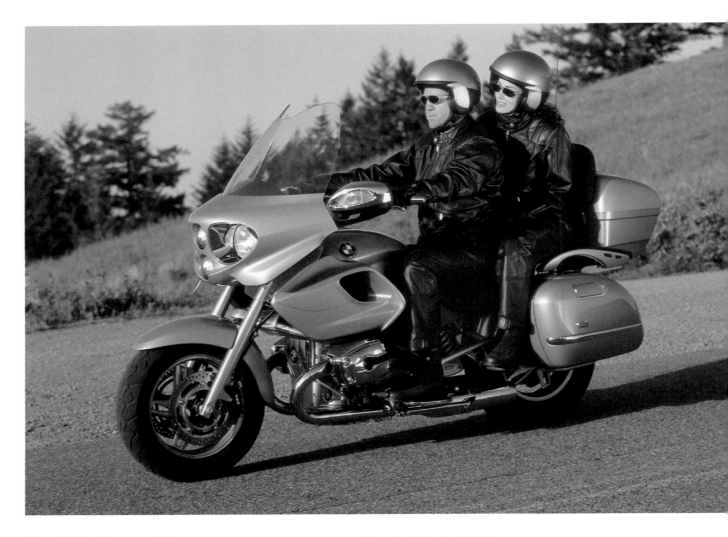

Above: The handlebar-mounted
fairing, and four headlights of
the R1200CL imparted a new
image. *BMW Group Press*

Opposite: While the R1200CL
was based on the R1200C
cruiser, the integrated luggage
and wide, 16in front wheel
signified a different focus. *BMW*

The 'CL' was the first boxer to receive the new six-speed transmission which soon found its way to the entire boxer line-up, except on the five-speed R1200C. The previous six-speed gearbox was never well liked, many actually preferring the earlier five-speed version, and the new gearbox was an attempt to silence the critics. While the previous basic structure was retained, the geometry of the new gears was modified, extending further upwards and providing a larger overlap. This resulted in a softer gear mesh, with less running noise. There were also developments to the gearshift operation through modification of the shifting forks and gear recesses. Not only did the gearbox mesh more precisely, but there was a reduction in weight of around 1kg (2.2lb).

Apart from the R1200C engine, rear-wheel drive, cast-aluminium front frame, and tiny, 17.5-litre fuel tank, most of the R1200CL design was new. Even when compared with the R1200C the steering geometry was extreme, with the front wheel raked out an incredible 33.5°, with an equally astonishing 184mm of trail. The wheelbase of 1,641mm (64.6in) was comparable to the cruiser. There were new, flatter, Telelever and wider forks legs to provide this cruiser geometry and accommodate the wide, 150/80 x 16in front tyre. The 144mm front shock absorber travel was the same as the cruiser, while the similar Monolever rear suspension set-up provided 20mm increased travel to 120mm. The entire rear frame and swingarm were new, while the Monolever was reinforced and modified to accept the K1200LT rear disc brake. The new rear frame was strengthened to accept footboards and luggage supports, and there were newly designed wheels, a 15in rear complementing the 16in front. The front brakes were the smaller, 305mm discs, with EVO calipers, and fully integrated ABS, as on the R1150RT, was an option.

Undoubtedly the most distinctive aspect of the R1200CL was the handlebar-mounted fairing which incorporated four headlights, two larger H4s for low beam and two smaller H1s for high beam. The alternator was uprated to 840 watts to power the extra lights, with a low-maintenance 19Ah battery. Although non-adjustable, the windshield was designed with a centre dip to provide a clear view of the road in all conditions, with the upper edge contoured to deflect air away from the rider. Two additional fairings on the side of the fuel tank were designed to create the look of a totally integrated fairing, and there was a deeply valanced front mudguard. Completing the touring cruiser image were wide handlebars, a stepped seat, and colour-coordinated integrated hard luggage. As expected of a luxury cruiser, there was a wide range of options, ranging from cruise control and heated handlebars, to intercom and CB radio. Undoubtedly, the R1200CL provided enough luxury to warrant its claim, along with the usual BMW ability to cover long distances in comfort (small fuel tank not withstanding). Yet, with a substantial weight of 308kg (679lb), and

considerably more when fully loaded, the 61bhp engine was surely to be taxed to the limit, even if it did possess a wide, flat torque curve. The R1200CL also spawned a cruiser during 2003, the Montauk. Designed to fill a gap between the R1200 Classic and R1200CL, this featured an R1200CL chassis with minimal cruiser equipment. The engine had twin-spark cylinder heads, and additionally there was a new five-speed gearbox.

The first 80 years of BMW motorcycle production saw the company rise and fall through several dramatic periods. BMW almost died after World War II, and again in 1959, and motorcycle production gradually slumped through the 1960s. Throughout this often-turbulent history, it has been the adherence to the traditional boxer engine layout that has seen the BMW motorcycle survive. With an increased proliferation of models, and the continual expansion of the range to meet new niches in the marketplace, by 2003 production levels were higher than ever. More than 75,000 motorcycles rolled out of the Spandau factory every year since 2000, a massive increase considering less than 5,000 emanated from the final year in Munich a little over 30 years earlier. Unlike the days gone by, BMW motorcycles are no longer outside the mainstream. In recent years, BMW has shown it can adapt to the modern competitive, and often fickle, motorcycle marketplace, yet still offer a unique product. The future will see new concepts, along with technical innovation, to further widen their appeal.

The new generation R1200GS
was significantly lighter and more
powerful than its predecessor.
BMW Group Press

8 NEW DIRECTIONS

Evidence of BMW's change in direction was noticeable from the 2004 Model Year. Although only two new models were released this year, one was arguably the most significant for a decade: the new 1,200cc R1200 GS boxer. Along with this landmark model, BMW rationalised its line-up by gradually phasing out the entire R1150-series, R1200C cruisers, and K1200RS. The F650-series and K1200LT received mid-cycle updates, but more significant was a future vision: unleashed with the new high performance K1200S. Motorcycle production increased to 93,836 during 2004, with 26,485 sales in Germany – a market share of nearly 20 per cent. This comfortably exceeded the previous year's figure of 89,745, and BMW were looking to consolidate and further expand. But with 17 new models about to be unleashed over the next three years, it was a big ask for them all to be wildly successful. And, as had happened previously with the K1, some of the new models released during this period completely missed the target.

R1200GS (2004-2007)

As in the past, BMW introduced the next generation boxer engine in the popular dual purpose GS model. The brief given to 40-year old Markus Braunsperger's development team was to refine and enhance the GS's capabilities, while retaining its distinctive character and class-leading performance. The project began soon after the 1150GS's launch, on December 9, 1999, the four-year development cycle beginning with a clean sheet of paper and resulting in an all-new motorcycle. The aim was to improve the power-to-weight ratio by boosting engine performance and shedding 30kg.

The air/oil-cooled boxer engine retained the previous high-cam single overhead camshaft layout, but now included a pair of gear-driven balancer weights. These were positioned on a single shaft at the rear of the cylinder block, and designed to reduce the 180-degree crankshaft's secondary imbalance. This had become more noticeable on the otherwise perfectly balanced flat twin boxer engine, as the capacity and rpm had increased. The 101x73mm bore and stroke was shared with the R1200C, but the new engine featured 15 per cent lighter cylinder heads with larger valves (36mm inlet and 31mm sodium filled exhaust). The box-type three-ring pistons weighed 410 grams (as opposed to

Below: The new 1,200cc
boxer engine retained the high
camshaft, four-valve layout but
now included a pair of balance
shafts. *BMW Group Press*

the previous 420 grams) and the newly cast crankcase
was 1.4kg lighter. The single plate clutch was 15mm
larger, but still 1.7kg lighter. The all-new Getrag six-
speed gearbox featured helical gears and sleeve and
roller gear selection. Weighing 12.5kg, 3kg less than
before, this mated to a 1.2kg lighter final drive. The
total engine weight was 46kg, 13kg lighter than before.

Like its predecessor, ignition was by twin spark
plugs per cylinder, but an uprated BMS-K engine
management system with a single injector per cylinder
now controlled this. With a 33 per cent lighter and
more efficient muffler the power increased to 100
horsepower at 7,000rpm, with an 18 per cent increase
in torque.

The boxer engine was still employed as the principal
load bearing chassis element, with the rear tubular

steel subframe bolted at four points, and the Telelever's
front triangular truss structure located at two points.
This delivered a 20 per cent stiffness-to-weight ratio,
but also positioned the rider lower and further forward
than before. As the R1200GS was significantly lighter
than the outgoing R1150GS, to improve stability the
wheelbase was lengthened slightly, to 1520mm. The
steering head angle was a conservative 27 degrees
with 110mm of trail. The rear shock absorber was
by White Power. The longer, 2.3kg lighter, swingarm
also featured a raised pivot. As the previous lower
torque rod was prone to damage off road the new
Paralever mounted the rod above the swingarm. This
also provided additional ground clearance and reduced
unsprung weight.

Braking was by twin 305mm front discs with four-

The Telelever and front frame of the new R1200GS. *BMW Group Press*

piston calipers and a rear 265mm disc with twin-piston caliper. This EVO braking system also included Partly Integrated ABS, and the lightweight wheels were either 2.50x19 and 4.00x17-inch cross spoke wire or alloy.

Also introduced with the R1200GS was single wire networking of electrical and electronic components in the motorcycle. Combining sophisticated electronics with CAN-bus technology (Controller Area Network), this innovative on-board network offered a wider range of functions than conventional on-board networks, at the same time reducing the number of cables to a single wire.

Lighter and more manoeuvrable than the R1150GS, the R1200GS was a landmark model. A true all-rounder, it was voted International Bike of the Year

by twelve of the world's leading motorcycle magazines (representing twelve countries). The R1200GS was also immediately successful, and with more than 90,000 examples sold between 2004 and 2007 the R1200GS became the most successful BMW motorcycle ever.

Alongside the new R1200GS, the existing range of 1150s continued much as before. The 1150s now featured dual plug cylinder heads, and joining them was a special black R850R Comfort built for the Italian market. Although the cruiser was in its final year, another version of the R1200C was available for 2004, the R1200C Montauk. Based on the R1200CL, but with a five-speed gearbox, this included a wide 150/80x16-inch front tyre and cast aluminium composite frame. This semi-naked version slotted in

The R1200C Montauk cruiser was derived from the R1200CL, and featured a wide 16-inch front tyre. *BMW Group Press*

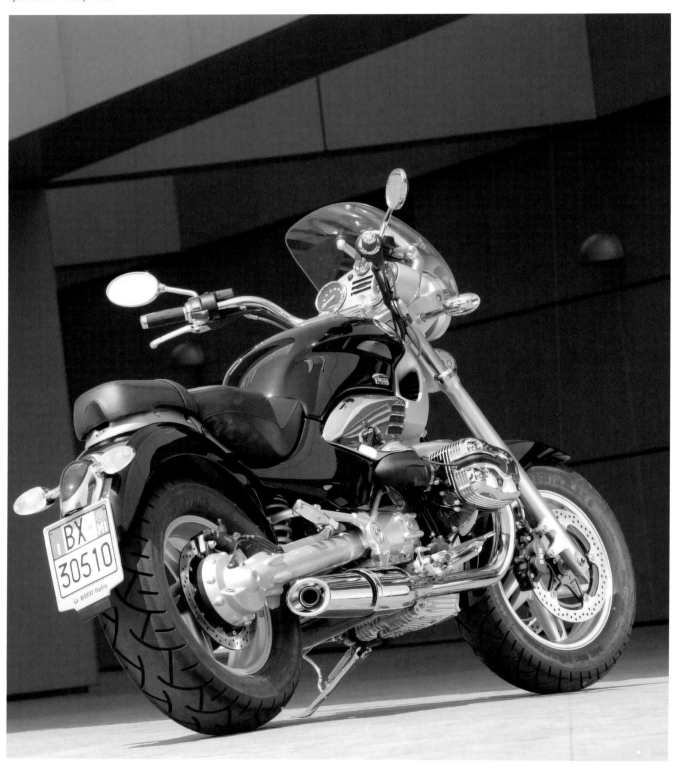

between the luxury R1200CL and basic R1200C. Becoming one of the more successful models in the line-up after five years, the K1200LT received a number of important updates for 2004. The highlight was a much-acclaimed electrohydraulic centre-stand, automatically raising the motorcycle with a button, while larger (36mm) throttles contributed to a 15 per cent power increase. The power was now 116 horsepower at 8,000rpm. An extended spring strut improved stability and a new lower seat helped shorter riders. Styling updates included a split headlight, a larger front mudguard, and a variety of chrome-plated items. Rolling on a 1,627mm wheelbase, the wet weight was up to 387kg.

K1200S, K1200R (2004-2008)

Another indication in BMW's change in focus at this time was the introduction of their second generation four-cylinder, the K1200S. As a company not known for producing high performance motorcycles, it was a bold move to take on the established Japanese open class heavyweights, notably the Suzuki Hayabusa, Kawasaki ZX-12R, and Honda CBR1100XX Blackbird. And as was to be expected from BMW, they took a unique and independent approach when creating their new multi-cylinder high performance sporting motorcycle. Created in secret design studios, the K1200S was released a little prematurely, and initial examples suffered from a lack of development.

The K1200S received an all-new across the frame four-cylinder engine, an all-new aluminium beam chassis, and a Hossack-inspired front end. It also included a state-of-the-art partially linked ABS, an electronically adjustable on-board suspension system, and shaft drive with a R1200GS Paralever rear end. Along with numerous weight saving and performance enhancing components, the K1200S was the most performance oriented BMW motorcycle to date.

The project commenced five years earlier under the direction of Franz Berkmann, aided by Markus Braunsperger (Head of R&D) and Markus Poschner (K-series Director). Engine development was the responsibility of Wolfgang Nehse (Head of Powertrain Development), Nehse coming to BMW from working on the McLaren F1 supercar. A low centre of gravity

was considered essential, and an across-the-frame four cylinder seen as the optimum solution for a high performance motorcycle. Thus the cylinders were canted forward 55 degrees to overcome the higher centre of gravity associated with this layout. With a bore and stroke of 79x59mm the four-cylinder engine displaced 1,157cc and produced 167 horsepower at 10,250rpm. The maximum torque of 96 lb-ft peaked at 8,250rpm – with more than 70 per cent of the engine's maximum torque available from just 3,000rpm. The engine unit (including the clutch and gearbox) weighed 81.3kg, and the engine was only 430mm wide.

Unlike the previous K-series, the engine specification began life as state-of-the-art. The forged one-piece crankshaft came with eight counterweights, 38mm con-rod bearing journals, and a crank angle of 180 degrees to provide consistent firing intervals. Two of the crankshaft counterweights served as gears for the primary clutch drive and to drive the two balance shafts. Oil was supplied to the crankshaft and bearings in a system carried over from Formula 1. Instead of feeding lubricant radially via the crankcase to each main bearing and via a ring groove to the con-rod bearings, lubricant was fed directly into the crankshaft in an axial flow. The lubricant then flowed through holes within the crankshaft to the con-rod bearings. This made the usual ring groove superfluous and allowed a slimmer and more compact bearing. The result was a short and compact crankshaft allowing minimum distances between the cylinders. Another advantage was the oil entering the crankshaft no longer acted against centrifugal forces. This allowed the oil pump to run at a much lower pressure.

The forged steel con-rods were 120mm long and weighed 413 grams. The upper bearing bush had a running life of more than 100,000km, and the connecting rods were split horizontally by proven crack technology. The flat-topped 299-gram three-ring pistons were box-type items, the surfaces cooled by oil injection nozzles in the crankcase. The compression ratio was a high 13:1.

The four-valve cylinder head design was also Formula 1 based, the 32 and 27.5mm valves set at a narrow 21-degree included angle. A chain from the crankshaft drove the exhaust camshaft, with the inlet camshaft driven by gear. With only one sprocket cylinder head, width was kept to a minimum. The

The K1200S and some of the development team. From left: David Robb, Kai Barbehoen, Markus Braunsperger, Markus Poschner, Wolfgang Nehse, Jürgen Bachmann, Horst Reichl, and Ralph Beier. *BMW Group Press*

Opposite top: The K1200S engine layout was completely new, the compact across-the-frame- four-cylinder engine mated to a cassette type gearbox and shaft final drive. *BMW Group Press*

Opposite bottom: Innovative design characteristics included the Duolever front fork, canted engine, single-sided Paralever swingarm, and low aluminium beam frame. *BMW Group Press*

camshafts were located directly above the valves, allowing a 1:1 ratio on the follower arms, thus keeping flex to a minimum and allowing the use of lightweight arms. Redline was 11,000rpm.

An oil reservoir for the dry sump engine was located in the frame triangle behind the engine, with an oil cooler in the front fairing beneath the headlight. For the first time on a BMW shaft drive motorcycle the clutch was a multiplate oil bath type. The six-speed gearbox was also a compact cassette type, with the two transmission shafts located above one another to aid compactness. As the final drive was by shaft and the engine fitted crossways, the output required two pivot points.

Developed in-house, and first fitted to the

R1200GS, the BMS-K (BMW Engine Management with Anti-Knock Control) featured fully sequential cylinder-specific fuel injection, rapid processing of comprehensive sensor signals, and self-diagnosis. Throttle butterflies were 46mm in diameter.

While the engine represented a significant innovation, the chassis specification involved even more radical and unique technical solutions. Two firsts were electronically adjustable suspension and a Hossack-style Duolever front end. Another first for BMW was the composite aluminium frame, this weighing only 11.5kg and consisting of internal high-pressure moulded elements (IHU) and extrusion pressed profiles together with die-cast head and the rear.

Continuing a BMW tradition of front suspension

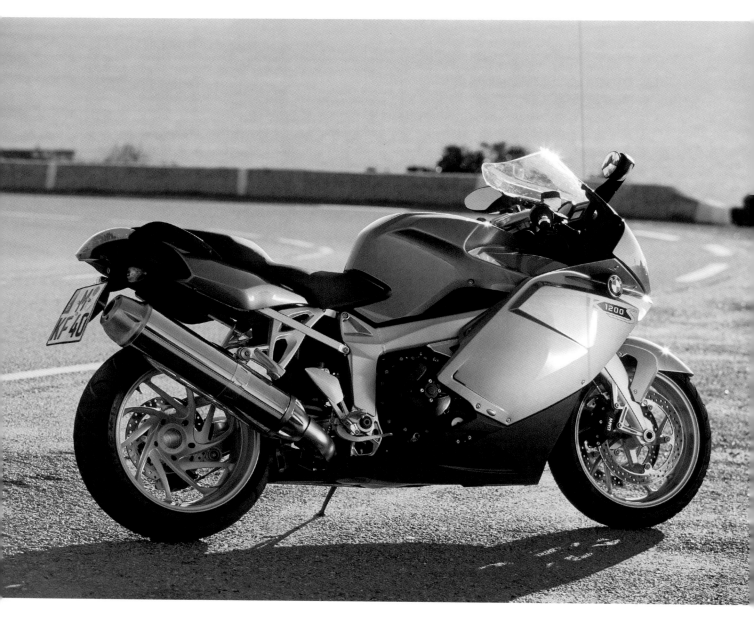

innovation, the telescopic fork (1937), Earles fork (1954), and Telelever (1993), the Duolever was another revolutionary concept. Inspired by Englishman Norman Hossack's design of 1979, this consisted of two longitudinal arms in a parallelogram arrangement. A rectangular pivot made up of two almost parallel longitudinal arms turning within the frame held the wheel bearing. The wheel bearing unit was a high-strength aluminium casting connected to the longitudinal arms by two ball bearings. The straight line connecting the two ball joints formed the steering axis, with an assembly resembling a pair of scissors conveying steering movements. The handlebar was mounted conventionally on the head of the frame and a central spring strut pivoting on the lower longitudinal arm provided the suspension and damping. Weighing

just 13.7kg, the entire construction was about 10 per cent lighter than a comparable Telelever. Through its kinematic configuration, the Duolever provided an anti-dive effect when braking, this remaining consistent throughout the entire path of spring travel.

The suspension system featured gas-pressure shock absorbers front and rear, with the rider able to adjust the suspension and damping by pressing a button on the handlebar. This ESA (Electronic Suspension Adjustment) was the first such system fitted to a production motorcycle.

The 3.50x17-inch and 6.00x17-inch cast alloy wheels were also specially designed for the K1200S, and braking was by BMW's own partly integrated EVO system. The front discs were 320mm with a 265mm at the rear. The CAN-bus electrical and

Opposite: With styling by David
Robb, the K1200S was an impressive
high-speed sporting motorcycle.
BMW Group Press

Below: When released, the naked
K1200R was the most powerful unfaired
motorcycle available. *BMW Group Press*

electronic system was a development of the R1200GS, this also integrating all control units through a single wire. And completing the sporting package was slim and compact aerodynamic bodywork, again provided by David Rodd's design department. While the K1200S undoubtedly provided class-leading performance, it still wasn't particularly small and lithe. Rolling on a long 1,571mm wheelbase, the wet weight was a hefty 248kg, and the K1200S was long and cumbersome.

For all its limitations, the K1200S was undeniably fast. Andy Sills of San Francisco set a new world land speed record for naturally aspirated 1000-1,350cc

stock motorcycles at Bonneville in 2005. Sills had amassed more than 300,000 miles on four BMW motorcycles within the previous seven years, and averaged 173.57mph (279.34km/h) on a stock K1200S. This nearly matched Henne's 1937 outright world speed record.

Joining the K1200S soon afterwards was the naked brutal-looking K1200R. The drivetrain, running gear, brakes, and on-board network were all shared with the K1200S. The engine and transmission were also basically identical, with the same camshafts and exhaust system. A new air intake, with only one snorkel leading to the airbox on the right-hand side

During 2005, BMW sponsored a
K1200R Power Cup racing series.
BMW Group Press

resulted in slightly less power of 163 horsepower at 10,250rpm.

The suspension and running gear were also modified slightly for the new model. The Duolever was slightly steeper, providing a 61-degree steering head angle, with 11mm shorter trail, at 101mm. This provided improved low speed handling. As the bodywork was simpler, the wet weight of 237kg was also less than the K1200S.

At the time, the K1200R was the most powerful naked bike available, and BMW sponsored a K1200R

Power Cup racing series instead of the BoxerCup. With a free flowing Lazer exhaust the race version sported 175 horsepower, and included White Power suspension and a number of carbon-fibre components. Italian Roberto Panichi won the seven-round 2005 series held as support races for MotoGP. BMW took a gamble with the second generation K-series. As with the first generation they ignored convention, thinking outside the square, but with the K1200S they took an even more risky approach. Ultimately the K1200S and R

The second new generation boxer was the impressive R1200RT. *BMW Group Press*

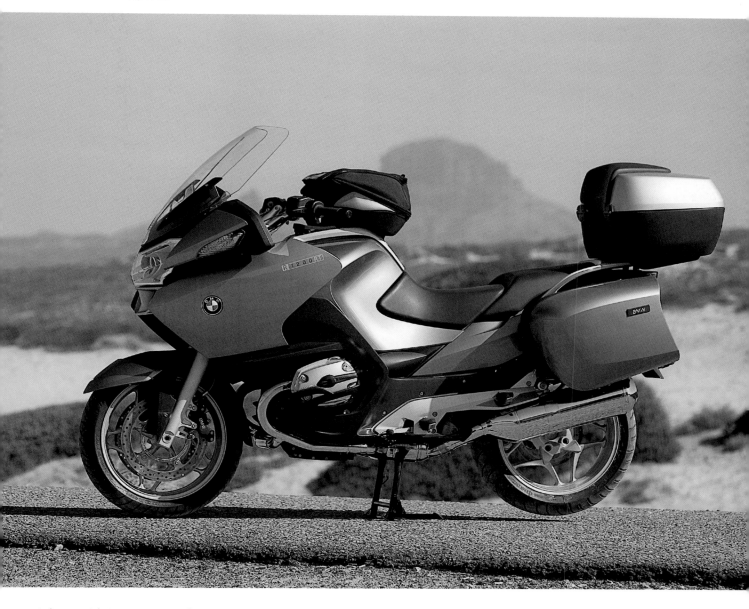

(along with its successor the K1300S, R and GT) were considered too unusual and oddball, and the second four-cylinder K-series lasted only eleven years.

R1200RT (2005-2009)

A second new generation boxer, the R1200RT, replaced the R1150RT for 2005. This was built on the technical specification established by the R1200GS in 2004. As with the R1200GS the design emphasis for the

R1200RT was to provide more power and less weight, this improving dynamic performance and agility.

The 1,170cc boxer twin engine was similar to the R1200GS, a new intake system, mufflers, camshafts and 12:1 compression ratio resulting in a power increase, to 110 horsepower at 7,500rpm. The BMS-K electronic engine management now featured anti-knock control and separate oxygen sensors for each cylinder. Also shared with the R1200GS was the helical gear six-speed transmission, but with a lower sixth gear.

177

The R1200ST was more
sporting, but the unusual front
styling proved unpopular.
BMW Group Press

Like the R1200GS, the two-piece main and rear
tubular steel space frame incorporated the engine
as a load-bearing unit. Designed specifically for the
R1200RT, the front frame was a welded steel structure,
with the rear frame of welded straight steel tubes. The
Telelever included a 35mm fixed tube and modified
longitudinal arm for superior road use, and the
R1200GS Paralever was modified to accept a wider

rear tyre. To improve agility the steering head angle
was a steep 26.6 degrees, with 109.9mm of trail.

The rear central shock absorber now incorporated
the R1150 GS Adventure's travel-dependent damper
technology (TDD), ensuring a progressive increase
in damper forces as a function of spring travel.
Also available as an option was the K1200S's ESA
(Electronic Suspension Adjustment). The five-spoke,

cast aluminium wheels measured 3.50 x 17 and 5.50 x 17 inches, allowing more modern tyre sizes of 120/70 ZR17 and 180/55 ZR17. BMW's proven EVO Integral ABS handled the braking, the front discs measuring 320mm and the rear a smaller 265mm. Also shared with the R1200GS was the single wire CAN-bus system, this allowing an efficient, comprehensive diagnosis of all relevant vehicle functions. Rider aids included an on-board computer.

New styling resulted in a higher and wider electrically adjustable windshield, ergonomically designed seat and controls, and standard integrated hard luggage. The result was a significantly more competent and refined replacement for the outgoing R1150RT. Surprisingly nimble and sure-footed for a 259kg fully equipped touring machine, the R1200RT resurrected BMW's reputation in the touring market it once called its own.

R1200ST (2005-2007)

Also released for 2005 was the R1150RS replacement, the R1200ST. This third iteration of the new generation boxer was aimed at more sporting touring riders. The R1200ST shared the 110 horsepower R1200RT engine and basic frame with a welded steel front section. Minor chassis differences saw the ST receive more conservative steering geometry, with a 27-degree steering head angle and 111.6mm of trail. The wheelbase was also slightly longer, at 1,502mm. While the wheels and brakes were also shared with the R1200RT, setting the ST apart was a distinctive new fairing with two vertically stacked H4 headlights. The R1200ST's most significant advantage over the RT was a reduction in weight, to 229kg wet (205kg dry). But while the new face was distinctive, it polarized opinion and wasn't universally accepted. As a result the R1200ST only lasted two years.

HP2 ENDURO (2006-2007)

By 2006, BMW were well on the way to rejuvenating their motorcycle line-up. The new 1,200cc boxer range was expanding, and the K1200S and K1200R allowed an entry into a new market, one that had previously eluded BMW. Unfortunately, sales of the

second generation K-series were slow and motorcycle production decreased slightly during 2005 to 92,012. Responding to this downturn, BMW released six new models for 2006, headed by the HP2 Enduro.

Heralding a new series of high performance (hence HP) low volume sports motorcycles was the HP2 Enduro. Developed by a small dedicated team of specialists, engineers and mechanics, the HP2 Enduro was BMW's first serious production sporting off-road motorcycle.

While based on the R1200GS, with the exception of the engine and the on-board network, nearly all the components were new. Saving weight and focusing on essential off-road ability were the main criteria. The power of the 1,170cc boxer twin engine was increased slightly, to 105 horsepower, with the balance shaft removed to reduce weight. The intake air snorkel was modified to deflect water from entering, while the muffler was 2kg lighter than the R1200GS.

The HP2 Enduro's frame and suspension was all new, the tubular steel spaceframe based on that of the R900R Dakar Rally machines of 1999-2001. Instead of the R1200GS's Telelever, the front suspension was by a long travel (270mm) 45mm upside-down fork with adjustable compression and rebound damping. The steering head angle was 29.5 degrees with 127mm of trail. The R1200GS's Paralever swingarm was redesigned, the swingarm now 30mm longer. Constructed of welded light alloy shells, this (and the entire drivetrain) was magnesium coloured. The rear shock absorber was developed in conjunction with Continental Automotive Systems, this notable for the air spring and damper system. Weighing only 2.3kg, the air spring strut featured a piston moving into a damper chamber, and acting on air forced through plate valves into a second chamber. The damping effect was achieved by throttling the flow of air, and as this was compressible the air within the chamber provided a spring effect and replaced a conventional spring. Along with easy adjustability, as it was fully sealed another advantage was the unit's resistance to dirt and contamination.

Further reflecting its off-road purpose, the aluminium wheels were cross spoke 1.85 x 21 and 2.50 x 17-inch, these fitted with specially developed Metzeler tubeless 'Karoo' tyres (90/90-21 and 140/80-17). The brakes were a single semi-floating 305mm disc with a sliding pin twin piston caliper at the front, and 265mm rear disc with the R1200GS's floating twin piston caliper. Unlike the R1200GS, the brakes were without ABS, this considered detrimental in off-road situations.

The bodywork was also new, with a 13-litre fuel tank nestling between the upper frame tubes. Quality detail touches included asymmetrically drilled handlebar clamps to provide two positions, a tapered aluminium handlebar with conical ends, and stainless steel serrated footpegs. With a claimed dry weight of only 175kg, the HP2 Enduro was the lightest large capacity boxer yet.

Testing was undertaken in extreme conditions, including the Baja California Desert race with Jimmy Lewis. BMW subsequently supported privately entered HP2 Enduros in the Erzberg race in Austria and the German Cross Country Championship (GCC) with current champion, the Finnish rider Simo Kirssi. The HP2 Enduro's success prompted BMW to offer further HP versions in the coming years.

R1200S (2006-2007)

When the 98 horsepower R1100S was launched in 1998, it was BMW's most powerful ever. But, unlike other boxers, it never grew to 1,150cc, and the R1100S remained largely unchanged throughout its eight-year life cycle. So, by 2006 a R1100S replacement was inevitable, and this took the form of the lighter and more powerful R1200S.

Powering the R1200S was another version of the new 1,170cc boxer twin, this now with a 12.5:1 compression ratio, longer duration, higher lift camshafts now running in three bearings, and stronger valve springs with reinforced rocker arms. Along with stronger alloy con-rods, the maximum engine speed was increased to 8,800rpm. This was a new upper rev limit for a BMW boxer engine.

The throttle butterflies, and intake and exhaust manifolds were enlarged in diameter by 5mm, to 52mm for the intake and 50mm for the exhaust. Retained from other production R1200s were the BMS-K engine management system, twin spark ignition, balance shaft, six-speed gearbox, and EVO Paralever swingarm. With a power output of 122 horsepower at 8,250rpm, the R1200S easily eclipsed the previous model.

The chassis specification provided a significantly improved sporting focus over the R1100S. While the wheelbase was up slightly (to 1,487mm), the Telelever geometry was more aggressive, a 24-degree rake and 87mm of trail providing lightning steering. This was one degree steeper and 13mm shorter than the R1100S. The Telelever tubes were 41mm in diameter.

The wheel and tyre dimensions were as expected for a large capacity sports machine, the 3.50 x 17-inch wheel at the front ran a 120/70 ZR 17 radial sports tyre, while the 5.50 x 17-inch wheel at the rear featured a 180/55 ZR 17 radial sports tyre. And as an option, the R1200 S was available factory-fitted with a six-inch rear wheel running a 190/50 tyre. The brakes were upgraded from the R1100S, with a pair of 320mm discs (4.5mm thick) with four-piston swing calipers on the front, a double-piston floating caliper, and 265mm disc on the rear. The ABS system was optimised for sports riding, the two-channel ABS acting without brake servo. The ABS could also be deactivated on request. Another factory option was Öhlins sports suspension.

With the exception of the HP2 Enduro, the R1200S was the lightest and most agile of all the new BMW boxers. Weighing 18kg less than the R1100S, the dry weight was 190kg and even fully-fuelled, the R1200S weighed only 213kg. As it was undeniably sporting focused, but with an emphasis on the street rather than the racetrack, BMW hoped to tempt riders away from the traditional Japanese and Italian Superbikes. Unfortunately this was an optimistic scenario. For all its excellence as a useable high performance sporting street bike it was still seen by conservative sportsbike buyers as an eccentric oddity. After two years the R1200S was discontinued, and BMW decided to follow a more conventional path with their next generation Superbike.

R1200GS ADVENTURE (2006-2009), R1200GS (2008-2009)

As the R1150GS Adventure was extremely successful it was inevitable a R1200GS Adventure would join the line-up. This was billed as the ultimate long distance adventure bike, and it was no idle claim. Based on the R1200GS, the Adventure included a host of standard equipment to improve outback performance. This included a 33-litre fuel tank, new windshield, height-adjustable seat, engine protectors and wider

Below: As the most powerful
and lightest sporting Boxer
yet, the R1200S promised
more than it could deliver, and
was dropped after two years.
BMW Group Press

Opposite: With more off-
road equipment standard
and optional, the R1200GS
Adventure was even more robust
and capable than the standard
R1200GS. *BMW Group Press*

rider footrests with adjustable gearshift and brake levers. Other features included 20mm longer travel suspension, wire spoked wheels with off-road tyres, partially integrated ABS, off-road tires and additional headlights. Offered with a wide range of accessories, including aluminium luggage by Tourtech and dedicated GPS, the R1200GS Adventure fulfilled every adventure motorcyclists' dream. The first R1200GS Adventure was offered during 2006, along with a white 25th Anniversary Special Edition. During 2007 Ewan

McGregor and Charley Boorman undertook their second adventure, *A Long Way Down*, riding R1200GS Adventures from John O'Groats, Scotland to Cape Agulhas in South Africa.

Both the R1200GS and R1200GS Adventure were slightly reworked for 2008. With a higher, 12:1 compression ratio, the power was increased slightly, to 105 horsepower at 7,000rpm. To improve traction and acceleration, the six-speed transmission now featured lower ratios, and larger bearings with the distance between the individual shafts modified. Other updates included optional off-road ESA, this achieved with an additional electrohydraulic adjustment of the spring base at the front suspension strut. Offered for the first time on an off-road motorcycle this comprehensive system provided a choice of six damping settings. It further cemented the R1200GS's status as the foremost large capacity dual-purpose motorcycle and both the R1200GS and R1200GS Adventure were extremely successful. The R1200GS Adventure was second only to the R1200GS as BMW's most popular model. Sales for the R1200GS during 2008 were 22,845 with 12,460 for the RG1200GS Adventure. These were 2,298 and 2,930 more than the previous year. Marking 15 years of the GS with the four-valve engine, an R1200GS Special Model was offered during 2009. This was white with black wire spoked wheels. The 500,000th GS also rolled off the production line in May. Although the R1200GS and R1200GS Adventure received the updated double overhead camshaft engine for 2010, a special 30th Anniversary commemorative edition based on the outgoing model was offered for the same year. This was painted in the original R80G/S colours.

K1200GT (2006-2008)

Following the introduction of the two new K-series K1200S and K1200R, it was inevitable a new K1200GT would replace the older style K model. Introduced for 2006, this completed a trio of new K-series bikes spanning sport, long distance sport touring, and high performance naked. Sharing the K1200S's chassis with Duolever front suspension, Paralever, and aluminium frame, the K1200GT was 17 per cent more powerful than its predecessor, and six per cent lighter.

Powered by the same engine as the K1200S and K1200R, the engine was tuned for less peak power and more mid range. The maximum power was now 152 horsepower at 9,500rpm but 75 per cent of the torque was now available from 3,000rpm. The chassis and front Duolever was the same as the K1200S, with identical geometry. The rear disc was increased in size to 294mm, and the rear wheel reduced to 5.50 x 17 inches. The usual EVO braking system included partly-integrated ABS, the front and rear brakes activated by the handlebar lever and the rear by the foot pedal. Standard equipment included an aerodynamic

fairing with an electrically adjustable windshield, and Electronic Suspension Adjustment (ESA) was optional. But despite its impressive specification, at 282kg fully wet the K1200GT was an intimidating grand tourer. This would be another short-lived model, lasting two years before its replacement in 2009 by the K1300GT.

F800S (2006-2010) AND F800ST (2006-2012)

In their boldest move since introducing the first K-series in 1983, BMW branched out into a completely new, fourth engine series with the F800. Introduced in 2006 and pitched at learners and mature riders returning to motorcycling, the F800 was BMW's first parallel twin. Rather than fill the void between the existing 650 singles and 1,200cc twins with shrunken versions of larger models as they had done in the past (with the K75 and R850), BMW took a fresh approach. In conjunction with the Austrian company Bombardier-Rotax, BMW's engineers started with a blank sheet of paper and the requirement for a small, light, agile, torque and innovative midrange motorcycle. Over a period of 47 months flat-twins, V-twins, singles and fours were rejected in favour of a parallel twin. Light, compact and with the preferred power characteristics, to go, feel, and sound right this required a 360-degree crank. As 360-degree twins vibrate noticeably, the engine included an innovative balancing system. Instead of conventional counterweight shafts, a system of pivots in the middle of the crankshaft offset the oscillating mass forces. An eccentric weight on the crankshaft, positioned 180 degrees underneath, incorporated a balance con-rod with a horizontal balance arm. This balance con-rod moved in the opposite direction to the two engine con-rods. The distribution of masses on the con-rod head and swinging arm ensured that the forces resulting from the swivelling movement acted against the oscillating forces on the crankshaft. This almost completely eliminated both the primary and secondary imbalance. To avoid splash the counter-balance system also required semi-drive sump lubrication.

The cylinders were inclined 30 degrees and the cylinder heads were similar to the new generation K-series. A silent chain drove twin overhead camshafts operating four valves per cylinder via follower

Despite its size and weight, the K1200GT was an extremely competent grand tourer.
BMW Group Press

Bottom right: The F800 was BMW's first parallel twin. Along with chain driven overhead camshafts and four-valves per cylinder, underneath the crankshaft was a con-rod and lever balancer. *BMW Group Press*

Opposite top: The sporting F800S featured a lower handlebar and half fairing. *BMW Group Press*

Opposite bottom: The F800ST had a larger fairing. Final drive for both F800s was by toothed rubber belt. *BMW Group Press*

arms. The valve sizes were 32 and 27.5mm, and the dimensions a nearly square 82x75.6mm. The compression ratio was 12:1 and injection was by the usual BMW-K system with intake manifold injection. With twin 46mm throttles the maximum power was 85 horsepower at 8,000rpm. 90 per cent of the maximum torque was available at 5,000rpm. A 34 horsepower version was also available to satisfy lower power requirements. Final drive was by a toothed rubber belt, this similar to the F650CS but slightly wider to accept the increased power. The engine was built by Rotax and shipped to Berlin for final assembly.

Also new was an aluminium frame, this made of welded extrusion-pressed profiles and die-cast components. The engine was incorporated as a load-bearing element, the crankcase acting as a mount for the single sided aluminium swingarm. To lower the centre of gravity the fuel tank was positioned beneath the seat. Front suspension was by a conventional 43mm telescopic fork with a single shock absorber at the rear. The wheels were a similar design to the K1200S, and braking was more as expected from a larger capacity motorcycle rather than a middleweight. This was a pair of 320mm discs and four piston calipers on the front and a single-piston floating caliper with a 265mm disc on the rear. Bosch two-channel ABS anti-lock braking was optional, this similar to the F650 in not requiring brake power assistance or an integral function.

The F800 was available in two versions: the sporting half-faired F800S and sports touring F800ST. Both shared the new engine and chassis, differences confined to a smaller screen, fairing and lower handlebar on the S. The wheel design also differed between the two. Compared with some recent BMW offerings both were styled conservatively and were arguably the best looking of BMW's range. They were also commendably light, the F800S weighing 182kg dry and the F800ST 187kg. Balancing power and weight with BMW individuality, the F800s were immediately successful and would spawn more models over the next few years. While some of the new models may have missed the mark, this expansion into more categories was paying off for BMW. Between the first new boxer in 1993 and the F800 of 2006 sales virtually tripled, from 35,219 to 100,064 units, breaking the magical 100,000 barrier for the first time.

HP2 MEGAMOTO (2007-2008)

Joining the HP2 Enduro as the second HP model for 2007 was the street oriented HP2 Megamoto. Aiming to despatch BMW's stodgy image completely, the light and agile HP2 Megamoto was the most focused street BMW ever. Based on the HP2 Enduro, a higher 12:1 compression ratio and Akrapovič exhaust helped to increase the power of the 1,170cc boxer engine, to 113 horsepower at 7,500rpm. The tubular steel space frame was similar to the HP2 Enduro, but a 28.6-degree rake and 95mm of trail provided more radical steering. BMW also provided the HP2 Megamoto with its own suspension and wheels. The front 45mm Marzocchi upside-down fork provided 160mm of travel, 10mm less than the Enduro, while a standard coil spring Öhlins shock absorber replaced the Enduro's air shock. The brakes were also

At the 85th running of the Pikes Peak International Hill Climb in 2007, Gary Trachy set a new record for motorcycles up to 1,200cc on the HP2 Megamoto. *BMW Group Press*

upgraded, with twin 320mm discs on the front with fixed four-piston Brembo calipers. The rear 265mm disc retained a floating twin-piston caliper. Completing the street specification were cast aluminium 3.50x17 and 5.50x 17-inch wheels, shod with high speed 120/70 ZR 17 and 180/55 ZR 17 tyres. The wheelbase was a stretched out 1,615mm but the dry weight only 179kg. Set off by a carbon-fibre tank and headlight fairing, the HP Megamoto was built to order and sold at a premium price.

R1200R (2007-2010)

After around 60,000 sales of the R1150R and R850R the more powerful and lighter R1200R replaced these for 2007. The final model in this boxer evolution, the R1200R continued the R1150R's naked style, but with 28 per cent more power and less weight, and for the first time the new generation of Integral ABS included optional ASC anti-spin control and tire pressure monitoring.

Replacing the R1150R, the R1200R completed the new boxer line-up. *BMW Group Press*

The 109 horsepower 1,170cc Boxer twin engine was shared with the R1200RT, but with the oil cooler fitted behind the front fork. The six-speed gearbox was also shared with the RT, but the drive shaft included a lower secondary transmission ratio, 2.75:1 compared to the RT's 2.62:1. This resulted in sixth gear as a performance gear and no longer an overdrive or economy gear.

Like the R1200RT and R1200ST, the BMW R1200R featured a two-piece frame integrating the engine as a load-bearing element. While the front half of the frame was from the RT, the steering head angle was raked out to 27.1 degrees with more trail of 119.1mm. The wheelbase was increased slightly, to 1,495mm. New for the R1200R was the rear tubular space frame. The suspension was by the usual Telelever and Paralever and the wheels the usual 3.50 and 5.50 x 17-inch. The ESA Electronic Suspension System was optional. The front braking system was upgraded to twin 320mm floating discs with two four-piston fixed calipers with a 265mm rear disc with floating twin-piston caliper. A factory fitted option was the latest generation Integral ABS with ASC (Automatic Stability Control). As on the other new R1200s the introduction of the Single-Wire-System simplified the structure and configuration of the on-board electrics, reducing the number of cables and connections. The updated styling provided a slightly more modern look and the 198kg dry weight saw the R1200R significantly lighter than its predecessor. With a wide range of optional equipment available the R1200R could also be configured as a touring model. The R1200R continued until 2010 as the final model featuring the high cam boxer four-valve engine. To maintain interest in the model prior to it incorporating the new generation double overhead camshaft engine a plain white R1200R Touring Special was offered for 2010. Special features included a new comfort seat, on-board computer, chrome exhaust, sports windshield and locking saddlebags.

G650XCHALLENGE, G650XMOTO, G650XCOUNTRY (2007-2009)

A further broadening of BMW's model line-up was particularly evident with the release of three new 650cc single cylinder models for 2007. Sharing the same technical foundation, each was specified with individual features and characteristics to create three distinct versions. While offering the smallest capacity engines in BMW's range, this trio of 650s weren't envisaged as traditional entry-level motorcycles, but higher specification models designed to entice a new clientele. The new G designation heralded a new range of sporting machines and the G650 Xchallenge Hard Enduro was a focused off-roader. The G650Xmoto Street Moto was totally at home in an urban environment, and the G650 Xcountry Scrambler able to satisfy road and mild off-road duties.

The single-cylinder engine was carried over from the existing F650, but modified for more power and less weight. Supplied by Rotax and developed in cooperation with Aprilia S.p.A., in Noale, Italy, the engine was assembled by Aprilia in their North Italian

Scorzè Plant. The upgraded four-valve engine now developed 53 horsepower at 7,000rpm, the response improved by the crankshaft running in anti-friction bearings and a lighter alternator. The balance shaft was retained, and the starter and alternator covers were now of magnesium. The dual ignition four-valve cylinder head with a timing chain, twin overhead camshafts and cup tappets remained unchanged. Engine management was provided by a BMS-C II electronic system. A new feature was the dry sump oil tank positioned on the left behind the cylinder, this contributing to an optimal mass concentration around the motorcycle's centre of gravity. While the five-speed gearbox was unchanged, the final drive on all three models was by an O-ring chain instead of toothed rubber belt.

The frame was also shared between all three models and consisted of four sections. The main frame was of welded steel sections with aluminium castings bolted around the swingarm mount. An aluminium lower section positioned the engine, and a forged aluminium rear frame bolted to the main frame and took up spring strut forces. The swingarm now pivoted on the main frame and not on the engine cases. The swingarm was a double-sided cast aluminium. Also identical on all three models was the 45mm Marzocchi upside-down fork, but each version was set up with different wheel travel and damping. The Xmoto and Xchallenge fork featured adjustable rebound and compression damping and different wheel mounting points. The rear suspension also varied between models, the Xchallenge with an HP2 Enduro type Continental air damping system, while the Xcountry featured a length adjustable spring shock absorber. The wheels were also tailored to each specific purpose, the Street Moto featuring 3.50 and 4.50x17-inch cast light-alloy rims, the Scrambler running on 2.50x19 and 3.50x17-inch spoke wheels, and the Xchallenge Hard Enduro featuring 1.60x21 and 2.50x18-inch spoke wheels with aluminium rims.

The braking systems also differed between models. The Xcountry and the Xchallenge had a 300mm single front disc with a twin piston floating brake caliper, while the Xmoto featured a four-piston brake caliper and a 320mm disc. The Xchallenge also featured a cross-wave type front disc, providing improved self cleaning. The rear disc on all models was 240mm with a single-piston floating caliper. Two-channel ABS was optional. Also shared between models was the 9.5-litre fuel tank positioned beneath the seat.

Below: Alluding to the classic scrambler, the G650Xcountry included a round headlight, a 'naked' cockpit without a fairing, a two-level seat and a close fitting front mudguard. *BMW Group Press*

Opposite top left: The fourth version of the new K1200 series was the half faired K1200R Sport. *BMW Group Press*

Opposite top right: The HP2 Sport cylinder head featured four radial valves and chain-driven double overhead camshafts. *BMW Group Press*

Opposite bottom: An official racing R1200S was entered in the 2007 Le Mans 24-hour race. Markus Barth, Thomas Hinterreiter and Rico Penzkofer won their class, and finished 16th overall. On the bike here is chief tester Stéphane Mertens. *BMW Group Press*

The weight of all three versions was commendably light. The Xchallenge dry weight was only 144kg, with the Xmoto weighing 147kg and the Xcountry 148kg. The G650Xchallenge soon proved a worthy addition to the stable, with Japanese rider Yoshio Ikemachi winning the 10-day 3,600km Ulaanbaatar to Uvs international cross-country rally on a one. But while the G650X was technically and functionally excellent, it was also a high priced entry in a very competitive market. The G650X was only available until 2009.

K1200R SPORT (2007-2008)

Ostensibly a half-faired version of the naked K1200R, with its high handlebars, comfortable riding position, and wind tunnel developed fairing, the K1200R Sport provided the best of the K1200R and K1200S. The

engine was the slightly lower power version of the K1200R and the wet weight was 241kg. Introduced in 2007 this would last only two years before the K1300R Sport replaced it.

HP2 SPORT (2008-2011)

By 2007 BMW's range restructuring was almost complete. This was the final year for the R1150, and the K1200LT was the only remaining version of the earlier K-series. Production increased slightly, to 104,396, with sales of 102,461. In April 2007, BMW also made an official return to road racing, with an entry in the Le Mans 24-hour race. On a modified R1200S, Markus Barth, Thomas Hinterreiter, and Rico Penzkofer won their class and finished 16th. This was especially encouraging in a field of faster and more powerful Japanese bikes. The team's next outing was in July at the non-championship Barcelona 24-hour

Below left: Only produced in limited quantities, the HP2 Sport was the highest performing boxer yet produced. *BMW Group Press*

Bottom: Aimed at an entry-level clientele, the F650GS was more road oriented. Both models were powered by an 800cc parallel twin, the cylinders more upright than on the F800S and ST. *BMW Group Press*

Below right: The F800GS had adventure-style wire spoked wheels and a beefy upside down front fork. *BMW Group Press*

race, run on the Catalunya GP circuit, but the bike was crashed eight laps into the race. At Oschersleben a month later for the 24-hour WEC race two bikes were entered, the second bike ridden by British rider Richard Cooper, German ex-GP star Peter Öttl and Spaniard José-Luis Nion. The German team finished fifth and the Euro team ninth, the two BMWs placing first and second in the open class. At the Bol d'Or 24-hour race season finale at Magni-Cours in September the BMWs were less successful. The Hinterreiter/Cooper/Penzkofer trio crashed three times, finishing 23rd, but still first in the Open class. The second bike of José-Luis Nion, American Boxer Cup-ace Brian Parriott, and Briton Barry Burrell rose to 14th place after eight hours before Nion crashed in the dark. With the suspension top triple clamp broken, they were forced to retire. This was a promising foray into endurance racing, and it led to the release of the third model in the High Performance range for 2008, the HP2 Sport. Ostensibly a street legal replica of the 2007 factory endurance racer, under the guidance of project leader Franz Berkmann the HP2 Sport would be the fastest, sportiest and lightest Boxer-engined sports bike yet.

Powering the HP2 Sport was an 1,170cc boxer engine with all-new double overhead camshaft cylinder heads. Replacing the high-cam and rocket arrangement of the R1200, the HP2 Sport received new four-valve cylinder heads with chain-driven double overhead camshafts. The more compact, flatter combustion chamber saw the inlet and exhaust valves disposed radially to each other at an 11-degree angle, these operated by conically ground camshafts. The inlet valves were 3mm larger, at 39mm, and the 33mm exhaust valves 2mm larger. The improved breathing and swirl negated the need for twin spark plugs, and ignition was via a single centrally mounted plug per cylinder with BMS-K injection and 52mm throttles. Also new were 12.5:1 Mahle forged pistons and steel connecting rods allowing the boxer twin to rev to 9,500rpm. The new cylinder heads were 10mm slimmer and the engine retained the twin gear-driven counterbalancers positioned on a single shaft at the rear of the cylinder block. With carbon fibre rocker covers the overall engine weight was 46kg. With a Euro 3 compliant titanium Akrapovič exhaust system the power was 128 horsepower at 8,750rpm. This was only slightly less than the factory endurance racer.

Along with improved porting, the cylinder heads were plumbed for superior oil cooling and an additional oil radiator was mounted in the nose. A deeper finned sump also aided lubrication. The helical gear Getrag six-speed gearbox was close ratio, and for the first time on a production BMW a racing power shift allowed open throttle clutchless gear changes. Incorporating this system with BMW's traditional single plate diaphragm dry clutch was no mean feat.

The chassis was similar to the discontinued R1200S, still employing the flat-twin engine as a stressed member, but with central and front tubular section steel frame sections matched to a self-supporting carbon-fibre rear subframe. This weighed just 2.2kg, saving 2kg over the R1200S aluminium unit. The Telelever front end included an Öhlins shock absorber, this now with adjustable compression damping via a remote knob at the front of the fuel tank. The Marzocchi built telescopic struts were housed in special milled aluminium triple clamps. Completing the race-oriented specification were forged alloy wheels, a 3.50x17-inch on the front and wide 6.00x17-inch on the rear. The front brakes were four-piston radial Brembo with 320mm discs, with a 265mm rear disc with single piston caliper. Another feature carried over from the racer was a MotoGP-inspired 2D dashboard. Only available in White and Black, the claimed dry weight was only 178kg. Around 1,000 examples of the HP2 Sport were available in 2008 but BMW wouldn't commit on numbers as its future was uncertain. With a 1,000cc four-cylinder Superbike already under development, the HP2 Sport was about be usurped as the ultimate BMW performance motorcycle.

F800GS, F650GS (2008-2012)

Two new enduro models powered by the F800S and ST twin cylinder engine replaced the single cylinder F650GS for 2008. The two enduros were distinctly individual, the F800GS more dual-purpose, combining road and off-road capability, while the F650GS was less adventure oriented. Although both models shared the 800cc parallel twin engine, the F800GS was envisaged as a smaller brother to the R1200GS, while the F650GS was seen as a successor to the F650 single cylinder series.

Although the already familiar F800S/ST 800cc

parallel twin engine powered the two new GSs, to allow for more suspension travel the engine cylinders were more upright. These were now canted forward 8.3 degrees instead of 30 degrees. A new die-cast aluminium lower engine housing provided an engine protection plate mount, while the cylinder head was reinforced for the frame attachment. Other modifications included a new clutch cover and water pump housing. Carried over were the 360-degree crankshaft, unique balancing system, and semi-dry sump lubrication. The F800GS received a wider oil cooler, with the F650GS retaining the narrower cooler of the F800S. The overall engine weight was also reduced a kilogram. While the F800GS featured the higher lift (9.64mm), longer duration F800S/ST camshafts, the F650GS included shorter duration, lower lift (7.2mm) camshafts, and a power-reducing valve. To meet Euro 3 compliance, the F800GS also received a secondary air system, this being unnecessary on the more mildly tuned F650GS. With a BMS-KP electronic injection system with twin 46mm throttle bodies, the power of both models differed significantly. The F800GS produced 85 horsepower at 7,500rpm and the F650 GS 71 horsepower at 7,000rpm. A 34 horsepower F650GS was also available for learner riders. As both the F800GS and F650GS were intended for off-road use, the final drive on both was by O-ring chain.

A tubular steel space frame of manganese-alloy steel was designed specifically for the two new GS models. A forged steel section brought the frame tubes together where they converged at the steering head and swingarm pivot. The slim steering head provided more steering lock (40 degrees for the 800 and 42 degrees for the 650) and each model received different suspension, wheels and brakes. To provide the best solution for 230mm travel, the F800GS received a 45mm upside-down front fork. With only 180mm of the travel, a conventional 43mm fork was deemed adequate for the F650GS. Both also featured a twin sided diecast aluminium swingarm with a single shock absorber, the F800GS with a R1200GS type WAD shock absorber with more travel (215mm) than the F650GS (170mm) with a gas assisted spring shock absorber.

The wheels also differed between each model. The F800GS received wire-spoked wheels with aluminium rims: a 2.15x21-inch on the front, and 4.25x17-inch

on the rear. The entry level F650GS received cast aluminium wheels, a 19x2.50-inch on the front and 17x3.5-inch on the rear. Both models were fitted with road-oriented enduro tyres as standard, somewhat negating the F800GS's off-road capability. The F800GS also received a more effective front braking system, with twin 300mm fully floating front discs with twin piston sliding Brembo calipers compared to the F650GS' single disc of the same specification. Both variants received an identical rear braking system, with a 265mm disc and single piston sliding Brembo caliper. Two channel ABS was an option and as on the sister F800 the electrical system was a single wire CAN bus type.

To appeal to shorter riders, a waisted seat was offered in two heights for both models, 880 or 850mm for the F800GS and 820 or 790mm for the F650GS. In addition, a lowering kit for the F650GS provided a 765mm seat height. Also separating the two were the fairings and windshield, the F650GS with more road-oriented equipment. While both shared a 26-degree steering head angle, as it was more street oriented, the F650GS' steering was lighter, with 97mm of trail compared to 117mm. At 171kg dry it was also significantly lighter than the 178kg F800GS.

Both were offered with a wide range of options, and the F800GS in particular could be outfitted into a serious adventure motorcycle. While the F650GS was an improvement over its predecessor, the F800GS provided a near impeccable balance between road and moderate off-road use. Its minimal weight and exceptional agility made it a perfect bike for many real world situations on a variety of terrains. Although not available until March 2008, the F800GS notched sales of 10,261 units, with the F650GS close behind with 9,644 sales. This placed them fifth in popularity in BMW's line-up. In tough market conditions BMW still recorded sales of 101,685 motorcycles in 2008. For 2010, F650GS and F800GS commemorative editions were available. Celebrating 30 years of the GS, these were in the original R80G/S colours.

G450X (2008-2011)

During 2007 BMW expanded their off-road involvement with 450cc 4-stroke prototypes to include the German Cross Country and World Enduro Championships, as well as the tough Australian

Four-Day Enduro. After a year of development in the hands of experienced riders like Sascha Eckert, Simo Kirssi and Joël Smets, BMW then introduced their first production competition Enduro motorcycle, the G450X. Although a rather eccentric offering in this conservative category, the G450X was already well developed and suitable for serious competition. Delivered ready to race, it also included a number of technologically advanced features.

Unlike the other singles that were designed in cooperation with outside companies, the 449cc water-cooled single cylinder engine was developed by BMW in-house. The bore and stroke was 98x59.6mm and the four-valve cylinder head design was similar to the K1200S, with intake valves operated by followers and the exhaust valves by tappets. Also unlike other models, the electronic fuel injection was Keihin, this including dual throttles. The crankshaft and con-rod ran in roller bearings and the forged piston included only two rings. To quell the single cylinder's vibration a balance shaft was driven from the crankshaft. The cable-operated multiplate wet clutch was mounted directly on the crankshaft with a clutch diaphragm. Compared to conventional geared down clutches, this allowed a smaller diameter unit with the same number of discs. Lubrication was wet sump, with two oil pumps: a pressure pump and a suction pump to lubricate the gearbox and crankshaft. An intermediate shaft transferred the power from the crank to the five-speed constant mesh gearbox, the engine turning backwards. The engine was mounted further back in the chassis than usual, allowing the cylinder to be canted forward by 30 degrees. This placed more weight on the front wheel and created the space for longer, straighter inlet tracts. As the compression ratio was a high 12:1, an automatic decompression function was fitted and starting was by electric start only. Although most off-road motorcycles ran two-piece radiators, this providing additional security if one was damaged, the G450X featured a single piece radiator. This included a thermo fan and the single radiator simplified plumbing. The air filter arrangement was also unusual. Instead of the usual foam filter arrangement, BMW adopted a cassette-style filter ahead of the motor. This compact engine weighed only 30kg and produced 50 horsepower at 9,000rpm.

The chassis also featured some innovative solutions, with the main frame section consisting of welded thin walled, stainless steel tubing and forged gussets. Weighing 8.6kg the swingarm and top suspension mount connected directly with the steering head. The 8.5-litre fuel tank was placed underneath the seat to lower the centre of gravity.

The double-sided aluminium swingarm also incorporated BMW's patented coaxial mount of the swingarm and countershaft. The swingarm pivot mounted through the hollow gearbox output, eliminating any change in chain length on compression and rebound over the entire spring travel. As the chain tension remained constant, the chain and sprockets were subject to less wear, which also resulted in reducing negative torque and improving traction. The swingarm was 30mm longer, without affecting the 1475mm wheelbase. One negative with this design was the requirement to remove the swingarm to replace the countershaft sprocket.

The high quality suspension consisted of a 45mm Marzocchi upside-down fork, with a generous 300mm spring travel, and a fully adjustable Öhlins central shock absorber providing 320mm travel. The steering geometry was also quite slow, with a 28.2 degree steering head angle and 119mm of trail. The wheels were similar to the G650Xchallenge, wire-spoked aluminium. On the front was a 1.60x21-inch with a 2.15x18-inch on the rear. The Brembo brakes included a single 260mm disc with a twin-piston floating caliper on the front, and 220mm disc with single-piston floating caliper on the rear. As it was intended for competition, ABS wasn't offered. Weighing only 111kg dry, the G450X was a serious enduro motorcycle, more than able to hold its own in a highly competitive market. Finnish rider Juha Salminen finishing runner-up in the 2008 Enduro World Championship E2 class, and Simo Kirssi winning the 2009 European Cross Country Championship was evidence of this. In the wake of this success, the G450X received a number of updates for 2010. These included a modified ECU, slip-on racing muffler, a new upside-down front fork, and recalibrated rear shock absorber. This wasn't enough to save it, unfortunately, and the G450X was discontinued after 2011.

During 2009 Europe was gripped by recession and BMW's new models were few. To celebrate 25 years of the K-series, the K1300 replaced the K1200. Other new models were the naked F800R, and single cylinder G650GS (primarily for the United States). Production dropped dramatically, to 93,243 motorcycles, and in June 2009 BMW celebrated forty years of motorcycle production in Berlin with 1,882,400 motorcycles leaving the Spandau factory over that period. This year also saw the establishment of the company's second motorcycle production facility, with motorcycles assembled from Completely Knocked Down (CKD) sets in Manaus, Brazil, in cooperation with local motorcycle producer DAFRA Motos.

K1300S, K1300R, K1300GT (2009-2016)

For 2009, the K1300 replaced the K1200, the three guises similar to before. While the basic engine configuration was carried over from the K1200, the cylinder bores were enlarged 1mm (to 80mm), and the stroke increased from 5.3mm to 64.3mm. The engine capacity increased 136cc, to 1,293cc. Other updates included lighter and shorter forged con-rods, 404 grams and 119mm compared with the K1200S' 413 grams and 120mm. These were also split horizontally with the same crack technology as before. Both the main and con-rod journals measured 38mm, as before. The new two-ring 80mm box-type pistons included a short piston apron, the weight with bolts and rings 287 grams, compared to the K1200S' 299 grams. Modified spray jets in the crankcase cooled the underside of the piston crown. The crankshaft was also rebalanced for the new pistons and the two gear driven balance shafts in front and behind the crankshaft provided an 86 per cent balance factor. The cylinder head design was unchanged but the exhaust camshaft timing was new as were the exhaust valve springs. The timing chain tensioning system was also revised. The maximum rpm was now 11,000rpm. The 13:1 compression ratio was unchanged as was the dry sump lubrication system. Also retained was the wet multiplate clutch, but with new linings and springs and larger diameter slave cylinder (34 instead of 32mm) to handle to engine's increased power and torque. The maximum power of the K1300S (BMW's most powerful motorcycle yet) was 175 horsepower at 9,250rpm, with maximum torque of 103 lb-ft at 8,250rpm. The K1300R produced slightly less: 173 horsepower at 9,250rpm and the K1300GT 160 horsepower at 9,000rpm. The engine unit weighed 82.8kg, and the BMS-K electronic fuel injection included D4 CVE (Central Vehicle Electronics) torque-based engine management with Alpha-n-control. This monitored the air drawn in via the throttle butterflies at a specific angle and engine speed. The engine operating efficiency was based on the throttle butterfly angle, this determined by a potentiometer, with additional engine and ambient parameters (engine temperature, air temperature, ambient air pressure) interacting with control maps installed in advance. The 46mm throttle butterflies came with a new, desmodromic operating system, each with an opening and closing cable. The K1300S and K1300R also received a revised stainless steel exhaust system, this with a significantly shorter muffler and an electronically controlled valve. The K1300GT muffler was carried over from the K1200GT but on all K1300s undercut gears, a revised shift fork and gear lever roller bearings added up to improved gear selection. A factory-fitted HP quick shift was also optional.

The aluminium frame, Paralever rear suspension, and Duolever front suspension were carried over from the K1200. New were firmer shock absorbers and the Duolever's lower longitudinal arm was now of light alloy instead of forged steel. This saved 1kg and the overall structure now weighed 12.7kg. The steering geometry was also revised, the K1300S with 29.6 degrees of fork rake and 104.4mm of trail. The wheelbase of the K1300S and K1300R was also stretched out to 1,585mm. The K1300R's geometry was identical to the K1300S, and the K1300GT had the same rake but 112mm of trail, along with a shorter 1,572mm wheelbase.

The aluminium Paralever swingarm was also redesigned for the K1300, to allow for the optional upgraded ESA II electronic suspension. ESA II allowed front and rear rebound damping adjustment, rear spring preload, and rear spring rate. This was simulated using a plastic element called Elastogran. As the spring was compressed, an electric motor and gears deflected the Elastogran element. Overall the ESA II system offered nine different settings. ASC anti spin control was also optional. While the wheels and brakes were unchanged the K1300S rear tyre was a slightly higher profile 190/55ZR17. The K1300R was now fitted with the previously optional 5.50x17-inch rear wheel with smaller 180x55ZR17 tyre.

Another feature for the K1300 was a new generation of smaller switches and controls that would soon feature across the range. While similar to the K1200S, the K1300S' fairing was slimmer, with different contours. The three new 1300s continued a similar style to their respective predecessors but along with the power the weight was also up considerably. The K1300S now weighed 228kg (dry), the K1300R 217kg, and the K1300GT a hefty 255kg. Fortunately the low centre of gravity belied their weight and the host of small updates ensured the K1300s were noticeably improved over the K1200s. An even more luxurious K1300GT Exclusive Edition was available for 2010, but with a 1,600cc six cylinder on the horizon the K1300GT's days were numbered. More special versions were offered for 2012, the HP package for the K1300S creating the sportiest K-series yet. Technical updates included a numbered badge, numerous HP carbon parts, an Akrapovič muffler, ESA II, ASC stability control, a speed gearshift and paddock stand. The 2012 K1300R included special paint, a carbon engine spoiler and the ESA II and ASC dynamics package. For 2013, marking the 30th anniversary of the K-series, the K1300S 30-Year featured special colours, ESA II and the RDC and ADC safety pack. Also included was an HP shift assistant and Akrapovič sports silencer. The K1300R's previously optional sports wheels were standard for 2013, and a K1300S Motorsport in white, red and blue was available for 2015. Although the K1300S and K1300R soldiered on until 2016, ultimately the K1300s were considered too unconventional and eccentric. As such, they never really achieved the success BMW envisaged.

Below: The aggressive looking
K1300R was BMW's most
powerful naked bike yet. *BMW
Group Press*

Opposite top: Full touring
equipment ensured the K1300GT
was a comfortable and effective
long distance motorcycle. *BMW
Group Press*

Opposite bottom: Based
on the F800S, the F800R's
styling mimicked the K1300R.
BMW Group Press

F800R (2009-2014)

Joining the existing range of 800cc parallel twins
for 2009 was the naked F800R. The impetus for
the F800R came from Christian Pfeiffer's success in
winning the European Stunt Riding Championship
three years in succession on a special F800R. Sharing
the style of the other two roadsters in the line-up, the
R1200R and K1300R, the F800R was designed for
dynamic urban riding, with an emphasis on fun. This
third in the Roadster series was based on the F800S
and continued the minimalist naked concept of less
weight and outstanding dynamics.

The parallel-twin engine was similar to the F800S
and ST, the cylinders canted 30 degrees with a 360
degree crankshaft, and the unique rod and pivot
balance system. Unchanged was the chain-driven double
overhead camshaft arrangement with four valves per
cylinder (32mm intake and 27.5mm exhaust). BMS-
KP engine management system included and two
46mm throttles. A new throttle valve kinematic system
featured on the F800R, this improving low end throttle
response. The new exhaust system included separate
catalytic converter, no longer integrated in the silencer
as on the F800S. The power was 87 horsepower at
8,000rpm. A 34 horsepower version was also available,
the reduction achieved through an altered throttle
valve. The lower three gear ratios were identical to the
F800S, with the top three gears lowered to improve
performance on tighter, twisting roads. Like the
F800GS, final drive was by O-ring chain rather than the
F800S and ST's belt final drive.

Also similar to the F800S was the welded and
diecast aluminium frame. The steering head angle
was a steep 25 degrees, with a short 91mm of trail.
The wheelbase was lengthened to 1,520mm. New for
the F800R was a double-sided aluminium swingarm.
Considering the generally high chassis specification, the
front suspension was, surprisingly, an older style 43mm
conventional front fork. The rear suspension was by
an adjustable shock absorber connecting directly to the
swingarm, while the cast alloy wheels were the 'Speed'
style of the F800S, these featuring useful side-mounted
tyre valves. Wheel sizes were 3.50x17-inch at the front
and a generous 5.50x17-inch at the rear, this allowing
a large 180/55ZR17 tyre.

As with the wheel sizes, the braking system was also
suitable for a larger displacement bike. At the front
were twin 320mm steel discs with Brembo 4-piston
fixed brake calipers. The front master cylinder was
also high spec, with an adjustable lever and remote
master cylinder. The rear brake was the usual 265mm
disc with single piston floating caliper. The optional
ABS had a readjusted pressure sensor that allowed
finer monitoring, particularly over bumps. The wheel
rotation sensors automatically monitored their distance
from the sensor wheel, enhancing safety. The overall
road dynamics were also enhanced by the relatively
light dry weight of 177kg.

The CAN-bus and single wire electrical system
was similar to other F800s, while the cockpit featured
analogue instruments and the switches were the new
generation type. Smaller and more compact, these
incorporated MID (Moulded Interconnect Devices)
with laser conductors instead of individual wiring.
Setting the F800R off was a pair of asymmetrical H7
headlamps, the aggressive face intentionally echoing the
K1300R design. Options extended to sport windshield,
radiator trim panels, passenger seat cover and an
engine spoiler. With four-time World and European
Stunt-Riding Champion Chris Pfeiffer convincingly
demonstrating the F800R's abilities, a special Pfeiffer
replica was available for 2010. Closely resembling
the competition version, ostensibly only the paint and
Akrapovič muffler separated the special edition from
the standard production model. The bespoke colour
scheme included a black drivetrain and swingarm, with
a Chris Pfeiffer signature and sponsor decals further
differentiating it. The F800R received a mid-cycle
update for 2012. Now slightly more aggressively styled,

the front and side trim served as radiator covers, and updated styling cues extended to new front fender, red rear shock absorber spring, and a body coloured sport windshield. A new version replaced it for 2015.

By the end of the 2000s, all motorcycle manufacturers were suffering, but, as Europe's premier motorcycle producer, BMW were optimistically planning for the future. In an endeavour to widen the marque's appeal, BMW decided to consciously target a younger clientele with a new Superbike and individualised boxers. With even more emphasis on competition, the next decade would see some of BMW's most impressive new models yet.

BMW entered a new era in
2009 with the racing S1000RR.
BMW Group Press

9 REDEFINING THE BRAND

BMW's motorcycle sales had gradually grown since the 2004 launch of the ground-breaking R1200GS, but while known for excellence, quality and innovation, BMW motorcycles were still generally considered idiosyncratic and individual. Only BMW made boxer twins and unusual front suspension like the Telelever, Duolever, and Paralever. Their take on the traditional parallel twin and single was also unique. All this changed with the new S1000RR Superbike, an uncompromising performance model embracing a conventional format. Although a succession of new high-performance models had gradually eroded BMW's staid image over the past few years, the S1000RR completely obliterated it. And BMW didn't stop there, presenting a six-cylinder concept at the end of 2009. Over the next few years, BMW would thus redefine their traditional touring category.

S1000RR (2009-2011)

In April 2008, BMW announced they would be developing a new 1,000cc inline four-cylinder Superbike in partnership with Alpha Technik. The intention was to compete in the 2009 World Superbike Championship, this also requiring at least 1,000 production versions to be built for the 2010 Model Year. BMW's first real Superbike since the R90S, the S1000RR offered unparalleled technical innovation and eye-watering performance, and immediately became the class-setting Superbike.

Unlike previous BMW designs, the S1000RR layout was surprisingly conventional. A water-cooled inline four-cylinder in an aluminium bridge frame was already established as the most efficient layout for a Superbike. Also proven was an upside-down front fork and linkage rear suspension. BMW then added their interpretation within this traditional framework. With the sportsbike sector accounting for more than 230,000 sales worldwide during 2008, BMW were intent on grabbing a significant slice by targeting a younger, more sporting customer.

Under Superbike project leader Rainer Bäumel, the primary objective was to create an extremely powerful narrow engine in a compact package. Sharing many characteristics of BMW's Formula One programme, the S1000RR was specifically designed for racing, and the initial version was a World Superbike racer. It was a dream kickoff for the S1000RR when it debuted at Phillip Island, Australia in March 2009. Troy Corser set the fastest lap and finished eighth in the first race, with the fastest speed (324km/h) through the trap in race two.

While the S1000RR's format was conventional, the 999cc engine featured the shortest stroke (49.7mm) on the Superbike grid. Only 463mm wide at the crankshaft, at just 59.8kg dry, the S1000RR engine was also the lightest in the class. The wet-sump engine featured Formula One-style, light, small finger cam followers, both the intake and the exhaust cam followers facing the rear, keeping the cylinder head narrower. The followers operated a pair of 33.5mm intake and 27.2mm titanium valves, and thanks to the larger 80mm bore, the valves were the largest of any 1,000cc four-cylinder Superbike. Set at a flat included angle of 24.5 degrees (11.2 degrees on the intake and 13.3 degrees on the exhaust), they provided a 50 per cent reduction in reciprocating mass, and when combined with the short stroke allowed for higher revs and more aggressive cam profiles. For the racing engine, the valves were from Del West in the USA, with stiffer Japanese NHK valve springs, two per valve. A toothed chain running on a secondary gear shaft just above the crankshaft on the right side of the engine drove the higher lift racing camshafts. The forged one-piece steel crankshaft was fitted with Pankl titanium race con-rods, while the two-ring forged pistons were also Pankl, with the Nikasil-bored cylinders inclined forward 32 degrees. Engine height was only 558mm. The compression ratio at the start of the season was 14:1, and three different engine specifications were tried during 2009.

Contributing to this impressive power claim was a home-brewed electronics package, and four 48mm Dell'Orto throttle bodies breathing though a 7.9-litre ram-fed airbox. BMW's own RSM5 engine management ECU monitored twin injectors per throttle body and variable length intakes via a ride-by-wire throttle. The six-speed gearbox featured stacked shafts to minimise engine length, with a choice of three options for each ratio. Completing the engine specification was an Akrapovič titanium 4-2-1 exhausts system, and the claimed power was 193 horsepower at 13,700rpm.

This impressive engine was rigidly mounted as a fully stressed component in a modular twin-spar chassis. Consisting of four cast aluminium members welded together, a 43mm Öhlins TTX25 front fork was set at 23.9 degrees, providing 102mm of trail. As on other World Superbike racers a pair of four-piston, four-pad Brembo Monobloc calipers gripped the 320mm Brembo floating front discs.

Swingarm experimentation resulted in three different versions, each retaining the long 593mm of the street version, but varying in rigidity. The wheelbase was a short 1,428mm. A choice of progressive rate linkages was also available for the Öhlins TT36X rear shock absorber. The Öhlins TT 'Twin Tube' suspension was the most sophisticated available and featured twin piggyback damper tubes offering separate adjustment for both compression and rebound. The OZ cast magnesium wheels were also standard World Superbike specification, the front a 16.5x3.25-inch and the rear a 16x6.25-inch.

Unfortunately, after the promising start to the season, things didn't go as smoothly in successive rounds. Ruben Xaus joined Corser in the team but he was sidelined through injury, and 2009 World Endurance Champion Steve Martin assumed the position as chief development rider. Although results picked up towards the end of the season, too many DNFs saw Corser ultimately finishing 13th overall, with Xaus 17th.

When the S1000RR went into production early in 2010, the engine specification was remarkably close to the 2009 World Superbike racer. The forged steel crankshaft retained 180-degree crank pins, and 34mm main and conrod journals, but with forged steel 103mm con-rods. These weighed 334 grams (with the bearings), the 17mm small end without a bearing bush. Two 45-degree lubrication openings in the upper eye ensured a reliable oil supply. The connecting rods were split horizontally by the proven cracking method. While the production engine retained Nikasil-coated cylinder liners the 253-gram forged box pistons included a third oil scavenger ring. To remove and dissipate heat, oil injection nozzles in the crankcase cooled the pistons underneath. The compression ratio of 13:1 was slightly less than the racer, but at the high limit for a production engine. The compact cylinder head design with finger cam followers was also identical to the racer. Valve adjustment was by small platelets running on the spring plates, aluminium on the intake. The production valves were still titanium,

Below left: The production
S1000RR chassis was similar
to the racer, but with Sachs
suspension and 17-inch wheels.
BMW Group Press

Below right: When released in
2010, the S1000RR immediately
set the standard for production
Superbikes. *BMW Group Press*

Opposite top: Corser's 2010
World Superbike racer featured
Nissin front brakes and a new
swingarm. *BMW Group Press*

Opposite bottom: With two
podium finishes, Corser had
a better season during 2010.
BMW Group Press

with unchanged sizes from the racer, with 5mm stems. Torque was transmitted from the crankshaft via a straight-toothed primary drive to an anti-hopping, 132.4mm diameter, 10-plate wet clutch.

Developed in-house, the BMS-KP Engine Management included Anti-Knock Control, and, as on the factory racer, variable length intake manifolds provided an optimum torque curve and increased maximum power. A ride-by-wire system also controlled the 48mm throttle bodies, and the exhaust system included two interference-type butterflies linking the two outer and the two inner manifolds in the immediate vicinity of the exhaust ducts. Also included in the electronic package was a choice of riding modes: Rain, Sport, Race and Slick. In the Rain mode, power was reduced to 150 horsepower; full power was available in Sport mode; Race provided more direct dynamic response, and Slick was intended for track use with slick tyres. A factory option was DTC (Dynamic Traction Control), and S1000RR was the first production motorcycle to combine Race ABS with Dynamic Traction Control. Producing 193 horsepower at 13,000rpm, and safe to 14,200rpm, the S1000RR also set a new standard for power with production Superbikes.

The 11.98kg production aluminium chassis was also very similar to the racing version, sharing the 27.9 degree steering head angle, but with 95.5mm of trail. The double-sided aluminium swingarm weighed only 6.22kg, and a 45mm range of rear axle adjustment

allowed for a wheelbase range from 1,414.5 to 1,459.5mm. Rather than the exotic Öhlins suspension of the racing version, the suspension on the production bike was via a 46mm upside-down Sachs front fork, and fully adjustable Sachs rear shock absorber. Also different for the production bike were 10-spoke cast aluminium wheels – 17x3.50-inch on the front and 17x6.50-inch on the rear. While the front brakes were a Brembo four-piston radial setup, with twin 320mm floating discs, the calipers had fixed 34mm pistons. A single piston floating caliper gripped the rear 220mm disc. Race ABS with four pressure sensors was available as an option. Weighing only 206.5kg with a full tank, the S1000RR was the lightest 1,000cc Superbike.

Although the S1000RR was a conventional Superbike in concept and execution, the quirky styling was typically BMW. Breaking with the norm the asymmetrical headlight arrangement was designed to emphasise an endurance-racing look. But looks aside the S1000RR was an exceptional motorcycle, winning a host of awards including the 'International Bike of the Year 2010.' It was also extremely successful in various road racing championships during 2010.

After a promising introduction during 2009, BMW worked hard at creating a competitive S1000RR racer for the 2010 season. Under the direction of Davide Tardozzi, and with Troy Corser and Ruben Xaus again riding, the engine was developed with Dell'Orto fuel-injection, and a ride-by-wire BMW RSM5 EFI system to produce 215 horsepower at 14,000rpm. With an

Öhlins 43mm TTX20 or TRVP25 front fork, RSP40 or TTX36 Monoshock, and a special aluminium swingarm, the S1000RR weighed right on the 162kg weight limit. The swingarm was unique as the top and bottom halves were glued together. The brakes this year were Nissin (Corser) or Brembo (Xaus) but the OZ magnesium 16.6 and 16-inch wheels were unchanged. The sophisticated electronics included BMW's race ABS system. As the basic credentials were sound, gradual development saw an improvement in race results. Corser finished on the podium at Monza and Misano, and 11th overall in the championship.

While it was an uphill struggle in World Superbike, in the Superstock 1000 FIM Cup Italian rider Ayrton Badovini rode a production-spec S1000RR to nine wins from ten races, and a comfortable title victory. Success in production-based national championships continued throughout Europe, with victories to Gregory Fastre (Belgium), Javier Fores Querol (Spain), Jon Kirkham (British Superstock Championship), Steve Brogan (British Superbike EVO Championship) Sami Penna (Finland), Martin Choi (Bulgaria), Maxim Averkin (Russia) and Erwan Nigon (France). In Germany, the S1000RR dominated several series, winning the DMV Road Racing Championship, Endurance Cup, and DMSB Endurance Championship.

After dominating sportsbike sales worldwide, apart from new grey and yellow colours and a slightly heavier crankshaft (on Troy Corser's recommendation), the production S1000RR was unchanged for 2011. And in their third season, BMW also hoped for more success in the World Superbike Championship. 2010 second placed finisher Leon Haslam was drafted alongside Corser. Haslam came brimming with confidence but found the S1000RR recalcitrant. Now 39, Corser was in the twilight of his illustrious World Superbike career and continued to struggle. Unfortunately, despite being well resourced the BMW team couldn't improve the S1000RR significantly from the previous year.

The basic engine architecture was unchanged, and still included Dell'Orto 48mm throttles with BMW's own RSM5 EFI. With a 14.1:1 compression ratio, the maximum power was over 220 horsepower at 14,000rpm, but, despite a new electronics package and revised crankshaft, this peak figure came at the expense of low down power. A short under-engine exhaust was tried early in the season but soon discarded. Chassis development included replacement of the racing swingarm with that of the stock street bike, and a return to Brembo Monobloc brakes. These were either EVO or lithium aluminium. The Öhlins suspension was a 43mm TRSP25 or TTX20 front fork and RSP40 rear shock absorber. Both OZ and Marchesini wheels used during the season, now a 17x3.50-inch on the front and 17x6.25-inch at the rear. While the S1000RR weighed right on the minimum 165kg, the balance was too front biased, and BMW introduced a new tank to move the rider towards the rear. Grappling with over complicated electronics, significant results remained elusive. Haslam managed only three podium finishes, and was beaten nine times by Badovini on the BMW Italia privateer S1000RR. Haslam finished the season in 5th overall, with Corser 15th. Although World Superbike results were disappointing during 2011, Sébastien Gimbert won the French Superbike title, Glenn Allerton took out the Australian Superbike Championship, and Team Motorrad France 99 came a close second in the FIM World Endurance Championship.

R1200GS (2010-2012), R1200GS ADVENTURE, R1200RT (2010-2013)

The popular R1200GS and R1200RT received an engine with updated double overhead camshaft cylinder heads for 2010. The engine layout and construction was similar to the HP2 Sport, with two chain-driven overhead camshafts per cylinder and the valves operated by light rocker arms. The four valves per cylinder were arranged radially and the valves increased to 39mm intake and 33mm on the exhaust. The valve lift was also increased to 10.8mm for both the intake and exhaust. Like the previous model (but unlike the HP2 Sport) ignition was by twin spark plugs. The bore and stroke of 101x73mm and 12:1 compression ratio was unchanged. While the crankshaft and con-rods were carried over, the cast aluminium pistons were redesigned to match the new combustion chamber shape. The throttle butterflies now measured 50mm (up from 47mm but smaller than the HP2's 52mm), and featured new air intake funnels. The power was increased to 110 horsepower

The R1200GS received a new
double overhead camshaft
engine for 2010, but was
otherwise basically unchanged.
BMW Group Press

at 7,750rpm with peak torque of 120Nm at 6,000rpm.
The maximum safe engine rpm also increased 500rpm,
to 8,500rpm. Setting the new engines apart were
magnesium-coloured cylinder head covers with two
instead of four fastening bolts. The exhaust system also
included an electronically controlled flap to provide

a throatier exhaust note. While the R1200GS chassis
was unchanged, Enduro ESA Electronic Suspension
Adjustment was now available as a factory-fitted
option. This offered both on-road and off-road modes
with damping, spring base and spring rate adjustable
with the touch of a button. Otherwise unchanged for

Also receiving the new boxer
engine was the R1200RT.
BMW Group Press

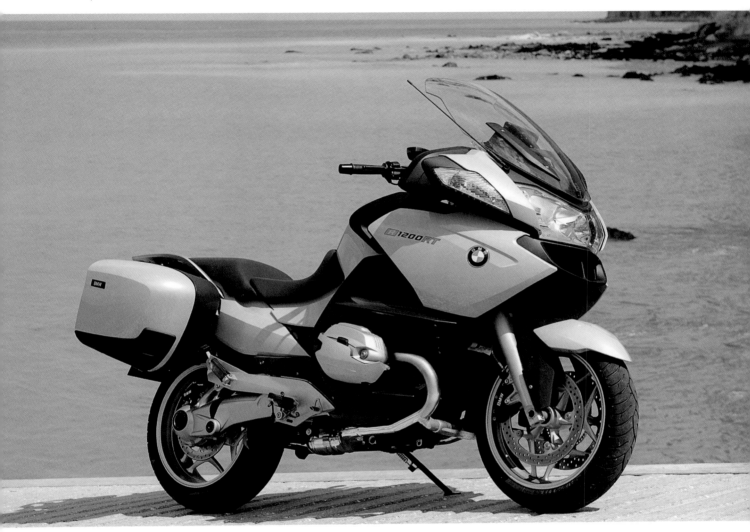

2011, joining the range this year was an R1200GS
Triple Black. A black fork, wheels and engine set this
limited edition model apart.

The R1200RT also received the same DOHC
engine as the R1200GS for 2010, and was available
with ESA II Electronic Suspension Adjustment. Partly
integrated ABS was standard. While the basic chassis
was unchanged, the fairing was redesigned to provide
improved protection. Along with a redesigned
cockpit, the electronically controlled windshield
provided reduced wind noise and visibility. The audio
system provided USB/MP3 and iPod connectivity.
Lockable 32-litre hard cases were standard. Along
with the S1000RR, the release of the new R1200GS

and RT contributed to a significant increase in
motorcycle sales, to 112,271 during 2010. For 2012,
a special version of the R1200GS Adventure, the
R1200GS Rallye was available. This included special
colours, a chrome exhaust system, and an onboard
computer.

K1600GT, K1600GTL (2011-2016)

BMW and motorcycle touring were historically
synonymous, and BMW consistently had several
extremely competent touring motorcycles in their

range. But while there were few complaints regarding the existing K1300GT and R1200RT, the release of the K1600GT and GTL grand tourers set a new benchmark. Six-cylinder inline engines had been a significant layout for BMW cars over the years, but six-cylinder motorcycle engines had always been either very long or very wide, compromising chassis geometry and weight distribution.

Derived from the existing four-cylinder K1300, BMW went to great lengths to keep the six-cylinder engine as compact as possible. To reduce width, the engine dimensions of 67.5x72mm were undersquare, and with only 5mm between the cylinder sleeves, the spacing between cylinders was only 77mm. Engine width was also minimised by moving the electrical ancillary units and their drive mechanisms behind the crankshaft, above the gearbox. Total engine width was 555mm, only slightly more than the K1300. Displacing 1,649cc, the engine, including clutch, gearbox and alternator weighed only 102.6kg, and it was the lightest ever production six-cylinder motorcycle engine. The maximum power was 160 horsepower at 7,750rpm, with maximum torque of 175Nm produced at 5,250rpm. Over 70 per cent of the maximum torque was available from 1,500rpm.

The forged steel crankshaft weighed only 12.9kg and featured the usual six-cylinder journal offset of 120 degrees. As the six-cylinder engine already possessed perfect primary balance, additional balance shafts weren't required. The main bearing journals were 42mm in diameter, with 40mm connecting rod journals. The con-rods measured 124.45mm, and, as on other models, benefited from crack technology. A hydraulically tensioned toothed chain on the right drove the twin overhead camshafts.

The four-valve cylinder head design differed to the K1300 as the valve operating mechanism featured bucket tappets. The included valve angle of 25 degrees (12 degrees on the intake and 13 degrees on the exhaust) was also slightly wider. Valve sizes were 29mm intake and 24.8mm exhaust, with 5mm stems. As on the K1300 the cylinders were tilted forward 55 degrees, aiding a lower centre of gravity, while three-ring slipper pistons provided a 12.2:1 compression ration. Unusually the aluminium crankcase was sandcast, this construction permitting thinner walls. The lubrication system was an integrated dry sump type, this without a conventional oil sump and

allowing a lower engine installation. The oil tank was integrated in the rear of the crankcase.

Torque was transmitted from the crankshaft to a 10-disc wet clutch via a straight-toothed primary drive. The helical-cut gearbox was a three-shaft type, the three gearbox shafts arranged one on top of the other and as on all large-capacity BMW touring bikes, final drive was by shaft.

A new electronic engine management system was introduced for the K1600, BMS-X. The Alpha-n torque-based system used the throttle valve angle and engine speed, along with various sensors and stored mapping characteristics to determine the injection volume and ignition timing. A ride-by-wire system controlled the 52mm central throttle valve. The central throttle enabled longer induction tracts with a consequent increase in lower and mid-range torque. Three different riding modes were also available (Rain, Road, Dynamic) with DTC (Dynamic Traction Control) available as an option.

The K1600's chassis was an evolution of the K1300 type, sharing the essential elements of an aluminium bridge-type frame, Duolever front suspension and Paralever rear suspension. Particular attention to mass concentration resulted in a static weight distribution of 52 per cent on the front wheel and 48 per cent on the rear. Thus with a pillion passenger the weight bias was still acceptable. The welded central bridge-type frame consisted of four heat-treated chill-cast parts with thin walls. As the engine was tilted heavily forward, the main frame ran above the cylinder head and could be kept narrow. The main frame weighed just 16kg, with the engine bolted at eight points. The 4kg rear subframe was constructed of welded aluminium extruded sections and bolted to the main frame at four points.

As on the K1300, the front suspension was by Duolever, with 115mm of spring travel, and an aluminium Paralever swingarm. This mounted directly on the main frame, the torque support still located above the swinging arm, with the brake caliper now mounted at the rear. A central adjustable shock absorber provided 135mm of spring travel. The light alloy wheels were ten-spoke, a 3.50 x 17-inch on the front and 6.0 x 17-inch on the rear. A factory option was Electronic Suspension Adjustment II (ESA II) that provided electronic adjustment for rebound damping and spring preload. This rather complicated system

Bottom: A host of luxury fittings differentiated the K1600GTL from the K1600GT. These included a topbox, chrome trim, fog lights and a taller screen. The rider's pegs were also set lower and further forward, with a lower seat. *BMW Group Press*

Below: Derived from the four-cylinder K1300, the compact six-cylinder K1600 engine featured chain-driven double overhead camshafts and four-valves per cylinder, with bucket-type tappets. *BMW Group Press*

included an electric motor and gear to vary the spring rate while small stepper motors altered the damping. Compression forces were absorbed by an elastomer element (Cellasto) combined with a conventional coil spring. An electrohydraulic mechanism moved an aluminium inner sleeve, this restricting the Cellasto element's expansion and adjusting the spring preload. Other electronic aids included partially integrated ABS. Including the alarm system, ABS and DTC there were 16 control units in the CAN communication network.

The braking system was similar to the K1300, with a pair of 320mm discs and four-piston calipers on the front, but with a larger 320mm disc and twin-piston caliper on the rear. DTC (Dynamic Traction Control) was also available as a factory option, this not only detecting rear wheel spin but also the banking angle. An 'Adaptive Headlight' was also available as an option, this using the traction control gyroscopes and two pitch sensors to direct the beam via a reflector mirror to provide the optimum spread of light, particularly when cornering.

Although the differences between the K1600GT and GTL were primarily in equipment, the GTL was also aimed at a different market. The riding position was more laid back on the GTL, and with the additional rear weight bias the steering was lighter. The GTL also received a longer and wider seat with a backrest on the standard topbox. As it was aimed at the luxury touring market, surprising omissions were a reverse gear and electric centre stand. Lighter and more agile, the GT was suitable for solo riding on more twisty roads. The K1600 exceeded all the design and engineering team's expectations, and set a new benchmark for touring motorcycles. Smooth, fast, and bristling with technology the K1600GT was arguably the ultimate fast tourer. It was no surprise that the K1600GT won the 'International Bike of the Year 2011' award. In a difficult retail environment BMW's sales were down slightly, to 104,286 motorcycles sold during 2011. On 6 May, BMW also celebrated the production of the two millionth motorcycle to roll off the Berlin production line.

For 2014, an even more opulent K1600GTL was available: the K1600GTL Exclusive. Based on the K1600GTL, standard equipment included central locking with an anti-theft alarm system, ESA II, DTC, Hill Start Control, and the obligatory ABS. A radio antenna was inserted in the top-box lid, while a new seat, a heated backrest and armrests improved pillion comfort. Also standard were LED auxiliary headlights, an adaptive xenon headlight, tyre pressure monitor, floor lighting, and, for the first time on a BMW motorcycle, Keyless Ride. From the fuel tank's aluminium moulding and fully chromed exhaust system to the new-look instrumentation, the Exclusive took luxury motorcycle touring to a new level. Also offered for 2014 was the more dynamic K1600GT Sport, this with black wheels, low windshield, and sports-style seat. Along with new colours for 2015, the K1600GT and GTL received Dynamic Traction Control (DTC), Hill Start Control, the GTL Exclusive instrument layout, and optional keyless start. For 2016, there were more new colours, and ABS Pro and the dynamic brakelight were standard. Considering the six-cylinder K-series was aimed at the luxury market, sales were surprisingly strong, totalling 4,866 during 2015.

R1200R, R1200R CLASSIC (2011-2014)

For 2011, the R1200R also received the HP2 Sport-derived double overhead camshaft boxer twin engine. Also joining the standard R1200R was the nostalgic R1200R Classic. The 110 horsepower engine and exhaust system (with 60mm shorter muffler) was shared with the R1200GS and R1200RT, and both R1200Rs received some chassis updates. While retaining the usual Telelever and Paralever designs, the new R1200R models were fitted with a completely redesigned fork structure, this now with 41mm tubes (up from 35mm). Distinguishing the R1200R Classic from the standard version were wire spoke wheels, while a chrome-plated exhaust replaced the standard brushed stainless steel unit. Continuing the retro theme on both versions were classical round instruments, augmented by an onboard computer. A tapered aluminium handlebar replaced the previous steel type and a centre stand was now standard. With an 18-litre fuel tank the R1200R fulfilled a role as a comfortable, fun, and practical road motorcycle, and with a pair of 17-inch wheels it was well suited to sporting street use. But the R1200R was always perceived as a niche model and never gained the following of the more popular dual purpose R1200GS. As such it was always the final model to receive updated engines, and while the R1200GS and R1200RT received the new water-cooled boxer engine in 2013 and 2014, the R1200R continued largely unchanged until the new model replaced it in 2015. To maintain interest in the model, an R1200R 'Dark White' special model was available for 2014. This included a standard sports windshield and sports seat.

G650GS, G650GS SERTÃO (2011-2016)

Although the single-cylinder G650GS (formerly the F650GS) was reintroduced for the United States as an entry-level model in 2009, it made a return to the general line-up for 2011. Last seen in 2007, and now built in Spandau, the 652cc four-stroke single cylinder engine was largely unchanged, retaining an 11.5:1 compression ratio, four valves per cylinder, double overhead camshafts, electronic fuel-injection, and twin-spark ignition.

Due to new Spanish licence regulations that would affect all other EU countries from 2013, the power output was reduced slightly, to 48 horsepower at 6,500rpm. The engine management was now by a BMS-CII system, and the gearbox remained a five-

The R1200R received the DOHC engine for 2011 and this R1200R Classic with wire-spoked wheels joined it. *BMW Group Press*

speed. As was usual for an enduro motorcycle, the secondary drive was by an O-ring chain.

The bridge steel frame with bolt-on rear subframe was inherited from the earlier F650GS, as were the conventional 41mm telescopic fork and double-sided steel swingarm with linkage Monoshock suspension. The front brake was a single 300mm disc with twin-piston floating caliper, with a 240mm rear disc and single piston floating caliper. ABS was optional. The cast alloy wheels were a new design, with the 17-inch rear widened from 3.0 to 3.5 inches.

The bodywork was completely redesigned, the front section now including an asymmetrical headlamp and extended front wheel cover. The coloured plastic bodywork and two-tone seat contrasted strongly with the black engine, exhaust, frame, swingarm, and fork legs. To appeal to a wider range of riders, three different seat heights for available: standard 800mm, low 770mm, and high 840mm. Although remarkably similar to the updated 2004 F650GS, and even the original 2000 version, the venerable five-speed G650GS proved there was still a market for a sensible, lightweight, low-cost passport to adventure, especially with a wide array of options available.

The G650GS was based on the earlier single-cylinder F650GS.
BMW Group Press

After being side lined since 2007, the previous F650GS Dakar made a comeback for 2012 as the G650GS Sertão. With the current trend of adventure bikes becoming more street oriented, the Sertão was designed for the genuine off-roader. Sharing the basic engine and chassis with the standard G650GS, the Sertão included longer travel suspension, 1.60x21 and 3.00x17-inch wire-spoked wheels, and an aluminium engine guard. Underpowered for pure street use, when the going got tough the well balanced Sertão could more than hold its own. Unfortunately, it was another model that underperformed in the marketplace and wasn't offered after 2014. The basic G650GS continued as a US model, and was offered with the option of wire-spoke wheels for 2016.

S1000RR (2012-2014)

Immediately after its launch in 2009 S1000RR Project Manager Ralf Schwickerath initiated a program of consulting racers and working to improve what was already the class leading Superbike. The culmination of this plan became evident two years later with the significantly updated S1000RR for 2012. Considering nearly 200 horsepower sufficient, BMW's engineers left the engine unchanged, but provided it with more mid-range torque and a more sensitive response through throttle reconfiguration. The previous four individual throttle curves were reduced to two: a gentle and sensitive throttle for Rain mode, and an immediately direct and spontaneous response for the Sport, Race, and Slick modes. In Rain mode, the S1000RR now delivered 163 horsepower, eleven more than previously. With three different torque curves instead of two, in Sport, Race, and Slick modes, the power could be raised significantly between 5,000 and 7,500rpm. Also introduced was overrun phase combustion control that converted braking torque and engine drag torque into retarding torque on the rear wheel. The stainless steel exhaust system included a redesigned catalytic converter, now integrated in the front silencer rather than the header pipes.

More significant were updates to the chassis. The aluminium frame featured a new steering head and tail section, and the air intake guide in the steering head was 20 per cent larger. The steering head angle was now 24 degrees (instead of 23.9 degrees) and the wheelbase shortened by 9.3mm to 1422.7mm. The front fork offset, provided by the milled and forged triple clamps, was 2.5mm shorter, at 29.5mm. The 46mm upside-down fork now featured a mid speed damping valve, and the shock absorber was longer. On the shock the piston rod diameter was increased from 14 to 18mm, allowing more oil to flow through the low/mid speed valve. The swingarm pivot was also positioned 4mm higher. Along with an adjustable mechanical steering damper, these frame and suspension modifications were instrumental in improving riding dynamics.

A number of new styling features also set the 2012 S1000RR apart from its predecessor. The tail section was leaner and the centre airbox cover featured new side aperture grilles. New aerodynamic winglet deflectors joined the characteristic asymmetrical side panels, these still with gills on the right and an air outlet on the left. The updated S1000RR steered with more precision and felt more nimble than the previous version. 35-year old Valerie Thompson, from Scottsdale, Arizona, vindicated the S1000RR's performance in June 2012 when she managed a measured top speed of 209.5mph at the Mojave Air and Space Port airfield in California. Apart from gearing and approved racing-fuel, Thompson's S1000RR was stock. Over the next few years, Thompson continued to set more records, achieving 217.7mph at the Texas Mile Speed Festival in October 2014.

After three years investment and development, the S1000RR finally tasted World Superbike success in 2012, with six race wins. Following Corser's retirement, Marco Melandri joined Leon Haslam on the factory S1000RR, the team headed by Bernhard Gobmeier. Melandri brought most of his Italian crew with him, including Andrea Dosoli as technical and rider manager and crew chief Silvano Galbusera. Giacomo Guidotti continued with Haslam.

Now based on the updated production version, the racing S1000RR featured the revised swingarm pivot, an aerodynamically and ergonomically improved fuel tank and seat, and improved BMW RSM5 electronics that smoothed the power delivery. The engine included a lighter crankshaft, with the power increased to around 225 horsepower at 14,900rpm. An underslung swingarm superseded the stock item, and the front brakes were Brembo EVO, with 320 or 328mm discs and T-type rotor mounts. The suspension was Öhlins as before, the front fork a slightly narrower 42mm TRSP25. Marchesini provided the new wheels (17x3.50 and 17x6.25-inch) and Gilles Tooling of Luxembourg produced many of the CNC-milled levers and pedals. With the required starter motor the weight was just over 165kg.

Melandri briefly led the series mid season, but some poor results towards the end saw him only finish third overall. Haslam had an even more disappointing season, his best result a second in race one at Donington before being taken out on the final corner in race two and denied a near certain victory. In other championships, Sylvain Barrier won the Superstock 1000 FIM Cup, Sébastian Gimbert the French Superbike Championship, and Erwan Nigon the German IDM Superbike championship. In the IDM series S1000RRs filled the top four positions. Again the BMW Motorrad France Team Thevant finished second in the FIM Endurance World Championship. The team of Nigon, Gimbert, Damian Cudlin and Hugo Marchand won the Doha 8-Hour race in Qatar, also finishing on the podium in the prestigious Le Mans 24-Hour race. This year also saw BMW's return to the Sidecar World Championship, with Jörg Steinhausen (son of 1975 and 1976 world champion Rolf Steinhausen) teaming with Grégory Cluze on an HP-supported LCR outfit. Powered by an S1000RR engine, Steinhausen and Cluze finished runner-up in the championship, with two race wins. It was BMW's first world championship three-wheeler race victory in 38 years.

BMW Motorrad ceased direct involvement in the World Superbike Championship for 2013,

An updated S1000RR was released for 2012, featuring a new tailpiece and aerodynamic winglets. *BMW Group Press*

Below: The new S1000RR formed
the basis of the much improved
2012 World Superbike racer.
BMW Group Press

Opposite top: Marco Melandri joined
the factory BMW team for 2012, and
provided the S1000RR with its first World
Superbike victories. *BMW Group Press*

Opposite bottom: Michael Dunlop won
three Isle of Man TTs in June 2014, on the
S1000RR. *BMW Group Press*

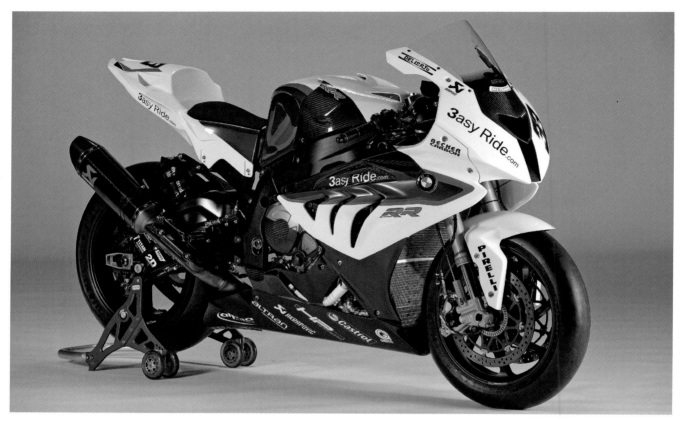

instead supplying engines and electronics to Andrea
Buzzoni's BMW Motorrad Italia. Buzzoni was
not only responsible for the racing team, but also
undertook testing and chassis development. Andrea
Dosoli continued as technical director and with
Serafino Foti as team manager the riders this year
were Marco Melandri and Chaz Davies. The power
was around 230 horsepower at 14,500rpm but both
riders struggled to find the optimum set up, the team
experimenting with many different chassis and Öhlins
suspension options. Davies took three race wins and
Melandri two, Melandri finishing fourth and Davies
fifth overall. During 2013 Andy Sills continued to set
world speed records at Bonneville on his S1000RR.
He managed 224.190mph, the fastest speed ever for a
BMW motorcycle.

After five seasons, as BMW still hadn't won the
World Superbike Championship, they decided not
to field a factory-supported team in 2014. Instead,
BMW realigned the racing program, increasing the
level of support offered to around 150 customer teams
worldwide and launching an innovative customer-
racing project, the BMW Motorrad Race Trophy. This

was very successful, highlighted by Michael Dunlop's
historic triple victory at the Isle of Man in June.
Celebrating the 75th anniversary of Meier's Senior TT
victory on the Type 255 Kompressor, BMW Motorrad
UK joined forces with Hawk Racing with the factory
supplying Superbike engines for Dunlop's S1000RR.
After winning the Superstock and Superbike races
at the North West 200 in May, 25-year-old Dunlop
won three TTs (Superbike, Superstock and Senior)
on the S1000RR, taking his total to 11 TT victories.
Dunlop's average speed for the six lap Senior TT was
128.680mph, with a new Senior TT lap record of
131.668mph.

Other notable victories this year included the
BMW Motorrad Italia SBK Team celebrating seven
victories in the EVO class of the Superbike World
Championship, and Ryuichi Kiyonari providing
BMW their first ever victory in the British Superbike
Championship. But the 2014 BMW Motorrad Race
Trophy went to 19-year-old Markus Reiterberger,
with three race wins in the German Superbike
Championship (IDM) and victory in the Superstock
class in the Oschersleben 8-hour race.

SCOOTERS C600 SPORT, C650GT, C EVOLUTION, C650 SPORT, C400X, C400GT (FROM 2012)

The C650GT (left) and C600 Sport (right) maxi scooters provided motorcycle capability. *BMW Group Press*

With half the world's population living in cities, BMW believed the demand for urban two-wheelers would rise steeply, and released two new maxi-scooters for 2012. More conservative in style than the earlier, but short lived, C1, the two contrasting models were aimed at different types of customer. The stripped-down C600 Sport was designed for a younger urban owner, with the more luxurious C650GT intended for the mature rider. Both were built at the BMW Motorrad plant in Berlin, the new parallel twin engine provided by Kymco in Taiwan.

Although the Sport was titled a C600 and the GT a C650, the mechanical platform was identical for both versions. With a 79mm bore and 66mm stroke, the displacement was 647cc. The cylinder head layout was similar to other BMW motorcycles, and consisted of four valves per cylinder, two 31.5mm intake and two 27.1mm exhaust. These were set at 12 degrees on the intake and 14 degrees on the exhaust. A toothed chain drove the twin overhead camshafts, and valve operation was by bucket tappets on shims. The compression ratio was 11.6:1.

To provide the optimal engine position, the cylinders were inclined 70 degrees, and the two crankpins were offset by 90 degrees. When coupled with the 270-degree ignition spacing and gear-driven balance shafts above and below, the crankshaft vibration was kept to a minimum. The engine was rigidly mounted in the frame, rather than on rubber, thus contributing as a stressed chassis member. Dry sump lubrication also enabled engine height to be reduced. BMS-E electronic fuel-injection, with two 38mm throttles, saw the engine deliver 60 horsepower at 7,500rpm, and peak torque of 66Nm at 6,000rpm.

Where the C-series differed to most motorcycles was the clutch and gearbox. The drive from the crankshaft was transmitted to an intermediate shaft with a torsion damper and primary chain to an automotive-style continuously variable transmission (CVT). This featured an automatic centrifugal dry clutch on the output shaft. The CVT was connected rigidly to the crankcase and the low maintenance chain final drive was housed in an oil bath.

BMW emphasized their scooters were designed by motorcycle engineers, and claimed they combined scooter convenience with motorcycle handling. To achieve this, the C-series featured a tubular steel twin spar chassis, the diecast aluminium single-sided swingarm pivoting on this rather than

the engine cases as on most scooters. The swingarm's centre of rotation was also coaxial with the output shaft, ensuring constant chain tension. The suspension was by a 40mm upside-down Marzocchi fork with single Sachs rear shock absorber and the 1,591mm wheelbase, 25.4 degrees of rake, and 92mm of trail, provided dimensions not dissimilar to a normal motorcycle. It was only the 15x3.5-inch and 15x4.5-inch wheels, albeit shod with wide low profile tyres, which provided a scooter flavour. Even the braking system was motorcycle inspired, with 270mm discs and twin piston calipers all round. ABS was standard.

The main difference between the two models was ergonomics. The Sport carried a lower, flatter handlebar and a taller, firmer seat. The GT on the other hand was more luxurious and relaxed, with a lower seat, and a higher pulled back handlebar. The GT also included a larger, electrically adjustable, windshield. The Sport received a Flexcase variable stowage concept under the seat while the GT included a more generous 60-litre storage system. BMW targeted ten per cent of the global maxi-scooter market in the first year, approximately 10,000 sales, these favouring the cheaper Sport 60/40. Both the C600 Sport and C650GT were mildly updated for 2014 and sales declined to 6,391. Sales declined further to 4,530 in 2015 before replacements for both were introduced for 2016.

Joining the conventionally powered maxi scooter C600 Sport and C650GT for 2014 was the electrically powered C evolution. In keeping with the BMW Group's sustainability strategy, this was BMW Motorrad's first electric mobility effort. Power was by a drivetrain swingarm with a liquid-cooled permanent magnet synchronous motor via a toothed belt and ring gearing. The rated power output was 15 horsepower, with a peak output of 47 horsepower enabling an electronically-limited top speed of 120km/h. The 8kWh capacity of the air-cooled lithium-ion high-voltage battery allowed a range of up to 100 kilometres. To conserve electrical energy, four ride modes were available. The

BMW's first electric motorcycle was the C evolution scooter.
BMW Group Press

central chassis component was the diecast aluminium battery casing with a tubular steel steering head support attached at the front, and a tubular steel single-sided swing arm at the rear. The suspension included an upside-down 40mm front fork at the front, and single shock absorber on the left. Standard equipment included 270mm disc brakes with twin piston calipers on the front and a single piston caliper on the rear. ABS was standard, with Torque Control Assist (TCA) optional. This was similar to the Automatic Stability Control featuring on BMW motorcycles powered by internal combustion engines. The wheels were 3.50x15 and 4.50x 15-inch. Other equipment included a reversing aid, LED daytime running light, and heated handlebar grips. Sales numbered 957 in 2015 and an updated C evolution was offered for 2017. This was now available in two variants, Long Range and European. These featured the new generation batteries as used in the current i3 car.

For 2016, the C650GT, was updated and the C650 Sport replaced the C600 Sport. While the conceptual emphasis of each was unchanged, the 647cc parallel twin engine received revised mapping and a new muffler to meet EU4 requirements. The CVT transmission received new clutch linings, a revised transmission ratio spread and modified centrifugal force weights. But for a more comfortable suspension setup the chassis was unchanged. Standard equipment included Bosch 9.1MB ABS and Automatic Stability Control (ASC). Side View Assist (SVA) to monitor blind spots when changing lanes was also available; a first for motorcycles. Other updates included new instruments, a new centre stand, and automatic daytime riding lights. While the C650 GT was moderately restyled, with new trim panels, the C650 Sport's new design emphasised sportiness.

Joining the maxi scooter C650 for 2018 was the mid-size

C400X. The new drive unit included a single cylinder engine, CVT gearbox, and secondary drive by a drivetrain swingarm. Displacing 350cc, with an 80 x 69.6mm bore and stroke, the four valves (32.5mm intake and 27.2mm exhaust) were set at an included angle of 27.5 degrees and operated by a chain-driven single overhead camshaft and forked rockers. The compression ratio was 11.5:1, and with a 40mm throttle and BMS-E2 engine management the maximum power was 34 horsepower at 7,500rpm. A counterbalance shaft was gear driven from the camshaft. To maintain a low centre of gravity, the cylinder was positioned horizontally, while drive was by an integrated CVT (Continuously Variable Transmission) gearbox.

The tubular steel frame included a cast-iron bearing support for the double-sided aluminium swingarm, and included rubber mounts to reduce vibration. The suspension featured a 35mm upside-down fork and twin rear shock absorbers, while the front wheel was a 3.5x15-inch, the rear was reduced to a 4.25x14-inch to allow the fitting of a Flexcase for storage. Front braking was by twin 265mm front discs with radial 28mm single piston floating calipers and the braking system included a Continental MK 100 MAB 2-channel ABS unit allowing independent control of the front and rear wheel circuits. As on the C650, the geometry and feel were designed to replicate motorcycle characteristics. The C400GT joined the C400X for 2019, this offering increased comfort and touring capability.

One of three 90th Anniversary boxers released for 2013 was this special R1200GS Adventure. This was still based on the previous model. *BMW Group Press*

During 2012, BMW became the first motorcycle manufacturer in the United States to offer ABS as standard on all models. Sales also increased this year to 106,358, with Germany (20,516) the predominant market followed by the United States (12,057). The most popular model worldwide was the about-to-be-superseded R1200GS. The following year BMW celebrated ninety years of the boxer motorcycle, introducing three special ninety-year editions. These '90 Jahre BMW Motorrad' ('90 years of BMW Motorrad') models included special versions of the

R1200GS Adventure, R1200R and R1200RT. These all continued with the earlier air-cooled engine and were ostensibly standard models with a black and grey finish, and a nickel-plated and polished brass plate on the upper fork bridge. Sales continued to increase, with an all time high of 115,215 motorcycles supplied during 2013. BMW also announced a partnership with India's fourth largest motorcycle manufacturer TVS to develop and build a range of entry-level bikes under 500cc.

R1200GS (2013-2018)

With more than 170,000 units sold, BMW's most impressive success story in the recent decade was undoubtedly the R1200GS. But, after getting a new engine in 2011, it received a ground up redesign for 2013. While retaining the 101 x 73mm bore and stroke, and 1,170cc displacement, the new boxer engine was totally new. According to Joseph Miritsch, Head of BMW Motorrad R-Series, the new engine would eventually power the entire range. And although the new engine was not BMW's most powerful boxer (that was still the HP2), there was more scope for future development. "The four-valve Boxer engine was built for 20 years and I think this new engine has 10-20 years development life in it. It will surely be good for 150-160 horsepower," said Miritsch at the R1200GS launch.

Work on the new engine under Project Director Antonius Ruhe began sometime earlier, in 2007. To meet anticipated noise and emissions requirements the most significant change was to the cooling system. However, a fully water-cooled solution was eschewed as it was considered too bulky. The boxer engine retained air/liquid cooling, but a glycol water mixture replaced the oil coolant. Cooling fluid flowed through the cylinder heads and part of the cylinders with heat dissipation via two radiators. The lower part of the cylinders retained air cooling. The new compact cooling system improved the heat cooling ratio from 22 per cent oil cooling and 78 per cent air cooling, to 35 per cent liquid cooling and 65 per cent air cooling. The new liquid cooling added a modest 2.7kg weight.

A significant change was to include vertical flow intakes with the exhaust exiting underneath rather than in front. This allowed for identical intake lengths for both cylinders, with the fuel injector in the intake port allowing fuel to be injected directly in front of the intake valves. As in the previous model, the two camshafts were arranged horizontally. But, by changing the through-flow direction from horizontal to vertical, it was now possible to have specific intake and exhaust camshafts rather than combined intake and exhaust.

As before, a chain running in the shaft behind the cylinders (on the right-hand side of the engine from the counterbalance shaft, and on the left from the crankshaft) drove the two respective camshafts.

This differed from the previous system where the chain drove both camshafts, the timing chain now driving an intermediate shaft between the intake and exhaust camshaft. A pair of spur gears then drove the camshafts. On each exhaust camshaft a de-compressor facilitated starting, allowing a lighter starter motor and battery.

A standard, pent roof four-valve combustion chamber replaced the previous radial valve arrangement. Set at 8 degrees on the intake and 10 degrees on the exhaust side, the valves were 1.0mm larger than before, at 40mm intake and 34mm exhaust. The compression ratio was increased to 12.5:1. As before, the valves were operated by light rocker arms, the design similar to the S1000RR. Valve clearance settings were by replaceable shims.

The crankshaft was also re-engineered. To reduce friction, the main bearing diameter was reduced from the 60mm to 55mm, while the narrower crankpins were enlarged from 48 to 50mm. As on the existing boxer, a counterbalance shaft ran at crankshaft speed to eliminate unwanted vibration. For the first time in a BMW boxer engine, the cylinders were no longer bolted to the crankcase, but were directly integrated. Also for the first time, the gearbox and clutch were integrated in the engine housing. Another boxer first was the multiplate wet clutch, this with eight friction discs instead of a single dry disc. This allowed a reduction in diameter to 147mm instead of 180mm. The clutch also included an anti-hopping mechanism for the first time on a boxer.

The BMS-X digital electronic engine management was new, the Alpha/n system drawing on a wide range of parameters. The throttle bodies were increased to 2mm, from 50mm, these with an electromotive throttle actuator system. The power output was 125 horsepower at 7,700rpm, with maximum torque of 125Nm at 6,500rpm. Electronic cruise control was also available, as was ASC with five selectable riding modes, 'Rain', 'Road', 'Dynamic', 'Enduro', and 'Enduro Pro' with three different throttle curves.

In contrast to all previous BMW boxers, the swingarm with integrated shaft drive and third generation EVO Paralever was now positioned on the left-hand side. While the previous frame consisted of an upper frame supporting the Telelever and the rear frame with integrated swingarm mount and welded on

Below: A new R1200GS was released for 2013. The water-cooled engine now featured top intake and underneath exhaust manifolds, and the driveshaft was on the left. Also new were the radial Brembo brakes. *BMW Group Press*

rear section, the new chassis consisted of a continuous steel bridge frame with a bolt-on rear subframe. The integration of the engine as a load-bearing element was retained, the engine housing supporting the forged aluminium swingarm. The Telelever was also refined, the fork tube diameter reduced from 41 to 37mm. The chassis geometry wasn't radically changed, the steering head angle increased slightly to 27.5 degrees, with 99.6mm of trail (down from 101mm). Despite the swingarm increasing in length from 535.6mm to 588mm the 1,507mm wheelbase was unchanged. The benefit of the longer swingarm was improved traction, particularly on loose off-road surfaces. To improve ride quality the wheel and tyre dimensions were also new. The 10-spoke alloy wheels were wider, a 19x3.0-inch on the front and 17x4.5-inch on the rear, allowing for a larger 120/70 R19 front and 170/60 R17 rear tyre. Cross spoke wire wheels were an option. While the front discs remained at 305mm, the front calipers were now radial Brembo Monobloc

with 32mm diameter pistons (instead of 34 and 36mm). The master cylinder diameter was reduced from 16 to 15mm. The rear brake retained a 2-piston floating caliper with 28mm pistons, but the brake disc diameter increased from 265 to 276mm. Integral ABS was standard.

New semi-active suspension included dynamic ESA monitors for vertical front and rear wheel movement, in addition to spring travel sensors to automatically adapt the damping. Damping adjustment was achieved through electrically controlled regulation valves. A new adjustable windshield offered improved protection, and the seat was adjustable for height and tilt angle. While slightly heavier than before at 238kg, BMW still managed to move the goalposts and stay ahead of the opposition. The new R1200GS was more agile than its predecessor, and the sophisticated electronics added to the safety and overall competence.

Alongside the obligatory colour changes, other developments over the next few years included the

In addition to water-cooling, the new boxer engine featured a revised double overhead camshaft drive system. The valves were no longer radially positioned, and the gearbox was incorporated in the engine unit. *BMW Group Press*

Opposite top: The HP4 was the first four-cylinder in the HP Series. The Competition Package included carbon panels and blue wheels. *BMW Group Press*

Opposite bottom: Sylvain Barrier won the 2013 FIM Superstock 1000 series on the new HP4. *BMW Group Press*

adoption of the heavier R1200GS Adventure and R1200RT crankshaft for 2015. Shift Assistant Pro and Keyless Ride were now an option. All these updates did was cement the R1200GS as BMW's most popular motorcycle. Sales during 2015 numbered 23,681 units and its success continued during 2016, with sales up 7 per cent to 25,336. Updates for 2016 included banking-optimised ABS Pro and a dynamic brakelight, with the Riding Modes Pro option, and the introduction of the R1200GS TripleBlack. The demand for an all-black finish saw this special model, with a black fuel tank, cross spoke wheels and fork offset by a grey engine, gearbox, swingarm, and side panels.

For 2017, all liquid-cooled boxers were EU4 compliant, and included a judder damper on the transmission output shaft. New features also included a revised drum actuator, transmission shafts, and transmission shaft bearing. The instrument panel was also redesigned. 2018 updates included a Connectivity option, with 6.5-inch TFT display.

HP4 (2013-2014)

Continuing BMW's HP series that began in 2006 with the HP2 Enduro, the HP4 was the first 4-cylinder motorcycle in the HP family. Built in modest numbers, each example was issued with an HP4 serial number engraved in the upper fork bridge. Under the direction of Project Leader Rudolf Schneider, most developments over the standard S1000RR were electronic and technological. These were primarily aimed at improving track performance. Standard features included Dynamic Damping Control DDC, this providing dynamic adaptive suspension damping for the 46mm Sachs upside-down fork and Monoshock. The front brakes included Brembo Monobloc calipers with 9x floating discs and a more refined race ABS. This retained four modes and included Dynamic Traction Control and Launch Control in 'Slick' mode. To further harness the improved traction the rear tyre was a larger 200/55 ZR 17.

Weight reduction was achieved through forged 2.4kg

lighter 7-spoke wheels, a lighter sprocket carrier, and a 4.5kg lighter titanium Akrapovič exhaust system. And while the engine power was unchanged, engine torque was increased between 6,000 and 9,750rpm and full power was available in all modes. Visually the HP4 emphasised a Monoposto look and included an elongated engine spoiler and tinted windshield. A Competition Package was also available, this with carbon panels, HP levers and rear sets, blue wheels, and a sponsor sticker kit. Designed primarily for racing, the HP4 was a homologation model for Superbike and Superstock racing, and Sylvain Barrier followed his 2012 FIM 1000 Superstock Cup victory on an S1000RR by riding an HP4 to victory in the 2013 series. The HP4 was discontinued after 2014, when the new S1000RR was released.

F700GS, F800GS, F800GS ADVENTURE (2013-2017)

Both the F650GS and F800GS were updated for 2013. As before, the F800GS was a more serious dual-purpose model, with the F700GS replacing the F650GS but continuing as an entry-level version geared more towards street use. The 798cc liquid-cooled 4-valve twin-cylinder engine with electronic fuel-injection, closed-loop catalytic converter, 6-speed gearbox and conrod balancer was largely as before. The power and torque of the F800GS was unchanged at 85 horsepower at 7,500rpm and 83Nm at 5,750rpm, but both power and torque were increased for the F700GS. The maximum power was now 75 horsepower at 7,300rpm and torque was 77Nm at 5,300rpm (up from 75Nm at 4,500rpm). The chassis, including a tubular steel frame, square section steel rear subframe, and chill-cast aluminium double-sided swingarm, and wheels and tyres, were unchanged from the previous versions. As on the F800GS, the F700GS now featured double 300mm floating front discs with dual piston floating calipers. The rear 265mm disc was also unchanged from the previous model. The F800GS retained an upside-down front fork, with the F700GS a conventional version. A hand wheel now adjusted the rear spring preload.

Most updates involved electronic safety aids.

Following BMW's 'Safety 360 degree' principle, two-channel ABS was standard on both models, with ASC (Automatic Stability Control) and the ESA (Electronic Suspension Adjustment) optional. To bring the twins more up to date, the styling was more dynamic. There was also an updated range of colours, and new instruments and switches. Important but not pivotal models in BMW's line-up, like the R1200GS, the new F800GS and F700GS, continued a developmental approach of evolution rather than revolution. They were also consistent sellers, with F700GS sales numbering 6,499 in 2014 and 6,282 in 2015. The F800GS sold 7,040 in 2014 and 6,603 in 2015.

Released midway through 2013 as an early release 2014 model, the F800GS Adventure provided a lighter and more agile alternative to the sometimes-intimidating R1200GS. Just as they did in 1980, BMW sensed an opportunity for a mid-range adventure bike, agile enough for novices but with enough power to satisfy experienced riders. Updates over the F800GS included a reinforced rear subframe to accommodate the larger, 24-litre fuel tank, a larger windshield, enduro footpegs, engine protection bar and pannier rack. The F800GS Adventure was first offered in a 'Launch Edition' of 1,000 units in Sandrover matt paint and three equipment packages: Comfort, Enduro and Special accessories. Offering excellent performance on a variety of road surfaces, the F800GS Adventure was almost the perfect all-rounder, a large dirtbike or touring streetbike; several bikes in one. F800GS Adventure sales were 4,278 in 2014 and 4,129 in 2015.

Updates to the F800GS for 2014 saw the Dynamic package replacing the safety package. This consisted of ESA, ASC, and an off-road mode for ABS. The only changes to all three models for 2015 were colours before the range received a mild cosmetic refresh for 2016. Along with a new fuel tank cover and colours were five possible seat heights with four seats and optional lowered suspension.

Although nearing the end of its model cycle, more changes were in store for the F700GS and F800GS for 2017. The 798cc engines were adapted for EU4 regulations, and distinguished from earlier versions by a new stainless steel muffler. The ride-by-wire system now operated directly from a sensor on the twist grip to the engine control system, this enabling the new standard riding modes 'Rain' and 'Road' to be used

Below: The F800GT offered more touring equipment and comfort than the previous F800ST. This colour, Valencia Orange Metallic, was only available for 2013 and 2014. *BMW Group Press*

Bottom: Mildly updated for 2017, the F800GT was now EU4 compliant. Unlike other F800s the GT retained the belt final drive. *BMW Group Press*

for riding on damp or dry surfaces as well as the modes 'Enduro' and 'Enduro Pro'. New instruments and colours completed the updates, while the F800GS Adventure received new galvanised radiator trim and a new intake silencer cover. With replacement imminent, 2018 updates were confined to colours.

F800GT (FROM 2013)

Replacing the F800ST for 2013 was the more powerful and better-equipped F800GT. While the twin-cylinder engine was basically unchanged, the power was increased to 90 horsepower at 8,000rpm. The exhaust manifold and silencer were shared with the F800R. A lighter titanium and stainless steel Akrapovič muffler was also an option. Final drive was still by toothed belt.

The chassis was also updated, with a 50mm longer swingarm, this combined with a slight reduction in rear shock absorber travel by 15mm, to 125mm, to improve ride stability. This also allowed a reduction in seat height from 840mm to 800mm. New, lighter wheels improved the handling but the tyre dimensions were unchanged. Rear spring preload adjustment was also now by a hand wheel. Along with standard dual-channel ABS, Automatic Stability Control (ASC) and the Electronic Suspension Adjustment (ESA) were also available for the first time on a mid-range touring bike. ESA offered a choice of three levels. New 20mm higher aluminium handlebars improved touring comfort as did rider's footpegs now 10mm further forward and 10mm lower. The standard seat was wider, the instrument cluster new, and standard equipment now included an onboard computer. Also available was a dedicated hard luggage system, the side cases providing 55 litres of storage with a load capacity of up to 10kg. But really setting the F800GT apart from the F800ST was the new full fairing. This provided significantly increased wind and weather protection with more modern styling. Continuing the style established by the excellent F800ST, the F800GT was a versatile all-rounder providing surprisingly nimble handling and enough power for most riders. Sales were steady and updates minimal over the next few years. But after selling 3,901 units in 2014 BMW only sold 2,631 in 2015. The only changes for 2016 were new colours but more revisions were evident for 2017. While the basic style was unchanged the F800GT was now EU4 compliant. This saw a new muffler, Ride-By-Wire system with 'Rain' and 'Road' modes, new instruments and windshield, and new colours.

R NINET, R NINET SCRAMBLER, R NINET RACER, R NINET PURE AND R NINET URBAN G/S (FROM 2014)

Following in the wake of three 90th special edition boxers in 2013 was the R nineT of 2014. Unlike the earlier special editions that were based on existing models, the R nineT, or nineT as it was also called, was specifically designed as a modular concept offering scope for customisation. The R nineT was thus marketed as the world's first production motorcycle designed as a basis for a custom: either Roadster, Café Racer or Bobber. Continuing from the 2013 Concept Ninety custom created in partnership with Roland Sands design, the nineT blended the boxer's iconic character and classic design of a bygone era with modern technology. The concept was also designed to enable individual tailoring. By combining traditional styling and manufacture with contemporary chassis components the result was extremely successful, and would eventually spawn an entire range of similar boxer twins.

Although it was a new design the R nineT retained the earlier air/oil cooled boxer engine, this still featuring the radial valve combustion chamber and chain-driven double overhead camshafts. The engine produced 110 horsepower at 7,750rpm and included a separate six-speed gearbox and shaft final drive on the right. The final drive gearing was lower and the left side exhaust featured twin blasted stainless steel mufflers. An Akrapovič titanium muffler was optional, and a longer or shorter connecting pipe allowed the muffler to be fitted lower or higher if required. The exhaust also included an electric acoustic valve to maximise the throatiness of the exhaust note.

The wide scope for customisation was largely due to the modular frame design. The tubular steel spaceframe still incorporated the boxer engine as a

Bottom: Celebrating 90 years of
the BMW boxer twin, the R nineT
combined classic features in a
modern framework and provided
a basis for customisation.
BMW Group Press

Opposite: Joining the R nineT
Roadster in 2017 was the R nineT
Scrambler. This example has the
optional wire-spoke wheels and
treaded tyres. *BMW Group Press*

load-bearing element, but saw the front frame section with an integral steering head and the rear section with the swingarm mount. The removable pillion frame allowed for solo or two-up use. To emphasise the R nineT's more traditional style the 46mm upside-down front fork of the S1000RR replaced the usual boxer Telelever. The rear suspension employed a Paralever single-sided swingarm with a central shock absorber. The swingarm also allowed for a wider 6-inch rear wheel can instead of the standard 5.50-inch version. Designed as a classic retro roadster, the nineT also featured wire-spoke wheels with black anodised alloy, non-flanged rims, black aluminium hubs and stainless steel spokes. Front braking was by a pair of radial 4-piston monobloc brake calipers and floating 320mm brake discs with BMW ABS. As it was designed with performance in mind the geometry was configured with nimble handling a priority. The rake was a steep 25.5 degrees, the trail 102.5mm, and the wheelbase 1,476mm.

With one of the styling objectives to reduce the bodywork as much as possible and to achieve a minimalist look, the sides of the 17-litre aluminium tank were hand brushed and coated. Further attention to detail saw the surfaces of many forged aluminium parts, including the triple and handlebar clamps, glass bead-blasted and then provided a natural anodised finish. Further homage to past models was evident by the round headlamp with central BMW emblem. Classic Black storm metallic paint with contrasting silver and metallic highlights also emphasised the classic character. The electrical system was also configured for flexibility, thereby facilitating the installation of alternative electrical components, such as headlights or turn indicators.

But while the R nineT employed styling cues from the past it wasn't really a retro bike. Instead, it synthesised state-of-the-art technical features from high-performance sports machines with classic principles derived from 90 years of the BMW boxer. Embodying the brand's values of 90 years, the R nineT uniquely summed the company's illustrious past, exuding style and cleverly allowing individual expressiveness. Individualization was becoming a growing phenomenon in motorcycling, one the R nineT looked set to capitalize on. This was soon evident with a long waiting list for an R nineT, even the factory workers in Berlin having to wait 18 months before delivery.

After a sell out for the 2014 Model Year (8,488 sales and BMW's fourth best seller) sales of the R nineT remained strong for 2015. Now a cult bike, the R nineT was BMW Motorrad's fifth best seller this year with 9,545 units sold. For 2016, the R nineT received a hand-brushed aluminium with either smooth or exposed welding seams before a more updated version was released for 2017. This was ostensibly identical to the previous model and still powered by the air/oil cooled boxer engine. Updates included the introduction of a fully adjustable 46mm upside-down front fork, the speedometer and tachometer now located in individual casings and a black swingarm and rear drive unit to match the black engine and frame.

Further variations on the R nineT theme were offered for 2017. These included the R nineT Scrambler, R nineT Racer, R nineT Pure and R nineT Urban G/S. As Ducati and Triumph had already achieved considerable with their new generation Scramblers, it wasn't surprising to see a Scrambler version of the R nineT become available. The Scramblers of the 1950s and 1960s were ostensibly modified street bikes, and were extremely successful before more specialised off-road motorcycles eclipsed them for competition and more serious off-road duties. BMW were also involved in the early Scrambler concept, offering a Scrambler high-rise exhaust for the classic R68 sports model. The R nineT Scrambler continued this theme, and while the basic air/oil-cooled 1,170cc boxer engine and modular tubular steel frame arrangement was similar to the R nineT roadster, the Scrambler received a raised exhaust with twin mufflers. The steering geometry was also altered to be more suitable for off-road use, the steering head raked out to 28.5 degrees, with 110.6mm of trail. The wheelbase was also lengthened to 1,527mm. The front suspension was now by a conventional 43mm telescopic fork with protective rubber gaiters, this providing 125mm of travel. The Paralever and single shock rear suspension provided 140mm of travel. The standard wheels were cast aluminium, a 19x3.0-inch on the front and 17x4.5-inch on the rear, but wire-spoked were optional. Road tyres in 120/70x19 and 170/60x17 sizes were standard but deep treaded off-road tyres were optional. ABS was standard and front braking was by axially mounted 4-piston brake calipers and 320mm discs. The Scrambler's riding position was also more relaxed than the Roadster, with higher handlebars and lower, and more rearward footpegs. The Scrambler's unladen weight of 220kg was slightly less than the Roadster.

New R nineT versions for 2017 included the R nineT Racer and R nineT Pure, these adding two specific new facets to BMW's heritage line. The Pure was a bare bones minimalist roadster, while the Racer was an old school half-faired café racer. Both concepts were popular in the 1960s and 1970s, and were designed to inspire nostalgia amongst older enthusiasts. When BMW showcased the BMW Concept Ninety at the Concorso d'Eleganza Villa d'Este in May 2013, it also evoked memories of the legendary R90S – a motorcycle that established BMW's more recent sporting reputation. The R nineT Racer continued this sporting theme, the frame-mounted fairing, hump seat, stub handlebars and rear set footpegs evoking 1970s café racers. The R nineT Pure provided a purist, minimalist, character by blending classical and modern elements.

As on other R nineTs the DOHC 110 horsepower air/oil cooled boxer engine powered both these new versions. Both also shared the modular tubular steel spaceframe, the three bolted components (main front, rear with integrated tail, and passenger) allowing for customisation. The steering geometry and wheelbase were tailored for the specific sporting capability of each, the Racer with a 24.4 degree steering head angle, 103.9mm of trail and a 1,491mm wheelbase. For the Pure, the rake was 24.6 degrees with 105mm of trail. The Pure's 1,493mm wheelbase was marginally longer than the Racer.

With its frame mounted fairing and hump solo seat the R nineT Racer replicated the 1970s café racer. *BMW Group Press*

The suspension on the Racer and Pure was by a conventional 43mm front fork, and rear Paralever with central shock absorber. Both also shared the five-spoke light alloy cast wheels, 3.5 x 17 and 5.5 x 17-inch, four-piston front brake calipers and 320mm floating front discs. ABS was standard with ASC (Automatic Stability Control) a factory option. The tyre sizes were the same as the R nineT, 120/70ZR17 and 180/55ZR17.

The R nineT Pure was a no frills design, combining a high quality finish with classical elements such as a circular headlight and circular analogue speedometer. Finished in BMW Motorsport colours, with analogue circular instruments and an Aluminium Silver frame contrasting the black drivetrain, the athletic R nineT Racer deliberately replicated the style of the 1970s sporting motorcycle. Last seen in 2004, during 2018 the BMW Motorrad BoxerCup made a comeback, now with factory prepared identical R nineT Racers. They featured Wilbers redesigned suspension, Ilmberger cylinder head covers, engine spoiler and rear panels, Akrapovič shock absorber and titanium manifold, BMW ABS racing software, Müller Präzision steering damper and uniform Metzeler tyres. The BoxerCup initially comprised six events, most as support races for the International German Motorcycle Championship (IDM).

As the R nineT embodied nostalgic concepts in a

The R nineT Pure was a
no-frills classic roadster.
BMW Group Press

modern package it wasn't surprising to see a version
replicate arguably the most significant boxer twin
of all: the G/S. Also released for 2017, the R nineT
Urban G/S drew on the design cues of the first G/S,
the 1980 R80G/S. While all R nineTs still shared the

earlier boxer engine and modular tubular steel frame,
the suspension and wheel specification was derived
from the Scrambler. This included identical steering
geometry, a 43mm conventional front fork and 19 and
17-inch cast alloy wheels. Cross-spoke wire wheels

Opposite top: Based on the R
nineT Scrambler, the Urban G/S
drew on the style of the 1980
R80G/S. *BMW Group Press*

Opposite bottom: For 2019, a wider range of
colours was available for the R nineT and its
variants. From the left is the Racer in Black Storm
Metallic/Aurum, R nineT in Pollux/Aluminium, Pure
in Black Storm Metallic/Light White, and R nineT in
Mars Red/Cosmic Blue. *BMW Group Press*

were an option. From its G/S ancestor came the white
and blue colours, red seat, high front mudguard and
headlamp mask. The new R nineT variants proved
extremely popular, boosting flat-twin boxer sales
by 9.6 per cent during 2017, to a total of 86,090
motorcycles. For 2019, the only changes to the R nineT
range were the inclusion of a dynamic brakelight and
new colours.

S1000R (FROM 2014)

With the hyper-naked market growing, the logical
extension of the S1000RR was to incorporate all
its state-of-the-art technology in a naked Roadster.
According to BMW Head of S and K Models, Bernd
Scherer, "With the S1000 Roadster we wanted to target
a younger customer and build a high-performance
roadster with as wide appeal as possible." BMW also
wanted to recoup some of the high S1000 development
costs, and as they envisaged sales of the S1000RR
Superbike to gradually decline over time, the Roadster
was designed to fill the void.

As current technology in high revving motorcycle
engines didn't allow for high horsepower at both high
and low rpm, BMW decided to emphasise lower and
mid-range power with the S1000R. This was to provide
ideal power for everyday use and sports road riding. At
the same time, maximum rpm was reduced by around
2,000rpm. The maximum power of 160 horsepower
was attained at 11,000rpm with peak torque of 112Nm
(83lb-ft) at 9,250rpm. Up to 7,500rpm, the S1000R
developed 10 Newton metres (7lb-ft) more torque than
the S1000RR, achieved with redesigned cylinder head
intakes, modified cam profiles, and a new BMS-X
engine management system. This supported an E-Gas
'throttle-by-wire' system and two riding modes (Rain
and Road) and ASC (Automatic Stability Control) were
standard. In 'Road' mode, Race ABS and ASC were
set up for dry road conditions and optimal throttle
response, while 'Rain' mode provided a softer throttle
response and earlier intervention of Race ABS and ASC.
The maximum power was limited to 136 horsepower at
9,500rpm and torque to 104Nm (77lb-ft) at 9,000rpm.
The Riding mode Pro option adds two further riding
modes, 'Dynamic' and 'Dynamic Pro', on top of the
standard specification. Dynamic Traction Control
(DTC) was available as a factory option, this including
riding mode Pro. With DTC an integrated lean angle

sensor replaced the standard ASC and the engine's
throttle response was more direct and the Race ABS
thresholds higher.

The 11.98kg aluminium alloy perimeter frame, with
the engine as a load-bearing component, was based on
the S1000RR. Also similar was the adjustable 46mm
upside-down front fork and a dual swingarm with
adjustable central Sachs shock absorber. The upside-
down fork featured inner cartridge inserts, with a
separate hydraulic piston-cylinder system allowing
adjustable compression and rebound damping. An
optional Dynamic Damping Control system (DDC),
first introduced on the HP4, allowed the compression
and rebound damping to be linked to the relevant
riding mode. But while the chassis specification was
similar to the S1000RR the steering geometry was
changed to provide specific Roadster requirements.
The steering head angle was raked out to 24.6 degrees
with 98.5mm of trail and the wheelbase lengthened
to 1,439mm. The cast aluminium 19-spoke 17x3.5-
inch and 17x6.0-inch wheels and front radial four-
piston Monobloc brakes with 320mm discs were also
unchanged from the S1000RR. Partially integral Race
ABS was standard.

While similar in style to the S1000RR, with its tail
up, nose down stance, the S1000R's styling emphasised
the aggressive sports roadster. The cockpit included
an LC display with analogue tachometer, along with
the gear display, riding mode and lap timer. The
S1000RR influence also continued with the distinctive
asymmetrical headlight arrangement. A wide, tapered
aluminium handlebar and repositioned footpegs
provided a relaxed seating position, suitable for
sports and long distance riding. Combining Superbike
dynamics and power with emotive roadster styling,
the S1000R replaced the powerful, but much heavier,
K1300R (in those markets where it was still available).
The S1000R was immediately successful, combining
with the S1000RR to number more than 10,000 sales
during 2014. S1000R sales totalled 6,473 during 2015
and 5,835 during 2016.

For 2017, the S1000R was updated to meet EU4
requirements. With a new HP titanium muffler
the power output increased to 165 horsepower at
11,000rpm. A new frame included a lighter main
section and contributed to a weight reduction, to
205kg wet. Other updates included vibration free
handlebars, a smaller fairing and new multifunction

instrument display. ABS Pro was now included in the optional 'Riding Modes Pro' and HP Shift Assistant Pro was an option. Other options included lighter HP forged aluminium wheels. Design Option Wheels with red rim lines were a new ex works option.

R1200GS ADVENTURE (2014-2018)

The third edition R1200GS Adventure was a follow on from the virtually all-new R1200GS released for 2013. Continuing as the quintessential long-distance and off-road all round touring motorcycle, the new R1200GS Adventure also built on the superior dynamics offered by the new generation R1200GS.

While the basic power unit was unchanged, to improve off-road rideability the flywheel was 950 grams heavier. To further improve low speed running an additional vibration damper was now incorporated

between the gearbox output and the driveshaft. The styling was new as was a 30-litre aluminium fuel tank (up 10 litres) that allowed for an increased range. Standard equipment included ABS, Automatic Stability Control (ASC), and two riding modes 'Rain' and 'Road'. Three further riding modes were available with the optional Riding mode Pro feature, this accompanied by Enduro ABS and Enduro ASC add-ons for off-road riding.

The chassis retained the R1200GS tubular steel bridge frame with bolt-on rear subframe, but the front Telelever and rear Paralever were re-engineered to increase torsional stiffness. The new chassis setup enhanced off-road performance, and provided an additional 20 millimetres of suspension travel, 10mm more ground clearance with new geometry for the longitudinal control arm. The steering head angle was also raked out one degree, to 24.5 degrees, with 92.7mm of trail. A steering damper was also standard as was a larger windshield with hand-

wheel adjustment while additional air flaps and hand
protectors increased weather protection. Wire wheels,
wide off-road foot pegs, adjustable reinforced foot
levers and engine and tank protectors completed
the off-road specification. While the new R1200GS
Adventure was arguably the most effective and
efficient big-bore adventure tourer, in every respect it
was larger than the R1200GS. The wet weight went
up to 260kg, the length by 40mm, width by 33mm
and the seat height by 40mm. But the combination
of all-round ability, comfort, weather protection, and
electronic wizardry saw the R1200GS Adventure
continue as the world's most popular large capacity
adventure bike. Production continued to increase,
to a new record of 123,495 motorcycles (and Maxi-
Scooters) delivered during 2014, a 7.2 per cent
increase. The R1200GS and GS Adventure continued
as the most successful models (24,380 R1200GS and
16,242 R1200GS Adventure sold), and in March
the 500,000th GS-series, an R1200GS, rolled off
the Berlin production line. Updates for 2015 were

minor, and now included the option of 30mm lower
suspension, R1200GS lower seat, Shift Assistant Pro
and Keyless Ride. Sales of the R1200GS Adventure
during 2015 totalled 18,011 units, second only to
the R1200GS in sales. With new colours and sharing
the electronic updates of the R1200GS, the R1200GS
Adventure was even more popular during 2016, with
sales increasing 18.8 per cent to 21,391 units. Updates
for 2017 included the transmission changes of the
R1200GS and a new instrument panel. Also new this
year was an R1200GS Adventure 'Triple Black' special
model. Following on from the 2016 R1200GS 'Triple
Black', this featured a black fuel tank cover, engine,
gearbox and swingarm, offset by a grey frame. With
50,281 sales of the R1200GS and R1200GS Adventure
during 2017, this was the first time in BMW's history
more than 50,000 units of any one model were sold.
2018 updates included optional Emergency Call and
Connectivity, a TFT screen, and expanded Riding Pro
modes with a new generation Dynamic ESA. Colour
options included Style Rallye in white and blue.

R1200RT (2014-2018)

The second R-series to receive the water-cooled boxer engine and updated drivetrain was the popular R1200RT. The 125 horsepower engine was basically unchanged from the R1200GS, but crankshaft and alternator mass were increased. The secondary transmission ratio was higher, and the throttle twist grip angle reduced to provide a more sensitive throttle response. Standard equipment included two riding modes, 'Rain' and 'Road', along with Automatic Stability Control (ASC). An optional Ride Mode Pro included a Hill Start Control function. The semi-integral ABS braking system allowed the rider to stop on an uphill slope with the engine running without depressing the brake lever. The rear brake could be operated individually and with the Hill Start Control activated pressure in the rear hydraulic brake unit held the motorcycle steady on an incline.

Gearshift Assistant Pro was another first for a production touring motorcycle. Although similar to the Gearshift Assistant already featured on the S1000RR, this was now adapted to the specific requirements of a touring bike. The system enabled upshifts and downshifts without the use of the clutch or throttle, and worked by employing a sensor on the gearbox output shaft to detect the rider's shift request and trigger the assistance mechanism.

The chassis was also similar to the R1200GS, the frame with more rigid Telelever and Paralever mounts. The springs were stiffer, and a 36-degree steering angle each side allowed a tighter turning circle and easier manoeuvring. The steering geometry was also considerably quicker than the GS, with a 26.4-degree rake, 116mm of trail and a 1,485mm wheelbase. Semi-active suspension with ESA (Electronic Suspension Adjustment) included spring travel sensors at both the front and the rear to monitor vertical wheel movement. This allowed the damping to be automatically adapted to riding situations. The brakes and wheels were also new for the R1200RT, with twin 320mm front discs and four-piston Brembo radial calipers, and a 276mm rear disc. The 10-spoke cast alloy wheels were 3.50x17 and 5.50x17-inch.

Further evolution was evident in the instrumentation. A large 7-inch TFT colour information display joined the traditional analogue instruments. This combined with the standard multi-controller to provide a wide array of functions. The standard onboard computer included information ranging from the oil level to the electrical voltage and gearshift indicator. Unlike other models that included more unusual asymmetrical headlight layouts the R1200RT was more traditional, with a new central front headlight unit flanked by two high-beam lights on the left and right. The audio system was similar to the high specification already found on the K1600.

Along with new styling and an impressive technical and electronic specification, the new R1200RT continued a trend already evident with the R1200GS Adventure: increased weight and general dimensions. Although the ergonomic triangle formed by the handlebars, seat and footrests was lowered 20mm compared with the previous model, the weight was up to a hefty 274kg. Fortunately, a lower centre of gravity and improved weight distribution offset this, allowing better manoeuvrability and sportier handling. While the 2014 updates didn't revolutionise the R1200RT, it now evolved into an even more accomplished tourer, with smoother power, class-leading electronics and a better chassis. BMW managed to retain all the points that made the older RT so good, while breathing new life into it. In the process it continued as their quintessential tourer. Buyers agreed, and during 2014 they bought 12,140 examples to put the R1200RT third on BMW's motorcycle sales chart. The R1200RT also remained BMW's third best seller during 2015, with 10,955 sales. The only update for 2016 was a new colour, Platin bronze, and sales declined 11.9 per cent, to 9,648 units. As on other liquid-cooled boxers for 2017, the R1200RT received a judder damper on the transmission shaft, and a revised selector drum, while optional features included banking optimised ABS Pro and a dynamic brakelight. For 2018, banking-optimised ABS Pro was standard, with two special colour schemes offered: a black Style Elegance and red Style Sport.

R1200R (2015-2018)

While the previous naked R1200R, and the earlier 1150 and 1100 versions, should have been amongst BMW's more popular models, sales were always below expectations. With the new R1200R BMW displayed their intention to change this. Except for the R nineT, this still continuing with the earlier air-cooled engine,

Along with the new engine and chassis, the 2014 R1200RT boasted more sophisticated electronics and new styling.
BMW Group Press

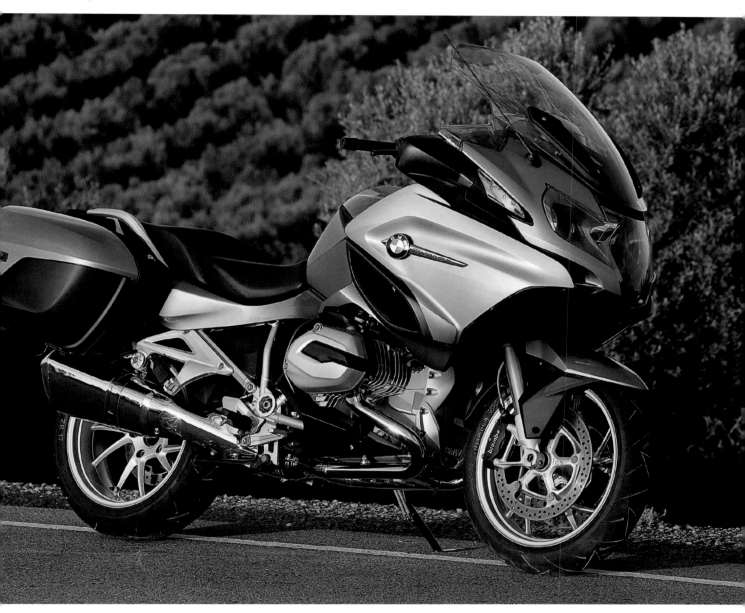

the R1200R was the final boxer to receive the new water-cooled unit. Apart from new gear ratios, these midway between the R1200GS and R1200RT, this was identical to the other models. The exhaust system was a 2-in-1 with a steeply angled rear silencer. A modified airbox, newly shaped air intake snorkels, and a centrally positioned radiator, also contributed to a narrower front profile. Along with the exhaust system these also allowed the engine to produce slightly more

torque at low rpm than the R1200GS, GS Adventure and RT. Standard equipment included two riding modes, 'Rain' and 'Road', ABS and Automatic Stability Control (ASC). The optional Riding Mode Pro, added Dynamic Traction Control (DTC) with banking detection and two additional riding modes, 'Dynamic' and 'User.'

The purpose-built chassis included a tubular steel bridge frame, this still incorporating the flat-twin

Opposite: The 2015 R1200R was more modern and aggressive-looking than previous models. This is the Sport model with red frame and colour-coded engine spoiler. *BMW Group Press*

Opposite bottom: Based on the R1200R, the R1200RS resurrected a famous name from the past. *BMW Group Press*

engine as a self-supporting element. In keeping with the classic roadster look, large frame sections were deliberately left exposed. The rear subframe was also tubular steel, and bolted to the main frame at four points, while the footpegs were forged aluminium. The steering geometry was significantly slower than both the R1200RT (this with a Telelever fork) and the R nineT, with a 27.6-degree rake, 125.6mm of trail and a long 1,515mm wheelbase. As on the R nineT the front suspension was now by a Sachs upside-down 45mm fork, this based on the S1000RR unit. The primary reason for the switch to a telescopic front fork was to improve packaging, the requirement for a narrow radiator and compact front profile effectively eliminating the Telelever at the early design stage. The same EVO Paralever with single shock absorber, as fitted to the other boxers, controlled both the front and rear with an ample 140mm of suspension travel, so the R1200R could comfortably manage well-worn backcountry roads. Recognised by gold-anodised stanchions and a white painted shock absorber spring, the latest generation Dynamic ESA (Electronic Suspension Adjustment) was also available. ABS was standard and braking by Brembo four-piston Monobloc calipers gripping 320mm solidly mounted discs on the front and a generous GS-style 276mm disc on the rear.

Redesigned under the direction of Christian Hahn-Wörnle, the new R1200R continued the style of the successful R nineT, balancing a dynamic look with classic elegance. Casting off the staid looks of its predecessor, with its low set headlight and jutting tail, the new R1200R gained a sportier profile and an aggressive stance. But as it was intended as a versatile all rounder, with significant touring potential, the R1200R owed more to the touring RT than the more focused S1000RR or even the retro R nineT. As pioneered with the R nineT, customizing was also an essential component of the new R1200R. Three models were initially offered: standard, Sport (with engine spoiler and fly-screen), and Exclusive (with a gold front fork and luggage rack). Although still quite heavy at 231kg, the new R1200R now appealed to a wider range of riders, and BMW anticipated it would contribute significantly to their sales expansion. These predictions were vindicated in the sales figures, the new R1200R selling 6,951 units during 2015, placing it sixth on the sales chart. The R1200R was unchanged

for 2016, but shared the transmission optional ABS Pro updates with other liquid-cooled boxers for 2017. With imminent replacement, an exclusive chocolate with gold brake calipers and a stainless steel tank cover was an option for 2018.

R1200RS (2015-2018)

Although the RS was historically important for BMW, the 1976 R100RS establishing a formula symbolizing consummate all-round sport touring, the RS had been absent from BMW's range for a decade. Then for 2015, BMW resurrected their great sports touring tradition with the R1200RS. Based on the R1200R the R1200RS was similar to earlier incarnations in that the primary difference between the RS and the standard model was a semi-fairing and sportier riding position.

The flat-twin boxer engine, narrow radiator, airbox and exhaust system were identical to the R1200R. Also shared were the 'Rain' and 'Road' riding modes, Bosch ABS and standard Automatic Stability Control (ASC). Riding mode Pro was optional with the added feature of Dynamic Traction Control (DTC) with banking detection. Gearshift Assistant Pro was also available, this allowing gear shifting without the operation of the clutch or throttle.

While similar to the R1200R frame, the R1200RS's tubular steel bridge frame was purpose-developed. The steering head angle was similar to the R1200R at 27.7 degrees but with significantly less trail of 114.8mm and a longer 1,530mm wheelbase. The static weight distribution was 51:49. Shared with the R1200R were the 45mm upside-down front fork and EVO Paralever Monoshock, both providing 140mm of travel. As on the R1200R dynamic ESA (Electronic Suspension Adjustment) was optional and recognised by gold-anodised fork stanchions and a white shock absorber spring. Also shared with the R1200R were the front radial four-piston Brembo calipers with 320mm discs and twin-piston floating caliper, and 276mm disc at the rear. The 3.5 and 5.50x 17-inch alloy were similar to the S1000RR, the front with a 'hub cage' enabling direct mounting of the brake discs without additional adapters.

Setting the R1200RS apart from the R1200R was the aerodynamically styled semi-fairing with twin asymmetrical headlights. These were placed either side of a vertical LED daytime running light. With a wide range of options, extending to hard luggage and navigation, the R1200RS was intended for the rider intimidated by a full-blooded sportsbike or adventure bike, but too young for a cruiser or maxi tourer. Somehow, BMW managed to once again find space in their line-up for another model without it having to compete directly with others in the range. This was no mean feat considering the boxer range already consisted of the R1200R and R1200RT, and the multi-purpose S1000XR was released simultaneously. Initial sales were also encouraging, the R1200RS finding 4,208 buyers during 2015. The R1200RS was unchanged for 2016, but shared the transmission and ABS Pro updates with other liquid-cooled boxers for 2017. Colour options for 2018 included a bronze/black, with gold brake calipers and a stainless steel fuel tank cover.

S1000XR (FROM 2015)

Following on from the S1000RR, HP4 and S1000R, BMW offered a fourth member of the four-cylinder S-class for 2015. Encompassing touring capability, sports performance and comfort, the S1000XR was designed to expand BMW's market share rather than encroach on their existing RR clientele. The inline-four-cylinder engine was derived from the S1000R roadster, providing 160 horsepower at 11,000rpm. Two riding modes and Automatic Stability Control (ASC) were standard, with the option of Dynamic Traction Control (DTC) and ABS Pro. Intentionally designed for use on public roads and previously confined to the HP4, with the S1000XR, ABS Pro made its debut on a series production model.

While the chassis was also based on the S1000R, the geometry was refined to suit the touring requirements. Built around a newly developed aluminium perimeter frame, welded from four segments, as on other S1000s, the engine was incorporated as a load-bearing element. To increase load carrying capacity the rear subframe was constructed from rigid pentagonal profile aluminium sections. This was bolted to the main frame at four points while a new double-sided swingarm was welded together from cast aluminium-alloy sections.

To provide optimum traction and handling along country roads, and high stability when loaded, the 25.5 degree steering head angle was 0.8 degrees shallower than the S1000R, while the trail of 117mm was 18.5mm longer. The swingarm was 65mm longer, at 670mm, and the wheelbase increased 109mm, to 1,548mm. The Sachs 46mm upside-down front fork and single adjustable shock absorber were also similar to the S1000R, these providing 150mm of front spring travel and 140mm at the rear. An optional lowering kit saw a reduction to 120mm of front suspension travel and 110mm at the rear. The 10-spoke die-cast aluminium wheels were similar to the S1000RR, these also with directly mounted floating steel 320mm front brake discs. The front braking system featured two radial Brembo four-piston fixed calipers while the rear brake disc increased to 265mm, with a twin-piston floating caliper. A steering damper was standard. The asymmetrical headlights were more subtly different than on the other S1000s, these featuring symmetrical apertures with asymmetrical reflectors. The 20-litre fuel tank was 2.5 litres larger than the S1000R and

The fourth incarnation of
the S1000 four-cylinder – the
multi-purpose S1000XR.
BMW Group Press

The F800R was restyled and re-engineered for 2015. The engine was more powerful, and the front end included an upside-down fork with radial brakes. *BMW Group Press*

the road-ready weight 228kg. Carving out a crossover niche, the versatile S1000XR provided RR thrills with real world usability and not surprisingly found 5,061 buyers during 2015.

But for a new colour scheme of light white and Granite Grey with red highlights and a dynamic brakelight, in conjunction with ABS Pro and Riding Modes Pro, the S1000XR continued unchanged for 2016. And, as demand for Sportsbikes waned, sales of the S1000XR blossomed, rising 74.6 per cent to 8,835 units. This placed it fifth on BMW's motorcycle sales chart. More changes were in store for 2017. Now meeting EU4 requirements, the power was increased to 165 horsepower at 11,000rpm. The payload increased 10kg, to 444kg, and vibration free handlebars increased comfort. For 2018, an HP Motorsport colour scheme was available, with a triple black for 2019.

F800R (FROM 2015)

For 2015, BMW took a fresh look at the long running F800R, pitching it at a younger, less experienced clientele. While the 800cc parallel twin engine had been around for nearly a decade, BMW managed to give it a new lease of life through revised ECU mapping, lowering overall gearing by a tooth on the countershaft sprocket, and lowering first and second gears. These modest updates resulted in a small power increase, to 90 horsepower at 8,000rpm, and a significantly more engaging ride. An optional Akrapovič titanium slip-on silencer, this saving 1.7kg, was an option while a lower 48 horsepower version was also available for novice riders.

It wasn't only the engine that was beefed up on the new F800R. A 43mm upside-down fork replaced the previous conventional fork and a set of radially mounted Brembo four piston calipers gripped the pair of 320mm front discs. Two-channel ABS was standard, with ASC (Automatic Stability Control) and ESA (Electronic Suspension Adjustment) optional. The wheel and tyre sizes were unchanged. Ergonomics were also more relaxed than on the outgoing model, with footpegs 10mm further forward and 10mm lower, a 790mm seat height, and a wider conical aluminium handlebar. The symmetrical headlight arrangement, radiator shields, front mudguard and wheels were redesigned to provide a new look, and BMW were rewarded with 5,971 sales during 2015 (up from 3,953 for the final year of the previous model). Mild updates for 2017 saw the F800R now EU4 compliant. The muffler was redesigned, the ride-by-wire system improved, and the instrument panel revised.

With five new model releases for 2015, this year would see BMW sell a record number of motorcycles: 136,963, up 10.9 per cent from 2014. Germany remained the single largest market, with 23,823 sales, followed by the USA with 16,501 sales. As always, the venerable R series boxers dominated, accounting for 73,357 vehicles (53.6 per cent of sales).

S1000RR (2015-2018)

With more than 50,000 sold, and 22 per cent of the over-800cc global sportsbike market since revolutionizing it in 2009, BMW released a significantly updated S1000RR for 2015. Effectively the limited edition HP4 transformed into volume production guise, the new S1000RR was designed to match new Japanese offerings, notably the updated Yamaha YZF-R1, in this hotly contested category. Demonstrating the level of development evident in just three years, the 2015 S1000RR was more powerful than the factory-supported HP4, Sylvain Barrier and Leon Camier campaigned in the 2014 World Superbike Evo class.

While the basic 999cc engine was as before, the cylinder head porting was reworked, the intake cams recountoured, and the intake valves two grams lighter. Each intake valve carried dual springs with the exhaust valve a single spring. To reduce friction, the cylinder barrels, still integrated in the top half of the engine block, were slide honed. To enhance midrange power, and increase torque particularly around 4,500rpm,

the intake manifold was shortened and the throttle valves repositioned closer to the cylinder head. A 0.2-litre larger airbox and full ride-by-wire (RBW) digital throttle completed the intake specification. The throttle no longer employed a cable to operate the remote RBW sender unit and worked directly off the twist grip. The new airbox was ram-fed from a central intake duct running either side of the steering head and was claimed to provide 30 bar pressure at 250km/h, boosting power by more than 5 horsepower at that speed.

The redesigned stainless steel exhaust system dispensed with the previous front silencer, and now featured a twin-pipe rear silencer. The manifold diameter was reduced, but exhaust backpressure lowered, increasing torque at medium revs and peak power. Retaining a pair of three-way catalytic converters and electronically controlled exhaust valves, the new throatier exhaust system saved 3kg.

The maximum power was increased to 199 horsepower at 13,500rpm, and the usable rev range was considerably wider. Near-peak torque was available between 9,500 and 12,000rpm. Electronic updates saw the new RR equipped with three standard riding modes, 'Rain', 'Sport', and 'Race', as well as Automatic Stability Control (ASC), this without a banking sensor. The optional Pro riding mode features two additional riding modes, 'Slick' and 'User', along with Dynamic Traction Control (DTC), this including a banking sensor.

Although the chassis was ostensibly the same as before, the frame, rear subframe and swingarm were all redesigned. The steering geometry was sharpened, the rake steepened by 0.5 degrees to 23.5 degrees. This was without any change in the triple clamp offset, while the fork overlap in the tubes was reduced by 6mm. This resulted in a reduction of trail by 2mm to 96.5mm. To increase squat, and improve grip, the swingarm pivot was lowered 3mm and the wheelbase lengthened by 15mm to 1,438mm.

Other chassis developments included a 5mm wider handlebar on each side, and a 40mm longer rear shock absorber spring. While the rebound damping range was unchanged, the compression damping range was slightly wider. The 46mm upside-down fork with cartridge inserts comprising separate hydraulic piston and cylinder systems was unchanged, but negative spring travel was reduced by 5mm. This saw the standard ride height increased for improved banking clearance. The optional electronically controlled suspension Dynamic Damping Control (DDC), first seen on the HP4 in 2012, was extensively reworked for the new S1000RR. While the Brembo braking system was also similar to the HP4, the front four-piston calipers were no longer the more expensive Monobloc type.

A new LCD dash display included 640 segments instead of the previous 320, and offered a near bewildering number of readouts. Also new was the bodywork, the dynamic nose-down, tail-up style of the previous model even further accentuated. The familiar asymmetrically styled side fairing sections continued, with distinctive gills on the right and a split face with an asymmetric headlight arrangement. The left cooling outlet was redesigned and the air-deflecting winglets

more neatly integrated into the new fairing. Along with a new windshield the asymmetrical headlights were swapped, with the dipped-beam lamp now on the right and the high beam on the left. While retaining the characteristic asymmetry the new RR stood out clearly from its predecessor. The new S1000RR raised the bar for production 1,000cc Superbikes and BMW were rewarded with 9,576 sales, putting it fourth on their sales chart. Unfortunately racing success wasn't as forthcoming during 2015. Still electing not to officially support the World Superbike Championship, BMW instead offered technical packages to several customer teams. The most successful was BMW Motorrad Italia, with Ayrton Badovini finishing 12th overall. Markus Reiterberger won the German IDM Superbike Championship, also taking out the BMW Motorrad Race Trophy. While not successful at the Isle of Man in 2015, Lee Johnston and Peter Hickman were victorious at the Ulster Grand Prix on S1000RRs. Following his success in the Brazilian Moto 1000 GP series, Matthieu Lussiana won the 2015 BMW Motorrad Race Trophy.

Apart from colours, the production S1000RR was unchanged for 2016, and while sales dropped 5.8 per cent to, 9,016, it still retained its fourth position in BMW's motorcycle ranking. This slight sales drop was more of a function of a general downturn in Sportsbike sales as S-series buyers turned to the more versatile S1000XR. On the racing front the S1000RR was still very successful. Michael Dunlop dominated the Isle of Man TT with wins in the Superbike and Senior Isle of Man TTs. In the process, he set a new outright lap record of 133.962mph (215.591km/h). Ian Hutchinson further cemented the S1000RR's dominance with a victory in the Superstock TT. Dunlop followed his TT success with four wins in Southern 100, also at the Isle of Man, a month later. At the Ulster Grand Prix, in the hands of Hutchinson, Dunlop and David Jackson, the S1000RR won five races. Hutchinson became the world's fastest road racer with a lap of 134.089mph.

Markus Reiterberger made the jump from IDM to World Superbike, joining Jordi Torres in the Althea Racing BMW team. They received factory supplied engines and electronics, but despite split throttles, Akrapovič support and the latest Öhlins RVP 42mm front forks, the S1000RR was outclassed. Torres was the most successful, finishing sixth overall. As a consolation Raffaele de Rosa won the Superstock 1000 FIM Cup on the Althea Racing S1000RR.

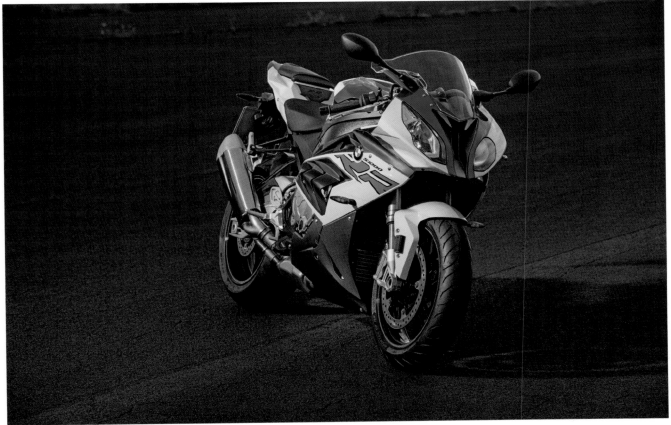

Ian Hutchinson won two Isle
of Man TTs in 2017 on the
S1000RR. *BMW Group Press*

The S1000RR dominated domestic Superbike racing around the world. A standout was Jordan Szoke, who defended his Canadian Superbike title, winning all seven races in the process. Szoke also won the 2016 BMW Motorrad Race Trophy from Vincent Lonbois and Michal Prášek.

As with the other S1000 models, the S1000RR was also adapted for EU4 requirements for 2017. ABS Pro was included in the optional 'Riding Modes Pro', and DTC was standard. Along with new colours, also standard was a passenger seat cover. Sales of the three S Series (S1000RR, S1000R and S1000XR) totalled 21,752 during 2017, providing this range a 13.3 per cent share of BMW motorcycle sales.

Racing success also continued during 2017. Alastair

Seeley took a hat trick of wins at the North West 200, and Ian Hutchinson won the Superbike and Superstock TTs at the Isle of Man. While extremely successful on street circuits BMW again struggled in the World Superbike, with Jordi Torres the leading BMW finisher in 9th overall on the Althea Racing BMW. After a disappointing start in World Superbike Reiterberger returned to the German IDM Championship, winning comfortably. Reiterberger also won his second BMW Motorrad Race Trophy. Amongst eight title wins for the S1000RR during 2017 were Jordan Szoke again winning the Canadian Superbike Championship and Kenny Foray taking the French Superbike Championship.

Apart from the option of an Akrapovič titanium exhaust, the S1000RR continued unchanged for 2018.

Peter Hickman at speed at Union
Mills on the Isle of Man in 2018.
Hickman set a record breaking
135.452mph lap in the Senior TT.
BMW Group Press

However, continued racing development resulted in even more success this year. The road racing series began well, Peter Hickman and Alastair Seeley winning the Superstock races at the North West 200. But the most impressive results were at the Isle of Man, and although marred by the death of Tyco BMW rider Dan Kneen, TT week was a great one for the S1000RR. After Michael Dunlop won the Superbike and Hickman the Superstock races, Hickman went on to set a new lap record of 135.452mph (217.989km/h) on his way to winning the Senior TT. While this was an astonishing speed, Hickman's 134.403mph (216.301km/h) lap on the Superstock race was arguably more impressive as it displayed the incredible capability of the production S1000RR. Hickman completed a spectacular season by winning his third

Macau Grand Prix in November. Jordan Szoke again won the Canadian Superbike Championship, Markus Reiterberger the FIM Superstock 1000 European Championship, and Ukrainian rider Ilya Mikhalchik clinched the German Championship (IDM). Tyco BMW rider Keith Farmer cemented the S1000RR's prowess in Superstock by winning the British Superbike Championship Superstock class. Winner of the BMW Motorrad Race trophy for 2018 was British rider Danny Webb. Webb dominated the International Road Racing Championship on his Wepol Racing by Penz13 S1000RR, securing the IRRC championship title at the penultimate round of the season in August. Alpe Adria Road Racing Championship Superstock champion Michal Filla came second, and Ilya Mikhalchik third.

G310R AND G310GS (FROM 2016)

During 2016, BMW sold more motorcycles and Maxi scooters than ever before, sales up 5.9 per cent to 145,032 units. Again, Germany was the largest market (24,894 sales), but all European countries showed strong growth. The USA received its second best sales result ever, with 13,730 units. With a stated intention of reaching 200,000 sales by 2020 it was no surprise to see the introduction of a sub-500cc model for 2016. Emphasising buyer loyalty, the G310R was designed to entice new customers to the brand before they progressed up the ownership ladder to larger and more expensive models. In Western markets it would be entry-level, while in Brazil and Asia it was positioned as a prestige model.

Designed and developed in Germany, the G310 was manufactured in Bangalore, India by TVS, India's fourth largest motorcycle manufacturer. With three factories in India, plus one in Indonesia, TVS built 2.15 million motorcycles in 2015. BMW signed an agreement with the Srinivasan family, TVS's owners, in April 2013 and development began in Munich under the supervision of project leader Jürgen Stoffregen.

Three years later, the G310R made it into production. According to Stoffregen, "The objective was to build a properly sized motorcycle, able to accommodate riders of all heights. Even though it was built in India it also had to be a true BMW." While 80 per cent of content was local, BMW went to length to ensure all the components met German standards. BMW also recruited Andreas Wimmer and Jörg Schüller from KTM, both involved with the establishment of KTM production in India with Bajaj.

Owing nothing to any previous BMW single, the G310 began with a clean sheet of paper, and the unusual capacity was chosen to separate it from the 250cc Japanese competition. With an 80 x 62.1mm bore and stroke, the liquid-cooled single cylinder engine displaced 313cc. The twin overhead camshaft cylinder head deign was based on the S1000RR, with light, DLC coated (Diamond Like Carbon) rocker arms and four valves (33.5mm inlet and 27.2mm exhaust). The valve angle was 11.2 degrees on the intake and 13.3 degrees on the exhaust side and the throttle valve was 42mm. DLC coating on the gudgeon pin allowed the pin to run directly in the connecting rod eye and the Nikasil cylinder was integrated in the upper half of the engine housing. Lubrication was by wet sump and power transmitted by multiplate wet clutch to a six-

Opposite: Markus Reiterberger on his way to winning the 2018 FIM Superstock 1000 European Championship on the S1000RR. *BMW Group Press*

Below: The first result of BMW's partnership with the Indian company TVS was the G310R. Here it is in Motorsport colours. *BMW Group Press*

speed gearbox. A rotating counterbalance shaft in front of the crankshaft suppressed excessive vibration. The most unusual feature was the backwards titled cylinder, with the cylinder head turned 180 degrees. Thus the intake was at the front and exhaust at the rear. This layout was unsuccessfully pioneered by Cannondale on its Motocross MX400 in 2001 and later adopted by Yamaha on the YZ450 dirtbike (2010-2013) but this was the first time it had appeared on a street bike. The reason BMW chose this layout was to place extra weight on the front wheel for improved grip. The rotated cylinder head allowed the engine to be positioned further forward, with a longer (650mm)

swingarm to improve stability. The rotated cylinder head also provided a shorter, straighter inlet charge, and allowed for a shorter exhaust pipe as required by EU4. With a Magneti Marelli BMS-E2 electronic injection and a secondary air system, the engine produced 34 horsepower at 9,500rpm with maximum torque of 28Nm at 7,500rpm.

The G310R engine sat in a tubular steel chassis, with a bolt-on rear subframe and die-cast aluminium swingarm. The conservative steering geometry provided a 25.1-degree steering head angle with 102.3mm of trail. The wheelbase was 1,374mm. In keeping with the entry-level budget nature, suspension was by a

Below: The second example
of the TVS partnership was
the G310GS. Released for
2017, the styling incorporated
the trademark GS beak.
BMW Group Press

non-adjustable 41mm Kayaba upside-down fork and
preload adjustable Kayaba Monoshock. Travel was
a generous 140mm on the front and 131mm on the
rear. Cast alloy five-spoke wheels, 3.0x17 and 4.0x17-
inch were shod with Michelin tyres (110/70R17 and
150/60R17) made in Thailand. A single front 300mm
disc with four-piston Bybre (ByBrembo, Brembo's
Indian subsidiary) radial caliper and rear 240mm disc
with twin-piston caliper handled the braking duties.
Two-channel Continental ABS was standard.

Weighing only 158.5kg, the styling and ergonomics
were intentionally sporty. A low 785mm seat height
ensured all riders could be accommodated, with

optional 760 and 815mm seats also available.
Standard equipment also included a Continental LCD
multi-function dashboard. As the first fruit of their
partnership with TVS, the G310R was impressive.
Dynamically and functionally the G310R met
expectations and the build quality was as expected of
a BMW. The G310R may have been inexpensive, but it
wasn't cheap.

The inevitable expansion of models on the G310
platform continued for 2017 with the G310GS. After
being involved with the K1200S, K1200R, HP2
Megamoto, R1200GS and Paris-Dakar racer, design
chief Edgar Heinrich worked with Bajaj in India

before returning to BMW in 2012. He was involved in developing the R nineT retro models before working on the G310GS. Heinrich said, "This was challenging as it was important to create a small capacity GS that lived up to the brand values."

While the engine and frame were unchanged from the street version, the seat height was increased 50mm, to 835mm (with 820 and 850mm seats also available), due to the longer travel dual-purpose suspension. Suspension travel was increased 40mm, to 180mm. The steering geometry was also relaxed to improve stability, with a longer 1,420mm wheelbase, 26.7-degree steering head angle and 98mm of trail. The 5-spoke light alloy die-cast wheels were 2.50 x 19-inch and 4.0 x 17-inch, with 110/80 R 19 and 150/70 R 17 tyres. The brakes were unchanged from the G310R. A broader, flatter handlebar on 60mm risers, along with lower mounted footrests, provided a more spacious riding position. The weight of 169.5kg was also up on the G310R. While the small capacity engine had to be worked quite hard to achieve maximum performance the G310GS was a versatile machine, setting a new standard of refinement in the mini-adventure segment.

The launch of the G310R and G310GS saw these two models achieving combined sales of 11,595 units during 2017. They proved not only popular in the anticipated growth markets of South America and Asia, but also Europe. Motorcycle sales reached another record high during 2017, up 13.2 per cent to 164,153 vehicles. The strongest growth was in Europe and again Germany was the largest market. While overall motorcycle sales in the US were down 3.2 per cent, BMW managed to buck the trend slightly, selling 13,546 motorcycles, 1.3 per cent lower than 2016.

HP4 RACE (2017)

BMW continued their commitment to innovation by releasing the exotic HP4 Race for 2017. Ostensibly a revival of the earlier HP4, the HP4 Race offered an even higher specification, and was available only in track-ready guise. Pushing the bounds of carbon-fibre componentry, the HP4 race was also incredibly light, built as a limited edition of 750 examples, and extremely expensive.

According to Rudolf Schneider, Head of four and six-cylinder Product Projects, "The HP4 Race engine is in World Superbike factory specification, individually crafted by a small, highly specialised team, ensuring the very highest level of quality in terms of power and reliability. The peak output of 215 horsepower at 13,900rpm is more than that used by Jordi Torres in the World Superbike Championship."

Along with new intake and exhaust camshafts, the compression ratio was raised to 13.7-13.9:1, and the engine fitted with intake funnels of varying length. These also had an enlarged cross section. On the HP4 Race the intake funnels were longer with an enlarged cross-section. The milled con-rods were from Pankl, the crankshaft lightened 200g, and the 4-in-2-in-1 exhaust system made of titanium. Apart from third gear all the gearbox ratios were new, and more suited to the race track than the standard S1000RR. The standard shift pattern was also reversed as generally favoured by racers while the HP Shift Assistant Pro allowed upshifting without the clutch.

Where the HP4 Race really set itself apart was with the carbon fibre frame, subframe and wheels. According to Christian Gonschor, HP4 Race Project manager, "The industrially produced carbon fibre frame opens a new chapter in motorcycle chassis construction. Here we are bringing together optimum technical qualities, consistent manufacturing quality and economy for the first time." When the project began in February 2015 a carbon fibre frame wasn't initially considered but with the volume carbon fibre construction introduced with the electric i3 and i8 cars it became possible to build a small series of carbon fibre motorcycle frames using the Resin Transfer Moulding (RTM) process. This provided consistent manufacturing quality, with each frame identical.

The main frame was a carbon fibre bridge type, a one-piece hollow monocoque made from a single piece, without seams and joints. The bulkhead partitions and metal inserts were bonded at the manufacturing stage. The self-supporting rear frame was also of carbon fibre, but not with the elaborate RTM process, but laminated with the classic hand-lay weave of carbon-fibre and epoxy resin. This was adjustable for three different seat heights: from 816 to 846mm. In order to achieve the optimal response, the frame was engineered with a degree of controlled flex. The total weight of the main frame was only 7.8kg, 4kg less than its aluminium counterpart.

Also constructed of carbon fibre were the 3.5x17 and 6.0x17-inch wheels. These were around 30

Produced as a numbered limited edition,
the HP4 Race also featured a carbon-fibre
frame and wheels. It was sold as a track-only
model. *BMW Group Press*

per cent lighter than conventional light alloy forged wheels, with a significant 40 per cent reduction in gyroscopic force. This translated into dramatically improved handling with faster changes of direction. The aluminium 604mm long swingarm was identical to the WSBK racer, with an adjustable swingarm pivot. Here, aluminium was considered sufficient, as it offered optimum performance in terms of weight, stiffness, traction and feedback.

The suspension was World Superbike Spec Öhlins, a 43mm FGR300 upside-down fork and a TTX 36 GP shock absorber. This was totally adjustable, with supplied offset triple clamps allowing for a steering head angle between 23.5 and 25.5 degrees with trail between 95 and 112mm. The Brembo brakes were also WSBK specification, with front GP4 PR monoblock fixed calipers with titanium pistons and a nickel-plated body. The floating T-type racing steel brake discs were 320mm and activated by a milled aluminium RSC 19 x 18 front master cylinder. The rear brake included a 220mm disc with 4-piston fixed caliper with titanium pistons. With a claimed dry weight of only 146kg, or 171.4kg fully fuelled, the HP4 Race was astonishingly light.

In the area of electronics the HP4 Racing also mirrored the WSBK racer. The extensive electronic control and assistance system package was geared specifically towards racing. This included adjustable Dynamic Traction Control (DTC), Wheelie Control, Engine Brake (EBR), Launch Control and a Pit Lane Limiter.

As an expensive numbered limited edition the HP4 Race was considered a future collectable, but without street or race homologation it was primarily an exhibition of BMW's technological prowess. Carbon fibre frames have been on the agenda for several decades, but were always limited by their cost effectiveness. With the RTM process, BMW finally found a commercially viable manufacturing technique, and while starting at the top, with an exclusive limited edition model, it was inevitable this technology would eventually filter down to other models.

A new model for 2017 was the K1600B Bagger, the long low lines reflecting this American custom style. *BMW Group Press*

K1600GT, K1600GTL, K1600B, K1600 GRAND AMERICA (FROM 2017)

After six years, the K1600GT and GTL were mildly updated for 2017. A third variation, the K1600B 'Bagger' was also available this year. This was primarily for the US market. While the power of the 1,600cc six-cylinder engine was unchanged, new engine mapping, a carbon canister for fuel tank ventilation, and a new catalytic converter allowed it to pass EU4 regulations. Also standard for all versions was electronically controlled suspension (ESA), with 'Road' and 'Dynamic' modes. Reverse assist and Shift Assistant Pro were optional. On both the K1600GT and GTL the instruments were new, and the bodywork received larger air deflectors and new side trim. While the K1600GT and GTL continued as a refinement of an already successful formula, the K1600B Bagger was the production realisation of the 'Concept 101' unveiled at the Concorso d'Eleganza Villa d'Este in 2015. This was BMW's interpretation of 'Grand American Touring' on endless highways. All black (Blackstorm metallic/black for the chassis and drivetrain), the K1600B took the form of a bagger, an exclusive American custom bike. Bagger characteristics included a drop-shaped silhouette, with the highest point the front fairing, and American style rear lights. A new rear frame significantly reduced the passenger seat height. The fixed side cases had slimmer covers and deeper bodies while the rear mudguard folded upwards to facilitate rear wheel removal. Completing the Bagger style were low-slung chrome mufflers, and a redesigned fairing with a short electrically adjustable windscreen. The success of the new K1600 series, particularly the K1600B Bagger in the US, resulted in a 50 per cent increase in sales during 2017, to 6,719.

Along with minor equipment updates to the K1600GT and GTL, a fourth K1600 variant was available for 2018: the K1600 Grand America. This was a full dresser developed specifically for the American touring market, and included a standard Audio system, GPS, Bluetooth, Floorboards, engine protection bars reverse assist, high windscreen, top case and K1600 Grand America nameplate. All K1600s received Hill Start Control Pro for 2019.

The K1600GT was updated for 2017. The engine now met EU4 and the bodywork was slightly restyled. *BMW Group Press*

The K1600 evolved into the full
dress Grand America for 2018.
BMW Group Press

F750GS, F850GS, F850GS ADVENTURE (FROM 2018)

After ten years of consistent model development, for 2018 the middleweight GS range was redesigned and reengineered. Replacing the F700 and F800GS, the F750GS even more street focused than before, and the F850GS offered improved off-road ability. To increase power and torque, the engine capacity was increased to 853cc, with a larger bore (84mm) and longer stroke (77mm). Unlike the previous engine that featured a 360-degree crankshaft with a conrod type balancer, the new 853cc engine featured a 270/450-degree crankshaft, the journal offset of 90 degrees providing a similar sound to a 90-degree V-twin. Two gear-driven opposed counterbalance shafts were positioned in front and behind the crankshaft. Lubrication was dry sump, with the separate oil tank contained within the crankcase.

New for 2018, the F750GS (left) and
F850GS (right) continued the style of
the previous F700GS and F800GS. The
fuel tank was in a more conventional
location, and the final drive was on the left.
BMW Group Press

The cylinder head still featured four valves per cylinder, these operated by double overhead camshafts and fixed rocker arms. The timing chain drive was on the right and the 33.5mm intake and 27.2mm exhaust valves set at a 24.5 degree included angle. The compression ratio was 12.7:1 and the electronic injection system the next-generation BMS-M. The maximum power for the F750GS was 77 horsepower at 7,500rpm, with the F850GS generating 95 horsepower at 8,250rpm. 48 horsepower versions of both were also available, primarily for A2 licence holders in the German market.

The six-speed transmission was also redesigned: the straight cut primary drive on the right, an anti-hopping wet clutch, with the final drive now on the left. As the final drive was on the left the exhaust system was on the right. Standard equipment included 'Rain' and 'Road' riding modes plus ABS and ASC, with Gearshift assistant Pro and riding Modes Pro (with Dynamic, Enduro and DTC) optional.

While retaining the engine as a stressed element, a welded sheet steel bridge monocoque frame replaced the previous tubular steel spaceframe. The fuel tank

Below: The F750GS and
F850GS engine now had a
270/450-degree crankshaft
and conventional balancers.
BMW Group Press

Bottom: A F850GS Adventure
joined the other F series GSs for
2019. *BMW Group Press*

was also no longer underneath the seat,
returning to the usual position between
the seat and steering head. This allowed
the rear section to be narrower and
improve overall packaging. A double-
sided aluminium swingarm completed
the frame specification.

The steering geometry was also
revised, with a flatter steering head
angle and more trail than before. The
F750GS head angle was 27 degrees and
the F850GS 28 degrees, compared to 26
degrees on the previous versions. The
trail went up to 104.5mm (F750GS) and
126mm (F850GS), up from 95.3 and
117mm for the F700GS and F800GS.
The wheelbase also increased slightly,
to 1,559mm (F750GS) and 1,593mm

(F850GS). The suspension was also new, the F750GS receiving a 41mm conventional fork and the F850GS a 43mm upside-down type. While the diameter was reduced from the previous model, response was improved and travel increased (151mm for the F750GS and 204mm for the F850GS). The adjustable rear shock absorber provided 177mm (F750GS) and 219mm (F850GS) travel.

As before, the road-oriented entry-level F750GS featured die-cast aluminium wheels, 2.50 x 19 and 4.25 x 17-inch. The F850GS was fitted with cross-spoke aluminium wheels, 2.15 x 21 and 4.25 x 17-inch. Both models were now fitted with tubeless tyres, 110/80 R19 and 150/70 R17 (F750GS) and 90/90 x 21 and 150/70 R17 (F850GS). The dual front discs measured 305mm and were gripped by two-piston floating calipers, with the single 265mm rear disc fitted with a single-piston floating caliper. On the F750GS, the 815mm standard seat height was unchanged, while the F850GS standard seat was reduced 20mm to 860mm. Optional seats were available to lower the F750GS seat to 770mm and the F850GS to 815mm.

The styling was also updated, with a new LED headlight and the option of an F850GS Rallye style variant. While the weight was increased to 224kg (F750GS) and 229kg (F850GS), the new middleweight GSs promised to continue and build on a successful formula. For 2019, the F850GS Adventure joined the line-up. This was based on the F850GS but with a 23-litre fuel tank (instead of 15 litres), a larger adjustable windscreen, hand protectors, enduro footpegs, engine protection bars, 15mm higher handlebars and a stainless steel luggage rack. The general dimensions were increased over the F850GS, the standard seat height an intimidating 875mm and the road ready weight a considerable 244kg. But, as it accentuated the style of BMW's GS Adventure family, the F850GS Adventure was already on the road to success.

S1000RR (FROM 2019)

With the S1000RR approaching its tenth anniversary BMW's design team embarked on a development program to significantly improve the Superbike's racetrack performance and reduce weight. ShiftCam was introduced to provide a wider range of useable power, this provided variable intake valve timing and valve lift. The system comprised a triple-section intake camshaft with two cams per valve, one partial-load and one full-load. The valves were titanium, and the intake valves hollow-bored to reduce weight. The DLC-coated rocker arms were also lighter, allowing maximum revs to increase from 14,200 to 14,600rpm. The engine unit was redesigned, also primarily to save weight. This saw the camshafts now driven directly from the crankshaft, without an idler gear, and the intermediate gear positioned inside the cylinder head. The oil and water pump were combined in a single, compact module, and, to reduce engine width by 12mm, a single crankshaft gear engaged the starter, this now integrated behind the cylinders. To reduce engine height, the con-rods were 4mm shorter, at 99mm. Although the ShiftCam system increased weight by 1.0kg, the complete engine unit now weighed 4kg less than before. The engine was also positioned 7.5mm to the left in the frame, with the drive chain moved 5mm left.

The new RR engine was fitted with variable length intakes, and the stainless steel exhaust system was 1.3kg lighter. While the peak power increased by 8 horsepower, to 207 horsepower, (205 horsepower in the USA), ShiftCam boosted torque between 5,500 and 14,500rpm. Along with two throttle curves (Country road and race track), standard linked riding modes included 'Rain', 'Road', 'Dynamic' and 'Race', with the option of Race Pro Modes. Also standard was the latest generation Dynamic Traction Control with a 6-axis sensor cluster, Shift Assistant Pro, Launch Control, and a Pit Lane Limiter.

The aluminium bridge frame was also revised and was now 1.3kg lighter. While still a welded structure of four chill cast elements with the engine integrated and tilted 32 degrees, the two top frame tubes, steering head and engine mounts now provided an increased load-bearing function. Also included in the design was a combination of stiffness and flexibility, this Flexframe design was also much narrower in the seat area to improve rider ergonomics. The steering head angle was slightly steeper, at 23.1 degrees, with the trail reduced to 93.9mm. With a new 606.6mm swingarm the wheelbase was increased to 1,441mm. The swingarm design was now derived from Superbike racing, with the shock absorber positioned as far from the engine as possible to reduce heat. The shock absorber piston diameter was increased to 46mm and the linkage ratio reduced from 1.9 to 1.6:1. Travel was also reduced

Unlike earlier versions, the
S1000RR headlight arrangement
for 2019 was more conventional.
BMW Group Press

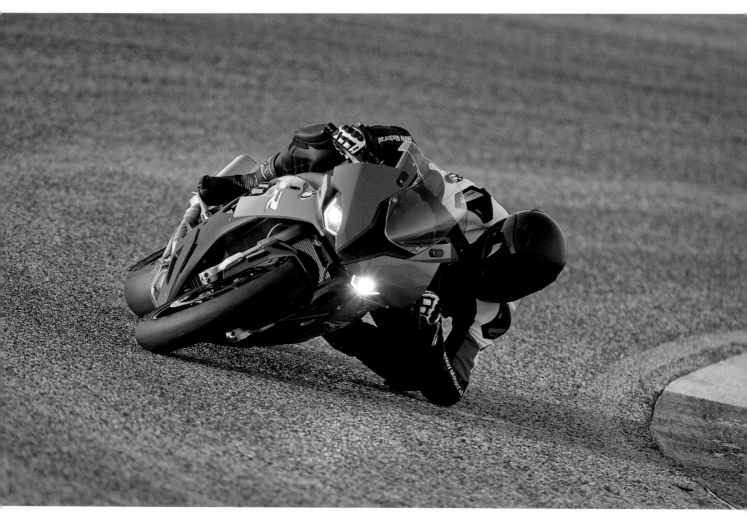

slightly, to 117mm. The upside-down front fork diameter was also reduced slightly, to 45mm, and was fitted with closed-cartridge inserts with separate rebound and compression damping systems. Travel was 120mm and a new generation electronic Dynamic Damping Control (DDC) was optional. Completing the specification package was a new multifunction 6.5-inch TFT screen.

Weight saving continued to the wheels and brakes, the 17-inch wheels 1.6kg lighter, and the 320x4.5mm front discs saving 0.5mm. ABS Pro now provided ABS when banked. These extensive weight reduction measures were reflected in an unladen, fully fuelled weight of only 197kg, or 193.5kg with the M Package (this available for the first time for a BMW motorcycle)

with front weight distribution increased from 52.3 to 53.8 per cent. The styling was also updated, the headlight layout no longer featuring the previously distinctive asymmetric arrangement.

This release of the third generation S1000RR also prompted BMW to return to the World Superbike Championship for 2019. In collaboration with the British-based Shaun Muir Racing team, BMW Motorrad Motorsport was responsible for the development of engine, electronics, chassis and aerodynamics, with Shaun Muir Racing organising testing and logistics. The riders were 2013 Champion Tom Sykes and recently-crowned FIM Superstock 1000 European Champion Markus Reiterberger.

The 2019 BMW Motorrad World SBK team.
From left: Marc Bongers (BMW Motorrad
Motorsport director), Markus Reiterberger,
Tom Sykes, Shaun Muir, and Dr Markus
Schramm (Head of BMW Motorrad).
BMW Group Press

Below: The 2019 S1000RR
was lighter, more powerful,
and fitted with a more
sophisticated electronics package.
BMW Group Press

Bottom: The third generation
S1000RR engine was more
compact than before.
BMW Group Press

R1250GS, GS ADVENTURE (FROM 2019)

With more than 700,000 of the various models built since 1980 the GS family had grown to be the most important in BMW's line-up. The R1200GS and R1200GS Adventure sat at the pinnacle of the series and their success had encouraged the growth of the maxi-enduro or Adventure Tourer market. As a result most other motorcycle manufacturers introduced competitive offerings. Although the R1200GS was established as the reference point for this increasingly

Setting the R1250 boxer engine apart from the previous R1200 was ShiftCam variable valve timing, and quieter, toothed camchains. *BMW Group Press*

popular category the rate of change from the competition was accelerating almost exponentially. To counter this, a new generation boxer was introduced for 2019. Unlike in previous years, where the R1200GS and R1200RT were introduced first with other versions following in successive Model Years, the new R1250 engine made it to the entire water-cooled boxer range.

With a larger bore of 102.5mm, and longer stroke of 76mm, the capacity of the boxer engine was increased to 1,254cc. Torque increased 14 per cent and power 9 per cent, and with a maximum output of 136 horsepower at 7,750rpm, the R1250 was the most powerful series production boxer yet. As on the new S1000RR, the improvement in power and torque across a wider rev range was largely as a result of ShiftCam variable valve control. This differed from the Vanos and Valvetronic variable valve lift system used in BMW cars, as it combined variable valve timing and differential valve lift to optimise cam timing and duration. The inlet camshaft included two cams per valve, one for partial load and one for full load. An electrically activated shifting gate linked to the throttle determined the camshaft selection. The switch between the two cam profiles also created more swirl, improving combustion and reducing fuel consumption by 4 per cent.

As on the previous engine the paired 40mm inlet and 34mm exhaust valves were set at a flat included angle of just 18 degrees and the compression ratio was 12.5:1. But new for the R1250 were dual knock sensors to permit the use of lower grade fuel in more remote areas. While the double overhead camshaft chain and gear drive system was as before, to reduce noise the camchains were a toothed type rather than roller. The fully sequential digital engine control was by a new BMW-O, with 52mm throttle bodies and new design twin-jet injector needles. The two-into-one exhaust system was a new design in stainless steel, and the air/oil cooling system and integral six-speed gearbox with wet clutch were carried over from the previous R1200. Standard equipment included two riding modes (Road and Rain), Automatic Stability Control, and Hill Start Control. With the optional 'Riding Modes Pro' the character could be further adapted to individual needs.

The Telelever front suspension still included a Sachs shock absorber and 37mm tubes, but the steering geometry was slightly revised, with a 27.1-degree steering head angle and 109mm of trail. The wheelbase also increased slightly to 1,525mm. Wheel travel of 190 and 200mm front and rear was unchanged. Due to the increased standard equipment, the weight went up five kilograms, to 249kg. The brakes were unchanged, but the four-piston calipers were either Brembo or BMW-branded American-made Hayes. Cast alloy 19 and 17-inch wheels were standard, with wire-spoked optional. Other standard equipment included the Connectivity feature with a 6.5-inch colour TFT screen and an LED headlamp. Optional seats, these offering seat heights between 800 and 900mm, were also available.

Alongside the basic version, special R1250GS variants were also available. The R1250GS Exclusive exuded a predominately black style and the R1250GS HP emphasised a sporting image. Longer travel sports suspension was also an option on the HP version, and the range of options for customisation for all versions was virtually endless.

Whereas with earlier R1200GS incarnations the Adventure version followed a year later, the R1250GS Adventure was released almost simultaneously with the R1250GS for the 2019 Model Year. This continued the style of its R1200GS Adventure predecessor, and like the R1250GS, was also available in Exclusive and HP versions. Small chassis changes over the R1250GS included longer travel suspension (210 and 220mm front and rear), revised steering geometry (24.9-degree steering head angle with 95.4mm of trail), and a shorter (1,504mm) wheelbase. The wet weight went up to 268kg, but some of this was due to the larger (30-litre) fuel tank.

It was a big ask to improve on the legendary R series GS, but BMW knew their clientele, and they knew GS owners would always want a newer and improved model. The GS had set the adventuring standard for several decades, and this wasn't about to change with the R1250GS and R1250GS Adventure.

R1250RT (FROM 2019)

Released concurrently with the R1250GS, the R1250RT shared the new 136-horsepower ShiftCam engine, but otherwise was very similar to the previous R1200RT. The tubular steel bridge frame, and Telelever and Paralever suspension was similar, and while the trail and wheelbase were unchanged the steering head angle of 25.9 degrees was 0.5 degrees steeper than on the outgoing model. Styling updates included new wheels (in the same sizes), redesigned engine spoiler, and an additional front spoiler. The R1250RT also now included two standard riding modes, Rain and Road, Hill Start Control, and a 5.7-inch TFT colour screen. An analogue speedometer and rev counter supplemented this and an emergency eCall system was available as an option. ABS Pro, with banking ABS, was standard, as was a dynamic brakelight, while the next generation ESA (Electronic Suspension Adjustment) was optional. Three different two-level seats were available, covering 90mm between the highest and lowest version. Offered in a choice of three colours and two styles, the basic R1250RT was available in White, Blue or Sparkling Storm, with the R1250RT Sport and R1250RT Elegance the two other variants.

R1250R AND R1250RS (FROM 2019)

Completing the R1250 range was the R1250R and R1250RS. These also shared the new ShiftCam boxer engine and included two riding modes, ASC and Hill Start Control as standard. Also standard was a 6.5-inch colour TFT multifunction display and the R1250RS received an LED headlamp. Styling updates for both models included a new front spoiler and cockpit cover. Alongside the standard black R1250R were two style variants, the R1250R HP and R1250R Exclusive. The R1250RS was available in three colours with R1250RS Exclusive and R1250RS Sport variants. The chassis specifications were also very similar to the outgoing versions, with an unchanged wheelbase and steering head angle, but the R1250R had slightly more trail (126.6mm) than before and the R1250RT less (110.8mm). The weight of both also increased, to 239kg and 243kg respectively.

Model changes in the mid-class segment resulted in BMW's motorcycle production decreasing 14.8 per cent in the first three quarters of 2018. However, following the release of the new five-model R1250 series, overall motorcycle sales increased 0.9 per cent, to 165,655 units. With these figures, BMW were certainly on track to achieve the goal of 200,000 sales in 2020. Germany, with 23,824 sales, remained the largest market, but France (16,615), Italy (14,110), USA (13,842), Spain (11,124) and the UK (9,224) all performed strongly. China (up 35 per cent) and Brazil (up 11 per cent) also portended the future. For the first time in BMW's history, the R1200/1250 GS and GS Adventure notched more than 51,000 sales, with the R series again dominating overall by accounting for 84,500 units. The S series sold 18.773 units, while the entry level G310R and GS were delivered to 24,363 customers. Largely due to the success of the Bagger, K1600 sales increased 25 per cent, to 8,306.

As BMW's centenary of motorcycle production approached the range embraced singles, twins, fours and sixes. But as had happened throughout this history the venerable boxer twin remained paramount, continuing to dominate sales and upholding its traditional position as the cornerstone of BMW's line-up. As improved technology resulted in motorcycling moving towards uniformity, BMW's success continued by offering a unique formula: one of individuality combining functional superiority and incomparable quality. This recipe would undoubtedly serve BMW well into the future, allowing them to maintain their position as Europe's premier motorcycle manufacturer.

APPENDICES
APPENDIX 1
BMW MOTORCYCLE PRODUCTION 1923-2008

Model	Year	Number	Model	Year	Number
R32	1923-26	3,090	R20	1937-38	5,000
R37	1925-26	152	R23	1938-40	8,021
R39	1925-27	855	R51	1938-40	3,775
R42	1926-28	6,502	R66	1938-41	1,669
R47	1927-28	1,720	R61	1938-41	3,747
R52	1928-29	4,377	R71	1938-41	3,458
R62	1928-29	4,355	R75	1941-44	18,000 approx
R57	1928-30	1,005	R24	1948-50	12,020
R63	1928-29	794	R25	1950-51	23,400
R11	1929-34	7,500	R25/2	1951-53	38,651
R16	1929-34	1,006	R25/3	1953-56	47,700
R2 Series 1	1931	4,161	R51/2	1950-51	5,000
R2 Series 2a	1932	1,850	R51/3	1951-54	18,420
R2 Series 2/33	1933	2,000 approx	R67	1951	1,470
R2 Series 3	1934	2,077	R67/2	1952-54	4,235
R2 Series 4	1935	2,700	R67/3	1955-56	700
R2 Series 5	1936	2,500	R68	1952-54	1,452
R4 Series 1	1932	1,101	R50	1955-60	13,510
R4 Series 2	1933	1,737	R69	1955-60	2,956
R4 Series 3	1934	3,671	R60	1956-60	3,530
R4 Series 4	1935	3,651	R26	1956-60	30,236
R4 Series 5	1936-37	5,033	R50/2 (incl. R50US)	1960-69	19,036
R3	1936	740	R60/2 (incl. R60US)	1960-69	17,306
R12	1935-42	36,000	R27	1960-66	15,364
R17	1935-37	434	R50S	1960-62	1,634
R5	1936-37	2,652	R69S (incl. R69US)	1960-69	11,317
R6	1937	1,850	R50/5	1969-73	7,865
R35	1937-40	15,386	R60/5	1969-73	22,721

Model	Year	Number	Model	Year	Number
R75/5	1969-73	38,370	K1	1989-93	6,921
R90S	1973-76	17,465	K100RS (4-valve)	1989-92	12,666
R90/6	1973-76	21,097	K75RT	1989-96	21,264
R75/6	1973-76	17,587	R100R and Mystic	1991-96	20,589
R60/6	1973-76	13,511	R80R	1992-94	3,593
R100RS	1976-84	33,648	K1100LT	1991-98	22,757
R100S	1976-78	11,762	K1100RS	1992-96	12,179
R100/7	1976-78	12,056	R1100RS	1993-2001	26,037
R75/7	1976-77	6,264	F650	1993-2000	50,990
R60/7	1976-78	11,163	R1100GS, R850GS	1993-2000	45,870
R80/7	1977-84	18,522	R1100R, R850R	1994-2000	53,685
R100RT	1978-84	18,015	R1100RT	1995-2001	53,092
R100T	1978-80	5,463	F650ST	1996-2000	13,349
R45	1978-85	28,158	R850C Classic/		
R65	1978-85	29,454	Avantgarde	1997-2001	1,505
R100	1980-84	10,111	R1150RS	2001-2005	7,309
R100CS	1980-84	4,038	R1150GS	1999-2003	58,023
R80 G/S	1980-87	21,864	R1150GS Adventure	2002-2005	17,828
R65LS	1981-85	6,389	R1200GS	2004-2007	90,142
R80ST	1982-84	5,963	R850R	2002-2007	15,013
R80RT	1982-84	7,315	R1150R	2001-2006	43,026
K100	1983-90	12,871	R1150RT	2001-2005	57,137
K100RS	1983-92	47,470	R1200C, R1200C Classic	1997-2003	29,788
K100RT	1984-89	22,335	R1200C Independent	2000-2003	6,010
R80	1984-95	13,815	R1200CL	2002-2004	5,160
R80RT	1984-95	22,069	R1200 Montauk	2003-2004	3,276
K75C	1985-90	9,566	R1100S	1998-2005	33,741
K75S	1985-95	18,649	R1200GS Adventure	2006-2007	18,320
R65	1985-93	8,260	HP2 Enduro	2005-2006	2,910
K75	1986-96	18,485	K1200RS	1997-2005	37,992
K100LT	1986-91	14,899	K1200GT	2002-2005	10,727
R100RS	1986-92	6,081	F650GS	2000-2008	85,194
R100GS	1987-96	34,007	F650GS Dakar	2000-2008	21,499
R80GS	1987-96	11,375	F650CS	2002-2005	20,845
R65GS	1987-92	1,727	C1	2000-2002	33,714
R100RT	1989-96	9,738			

APPENDIX 2
SPECIFICATIONS OF PRODUCTION BMWs 1923-2019

Model	Years	Engine	Bore (mm)	Stroke (mm)	Displ (cc)	Comp ratio	Carburettor	HP
R32	1923-26	Twin Cyl SV	68	68	494	5.0:1	BMW 22mm	8.5 @ 3,200 rpm
R37	1925-26	Twin Cyl OHV	68	68	494	6.2:1	BMW 26mm	16 @ 4,000 rpm
R39	1925-27	Single Cyl OHV	68	68	247	6.0:1	BMW 20mm	6.5 @ 4,000 rpm
R42	1926-28	Twin Cyl SV	68	68	494	4.9:1	BMW 22mm	12 @ 3,400 rpm
R47	1927-28	Twin Cyl OHV	68	68	494	5.8:1	BMW 22mm	18 @ 4,000 rpm
R52	1928-29	Twin Cyl SV	63	78	486	5.0:1	BMW 22mm	12 @ 3,400 rpm
R62	1928-29	Twin Cyl SV	78	78	745	5.5:1	BMW 22mm	18 @ 3,400 rpm
R57	1928-30	Twin Cyl OHV	68	68	494	5.8:1	BMW 24mm	18 @ 4,000 rpm
R63	1928-29	Twin Cyl OHV	83	68	736	6.2:1	BMW 24mm	24 @ 4,000 rpm
R11	1929-34	Twin Cyl SV	78	78	736	5.5:1	BMW 24mm Sum 24mm 2 Amal 25mm	18 @ 3,400 rpm (20 @ 4,000 rpm)
R16	1929-34	Twin Cyl OHV	83	68	745	6.5:1 (7:1)	BMW 26mm 2 Amal 25mm	25 @ 4,000 rpm (33 @ 4,000 rpm)
R2	1931-36	Single Cyl OHV	63	64	198	6.7:1	Sum 19mm Amal 18.2mm	6 @ 3,500 rpm (8 @ 4,500 rpm)
R4	1932-37	Single Cyl OHV	78	84	398	5.7:1	Sum 25mm	12 @ 4,000 rpm (14@ 4,000 rpm)
R3	1936	Single Cyl OHV	68	84	305	6.0:1	Sum 25mm	11 @ 4,200 rpm
R12	1935-42	Twin Cyl SV	78	78	745	5.2:1	Sum 25mm (2 Amal 24mm)	18 @ 3,400 rpm (20 @ 4,000 rpm)
R17	1935-37	Twin Cyl OHV	83	68	736	6.5:1	2 Amal 25.4mm	33 @ 5,000 rpm
R5	1936-37	Twin Cyl OHV	68	68	494	6.7:1	2 Amal 22.2mm	24 @ 5,800 rpm
R6	1937	Twin Cyl SV	70	78	596		2 Amal 22.2mm	18 @ 4,500 rpm
R35	1937-40	Single Cyl OHV	72	84	342	6.0:1	Sum 22mm	14 @ 4,500 rpm
R20	1937-38	Single Cyl OHV	60	68	192		Amal 18.2mm	8@ 5,400 rpm
R23	1938-40	Single Cyl OHV	68	68	247		Amal 18.2mm	10@ 5,400 rpm
R51	1938-40	Twin Cyl OHV	68	68	494	6.7:1	2 Amal 22.2mm	24 @ 5,800 rpm
R66	1938-41	Twin Cyl OHV	69.8	78	597	6.8:1	2 Amal 23.8mm	30 @ 5,300 rpm
R61	1938-41	Twin Cyl SV	70	78	596	5.7:1	2 Amal 22.2mm	18 @ 4,800 rpm
R71	1938-41	Twin Cyl SV	78	78	745	5.5:1	2 Graetzin 24mm	22 @ 4,600 rpm
R75	1941-44	Twin Cyl OHV	78	78	745	5.8:1	2 Graetzin 24mm	26 @ 4,000 rpm
R24	1948-50	Single Cyl OHV	68	68	247	6.75:1	Bing 22mm	12@ 5,600 rpm
R25	1950-51	Single Cyl OHV	68	68	247	6.5:1	Bing 24mm	12@ 5,600 rpm
R25/2	1951-53	Single Cyl OHV	68	68	247	6.5:1	Bing 22mm or SAWE 22mm	12@ 5,800 rpm
R25/3	1953-56	Single Cyl OHV	68	68	247	6.5:1	Bing 24mm or SAWE 24mm	12@ 5,600 rpm
R51/2	1950-51	Twin Cyl OHV	68	68	494	6.4:1	2 Bing 22mm	24 @ 5,800 rpm
R51/3	1951-54	Twin Cyl OHV	68	68	494	6.3:1	2 Bing 22mm	24 @ 5,800 rpm
R67	1951	Twin Cyl OHV	72	73	594	5.6:1	2 Bing 24mm	26 @ 5,500 rpm
R67/2	1952-54	Twin Cyl OHV	72	73	594	6.5:1	2 Bing 24mm	28 @ 5,600 rpm
R67/3	1955-56	Twin Cyl OHV	72	73	594	6.5:1	2 Bing 24mm	28 @ 5,600 rpm
R68	1952-54	Twin Cyl OHV	72	73	594		2 Bing 26mm	35 @ 7,000 rpm
R50	1955-60	Twin Cyl OHV	68	68	494	6.8:1	2 Bing 24mm	26 @ 5,800 rpm
R69	1955-60	Twin Cyl OHV	72	73	594		2 Bing 26mm	35 @ 7,000 rpm
R60	1956-60	Twin Cyl OHV	72	73	594	6.5:1	2 Bing 24mm	28 @ 5,600 rpm
R26	1956-60	Single Cyl OHV	68	68	247	7.5:1	Bing 26mm	15@ 6,400 rpm
R50/2	1960-69	Twin Cyl OHV	68	68	494	7.5:1	2 Bing 24mm	26 @ 5,800 rpm
R60/2	1960-69	Twin Cyl OHV	72	73	594	7.5:1	2 Bing 24mm	30 @ 5,800 rpm
R27	1960-66	Single Cyl OHV	68	68	247	8.2:1	Bing 26mm	18@ 7,400 rpm
R50S	1960-62	Twin Cyl OHV	68	68	494	9.5:1	2 Bing 26mm	35 @ 7,650 rpm
R69S	1960-69	Twin Cyl OHV	72	73	594	9.5:1	2 Bing 26mm	42 @ 7,000 rpm
R50US	1967-69	Twin Cyl OHV	68	68	494	7.5:1	2 Bing 24mm	26 @ 5,800 rpm
R60US	1967-69	Twin Cyl OHV	72	73	594	7.5:1	2 Bing 24mm	30 @ 5,800 rpm
R69US	1967-69	Twin Cyl OHV	72	73	594	9.5:1	2 Bing 26mm	42 @ 7,000 rpm
R50/5	1969-73	Twin Cyl OHV	67	70.6	498	8.6:1	2 Bing 26mm	32 @ 6,400 rpm
R60/5	1969-73	Twin Cyl OHV	73.5	70.6	599	9.2:1	2 Bing 26mm	40 @ 6,400 rpm
R75/5	1969-73	Twin Cyl OHV	82	70.6	745		2 Bing CV 32mm	50 @ 6,200 rpm

Trans	Front Suspension	Rear Suspension	Front tyre	Rear tyre (mm)	Wheelbase (kg)	Weight
3 speed	Cantilever Spring	Rigid	26x3	26x3	1380	122
3 speed	Cantilever Spring	Rigid	26x3	26x3	1380	134
3 speed	Plate Spring	Rigid	27x3.5	27x3.5	1232	110
3 speed	Plate Spring	Rigid	26x3.5	26x3.5	1410	126
3 speed	Plate Spring	Rigid	26x3	26x3	1410	130
3 speed	Plate Spring	Rigid	26x3.5	26x3.5	1400	152
3 speed	Plate Spring	Rigid	26x3.5	26x3.5	1400	155
3 speed	Plate Spring	Rigid	26x3.5	26x3.5	1400	150
3 speed	Plate Spring	Rigid	26x3.5	26x3.5	1400	152
3 speed	Plate Spring	Rigid	26x3.5	26x3.5	1380	162
3 speed	Plate Spring	Rigid	26x3.5	26x3.5	1380	165
3 speed	Cantilever Spring	Rigid	25x3	25x3	1320 (1303)	130
3 speed (4 speed)	Plate Spring	Rigid	26x3.5	26x3.5	1300	137
4 speed	Cantilever Spring	Rigid	26x3.5	26x3.5	1320	149
4 speed	Telescopic Fork	Rigid	3.5x19	3.5x19	1380	185
4 speed	Telescopic Fork	Rigid	3.5x19	3.5x19	1380	183
4 speed	Telescopic Fork	Rigid	3.5x19	3.5x19	1400	165
4 speed	Telescopic Fork	Rigid	3.5x19	3.5x19	1400	175
4 speed	Telescopic Fork	Rigid	3.5x19	3.5x19	1400	155
3 speed	Telescopic Fork	Rigid	3x19	3x19	1330	130
3 speed	Telescopic Fork	Rigid	3x19	3x19	1330	135
4 speed	Telescopic Fork	Plunger	3.5x19	3.5x19	1400	182
4 speed	Telescopic Fork	Plunger	3.5x19	3.5x19	1400	187
4 speed	Telescopic Fork	Plunger	3.5x19	3.5x19	1400	184
4 speed	Telescopic Fork	Plunger	3.5x19	3.5x19	1400	187
4 speed + Rev	Telescopic Fork	Rigid	4.5x16	4.5x16	1444	400 With SC
4 speed	Telescopic Fork	Rigid	3x19	3x19		130
4 speed	Telescopic Fork	Plunger	3.25x19	3.25x19		140
4 speed	Telescopic Fork	Plunger	3.25x19	3.25x19	1335	142
4 speed	Telescopic Fork	Plunger	3.25x18	3.25x18	1365	150
4 speed	Telescopic Fork	Plunger	3.5x19	3.5x19		185
4 speed	Telescopic Fork	Plunger	3.5x19	3.5x19	1400	190
4 speed	Telescopic Fork	Plunger	3.5x19	3.5x19	1400	192
4 speed	Telescopic Fork	Plunger	3.5x19	3.5x19	1400	192
4 speed	Telescopic Fork	Plunger	3.5x19	3.5x19 4.00x18	1400	192
4 speed	Telescopic Fork	Plunger	3.5x19	3.5x19	1400	190
4 speed	Swingarm	Swingarm	3.5x18	3.5x18	1415	195
4 speed	Swingarm	Swingarm	3.5x18	3.5x18	1415	202
4 speed	Swingarm	Swingarm	3.5x18	3.5x18	1415	195
4 speed	Swingarm	Swingarm	3.25x18	3.25x18	1390	158
4 speed	Swingarm	Swingarm	3.5x18	3.5x18	1415	195
4 speed	Swingarm	Swingarm	3.5x18	3.5x18	1415	195
4 speed	Swingarm	Swingarm	3.25x18	3.25x18	1390	162
4 speed	Swingarm	Swingarm	3.5x18	4.0x18	1415	198
4 speed	Swingarm	Swingarm	3.5x18	4.0x18	1415	202
4 speed	Telescopic Fork	Swingarm	3.5x18	4.0x18	1427	195
4 speed	Telescopic Fork	Swingarm	3.5x18	4.0x18	1427	195
4 speed	Telescopic Fork	Swingarm	3.5x18	4.0x18	1427	199
4 speed	Telescopic Fork	Swingarm	3.25x19	4.0x18	1385 (1435)	205 (200)
4 speed	Telescopic Fork	Swingarm	3.25x19	4.0x18	1385 (1435)	210 (205)
4 speed	Telescopic Fork	Swingarm	3.25x19	4.0x18	1385 (1435)	210 (205)

Model	Years	Engine	Bore (mm)	Stroke (mm)	Displ (cc)	Comp ratio	Carburettor	HP
R90S	1973-76	Twin Cyl OHV	90	70.6	898	9.5:1	2 Dell'Orto 38mm	67 @ 7,000 rpm
R90/6	1973-76	Twin Cyl OHV	90	70.6	898		2 Bing CV 32mm	60 @ 6,500 rpm
R75/6	1973-76	Twin Cyl OHV	82	70.6	745		2 Bing CV 32mm	50 @ 6,200 rpm
R60/6	1973-76	Twin Cyl OHV	73.5	70.6	599	9.2:1	2 Bing 26mm	40 @ 6,400 rpm
R100RS	1976-84	Twin Cyl OHV	94	70.6	980	9.5:1	2 Bing CV 40mm	70 @ 7,250 rpm
R100S	1976-78	Twin Cyl OHV	94	70.6	980	9.5:1	2 Bing CV 40mm	65 (70) @ 6,600 (7250)
R100/7	1976-78	Twin Cyl OHV	94	70.6	980		2 Bing CV 32mm	60 @ 6,500 rpm
R75/7	1976-77	Twin Cyl OHV	82	70.6	745		2 Bing CV 32mm	50 @ 6,200 rpm
R60/7	1976-78	Twin Cyl OHV	73.5	70.6	599	9.2:1	2 Bing 26mm	40 @ 6,400 rpm
R80/7	1977-84	Twin Cyl OHV	84.8	70.6	797	9.2:1 (8:1)	2 Bing CV 32mm	55 (50) @ 7,000 (7250)
R100RT	1978-84	Twin Cyl OHV	94	70.6	980	9.5:1	2 Bing CV 40mm	70 @ 7,250 rpm
R100T	1978-80	Twin Cyl OHV	94	70.6	980	9.5:1	2 Bing CV 40mm	65 @ 6,600 rpm
R45	1978-85	Twin Cyl OHV	70	61.5	473	9.2:1 (8.2:1)	2 Bing CV 28mm (26mm)	35 (27) @ 7,250 (6500)
R65	1978-85	Twin Cyl OHV	82	61.5	649	9.2:1	2 Bing CV 32mm	45 (50) @ 7,250 rpm
R100CS	1980-84	Twin Cyl OHV	94	70.6	980	9.5:1	2 Bing CV 40mm	70 @ 7,250 rpm
R100	1980-84	Twin Cyl OHV	94	70.6	980	8.2:1	2 Bing CV 40mm	67 @ 7,000 rpm
R80G/S	1980-87	Twin Cyl OHV	84.8	70.6	797	8.2:1	2 Bing CV 32mm	50 @ 6,500 rpm
R65LS	1981-85	Twin Cyl OHV	82	61.5	649	9.2:1	2 Bing CV 32mm	50 @ 7,250 rpm
R80ST	1982-84	Twin Cyl OHV	84.8	70.6	797	8.2:1	2 Bing CV 32mm	50 @ 6,500 rpm
R80RT	1982-84	Twin Cyl OHV	84.8	70.6	797	8.2:1	2 Bing CV 32mm	50 @ 6,500 rpm
K100	1983-90	Four Cyl DOHC	67	70	987	10.2:1	Bosch LE Injection	90 @ 8,000 rpm
K100RS	1983-92	Four Cyl DOHC	67	70	987	10.2:1	Bosch LE Injection	90 @ 8,000 rpm
K100RT	1984-89	Four Cyl DOHC	67	70	987	10.2:1	Bosch LE Injection	90 @ 8,000 rpm
R80	1984-95	Twin Cyl OHV	84.8	70.6	797	8.2:1	2 Bing CV 32mm	50 @ 6,500 rpm
R80RT	1984-95	Twin Cyl OHV	84.8	70.6	797	8.2:1	2 Bing CV 32mm	50 @ 6,500 rpm
R65	1985-93	Twin Cyl OHV	82	61.5	649	8.7:1 (8.4:1)	2 Bing CV 32mm (26mm)	48 (27) @ 7,250 rpm
K75C	1985-90	Three Cyl DOHC	67	70	740		Bosch LE Injection	75 @ 8,500 rpm
K75S	1985-95	Three Cyl DOHC	67	70	740		Bosch LE Injection	75 @ 8,500 rpm
K75	1986-96	Three Cyl DOHC	67	70	740		Bosch LE Injection	75 @ 8,500 rpm
K100LT	1986-91	Four Cyl DOHC	67	70	987	10.2:1	Bosch LE Injection	90 @ 8,000 rpm
R100RS	1986-92	Twin Cyl OHV	94	70.6	980	8.45:1	2 Bing CV 32mm	60 @ 6,500 rpm
R100GS	1987-96	Twin Cyl OHV	94	70.6	980	8.5:1	2 Bing CV 40mm	60 @ 6,500 rpm
R80GS	1987-96	Twin Cyl OHV	84.8	70.6	797	8.2:1	2 Bing CV 32mm	50 @ 6,500 rpm
R65GS	1987-92	Twin Cyl OHV	82	61.5	649	8.4:1	2 Bing CV 26mm	27 @ 5,500 rpm
R100RT	1987-96	Twin Cyl OHV	94	70.6	980	8.45:1	2 Bing CV 32mm	60 @ 6,500 rpm
K1	1989-93	Four Cyl DOHC 4v	67	70	987		Bosch Motronic Injection	100 @ 8,000 rpm
K100RS	1989-92	Four Cyl DOHC 4v	67	70	987		Bosch Motronic Injection	100 @ 8,000 rpm
K75RT	1989-96	Three Cyl DOHC	67	70	740		Bosch LE Injection	75 @ 8,500 rpm
R100R (Mystic)	1991-96	Twin Cyl OHV	94	70.6	980	8.5:1	2 Bing CV 40mm	60 @ 6,500 rpm
R80R	1992-94	Twin Cyl OHV	84.8	70.6	797	8.2:1	2 Bing CV 32mm	50 (34,27) @ 6,500 rpm
K1100LT	1991-98	Four Cyl DOHC 4v	70.5	70	1092		Bosch Motronic Injection	100 @ 7,500 rpm
K1100RS	1992-96	Four Cyl DOHC 4v	70.5	70	1092		Bosch Motronic Injection	100 @ 7,500 rpm
R1100RS	1993-2001	Twin Cyl OHV 4v	99	70.5	1085	10.7:1	Bosch Motronic Injection	90 @ 7,250 rpm
F650	1993-99	Single Cyl DOHC 4v	100	83	652	9.7:1	2 Mikuni 33mm	48 (34) @ 6,500 rpm
R1100GS	1993-99	Twin Cyl OHV 4v	99	70.5	1085	10.3:1	Bosch Motronic Injection	80 @ 6,750 rpm
R1100R	1994-2000	Twin Cyl OHV 4v	99	70.5	1085	10.3:1	Bosch Motronic Injection	80 @ 6,750 rpm
R850R	1994- 2002	Twin Cyl OHV 4v	87.5	70.5	848	10.3:1	Bosch Motronic Injection	70 (34) @ 7,000 rpm
R1100RT	1995-2001	Twin Cyl OHV 4v	99	70.5	1085	10.7:1	Bosch Motronic Injection	90 @ 7,250 rpm
F650ST	1996-99	Single Cyl DOHC 4v	100	83	652	9.7:1	2 Mikuni 33mm	48 (34) @ 6,500 rpm
K1200RS	1997-2004	Four Cyl DOHC 4v	70.5	75	1171		Bosch Motronic Injection	130 (98)@ 8,750 rpm
R1200C	1997-2005	Twin Cyl OHV 4v	101	73	1170	10.0:1	Bosch Motronic Injection	61 @ 5,000 rpm
R1100S (Boxer Cup)	1998-2005 (2003)	Twin Cyl OHV 4v	99	70.5	1085	11.3:1	Bosch Motronic Injection	98 @ 7,500 rpm
R850GS	1998-2003	Twin Cyl OHV 4v	87.5	70.5	848	10.3:1	Bosch Motronic Injection	70 (34) @ 7,000 rpm
K1200LT	1999-2010	Four Cyl DOHC 4v	70.5	75	1171	10:8 (11.5:1)	Bosch Motronic Injection	98 @ 6,750 rpm (116@8,000rpm)
R1150GS (Adventure)	1999-2005	Twin Cyl OHV 4v	101	70.5	1130	10.3:1	Bosch Motronic Injection	85 @ 6,750 rpm
R850C	1999-2002	Twin Cyl OHV 4v	87.5	70.5	848	10.3:1	Bosch Motronic Injection	50 (34) @ 7,000 rpm
F650GS (Dakar)	2000-07	Single Cyl DOHC 4v	100	83	652	11.5:1	BMS	50 (34) @ 6,500 rpm
R1150R	2000-06	Twin Cyl OHV 4v	101	70.5	1130	10.3:1	Bosch Motronic Injection	85 @ 6,750 rpm
C1	2000-02	Single Cyl DOHC 4v	56.4	50	125		BMS	15@ 9,250
R1150RT	2001-04	Twin Cyl OHV 4v	101	70.5	1130	11.3:1	Bosch Motronic Injection	95 @ 7,250 rpm
C1 200	2001	Single Cyl DOHC 4v	62	58.8	176	11.5:1	BMS	18@ 9,000
R1150RS	2002-04	Twin Cyl OHV 4v	101	70.5	1130	11.3:1	Bosch Motronic Injection	95 @ 7,250 rpm

Trans	Front Suspension	Rear Suspension	Front tyre	Rear tyre (mm)	Wheelbase (kg)	Weight
5 speed	Telescopic Fork	Swingarm	3.25x19	4.0x18	1465	215
5 speed	Telescopic Fork	Swingarm	3.25x19	4.0x18	1465	210
5 speed	Telescopic Fork	Swingarm	3.25x19	4.0x18	1465	210
5 speed	Telescopic Fork	Swingarm	3.25x19	4.0x18	1465	210
5 speed	Telescopic Fork	Swingarm	3.25x19	4.0x18	1465	230
5 speed	Telescopic Fork	Swingarm	3.25x19	4.0x18	1465	220
5 speed	Telescopic Fork	Swingarm	3.25x19	4.0x18	1465	215
5 speed	Telescopic Fork	Swingarm	3.25x19	4.0x18	1465	215
5 speed	Telescopic Fork	Swingarm	3.25x19	4.0x18	1465	215
5 speed	Telescopic Fork	Swingarm	3.25x19	4.0x18	1465	215
5 speed	Telescopic Fork	Swingarm	3.25x19	4.0x18	1465	234
5 speed	Telescopic Fork	Swingarm	3.25x19	4.0x18	1465	215
5 speed	Telescopic Fork	Swingarm	3.25x18	4.0x18	1400	205
5 speed	Telescopic Fork	Swingarm	3.25x18	4.0x18	1400	205
5 speed	Telescopic Fork	Swingarm	3.25x19	4.0x18	1465	220
5 speed	Telescopic Fork	Swingarm	3.25x19	4.0x18	1465	218
5 speed	Telescopic Fork	Monolever Swingarm	3.00x21	4.0x18	1465	186 (205)
5 speed	Telescopic Fork	Swingarm	3.25x18	4.0x18	1400	207
5 speed	Telescopic Fork	Monolever Swingarm	100/90x19	4.0x18	1446	198
5 speed	Telescopic Fork	Swingarm	3.25x19	4.0x18	1465	235
5 speed	Telescopic Fork	Monolever Swingarm	100/90x18	130/90x17	1516	239
5 speed	Telescopic Fork	Monolever Swingarm	100/90x18	130/90x17	1516	249
5 speed	Telescopic Fork	Monolever Swingarm	100/90x18	130/90x17	1516	253
5 speed	Telescopic Fork	Monolever Swingarm	90/90x 18	120/90x18	1447	210
5 speed	Telescopic Fork	Monolever Swingarm	90/90x 18	120/90x18	1447	227
5 speed	Telescopic Fork	Monolever Swingarm	90/90x 18	120/90x18	1447	205
5 speed	Telescopic Fork	Monolever Swingarm	100/90x18	120/90x18	1516	227
5 speed	Telescopic Fork	Monolever Swingarm	100/90x18	130/90x17	1516	229
5 speed	Telescopic Fork	Monolever Swingarm	100/90x18	120/90x18	1516	227
5 speed	Telescopic Fork	Monolever Swingarm	100/90x18	130/90x17	1516	283
5 speed	Telescopic Fork	Monolever Swingarm	90/90x 18	120/90x18	1447	229
5 speed	Telescopic Fork	Paralever Swingarm	90/90x 21	130/80x17	1514	210 (236)
5 speed	Telescopic Fork	Paralever Swingarm	1.85x21	130/80x17	1514	210
5 speed	Telescopic Fork	Monolever Swingarm	1.85x21	4.0x18	1465	198
5 speed	Telescopic Fork	Monolever Swingarm	90/90x 18	120/90x18	1447	229
5 speed	Telescopic Fork	Paralever Swingarm	120/70x17	160/60x18	1565	234
5 speed	Telescopic Fork	Paralever Swingarm	120/70x17	160/60x18	1565	235
5 speed	Telescopic Fork	Monolever Swingarm	100/90x18	130/90x17	1516	258
5 speed	Telescopic Fork	Paralever Swingarm	110/80x18	140/80x17	1495	218 (215)
5 speed	Telescopic Fork	Paralever Swingarm	110/80x18	140/80x17	1495	217
5 speed	Telescopic Fork	Paralever Swingarm	110/80x18	140/80x17	1565	290
5 speed	Telescopic Fork	Paralever Swingarm	120/70x17	160/60x18	1565	268
5 speed	Telelever Fork	Paralever Swingarm	120/70x17	160/60x18	1473	239
5 speed	Telescopic Fork	Rising rate Swingarm	100/90x19	130/80x17	1480	189 (191)
5 speed	Telelever Fork	Paralever Swingarm	110/80x19	150/70x17	1509	243
5 speed	Telelever Fork	Paralever Swingarm	120/70x17 110/80x18	160/60x17 150/70x17	1487	235
5 speed	Telelever Fork	Paralever Swingarm	120/70x17 110/80x18	160/60x17 150/70x17	1487	235
5 speed	Telelever Fork	Paralever Swingarm	120/70x17	160/60x18	1485	282
5 speed	Telescopic Fork	Rising rate Swingarm	100/90x18	130/80x17	1465	191
6 speed	Telelever Fork	Paralever Swingarm	120/70x17	170/60x17 180/55x17	1555	285
5 speed	Telelever Fork	Monolever Swingarm	110/90x18	170/80x15	1650	256
6 speed	Telelever Fork	Paralever Swingarm	120/70x17	170/60x17 (180/55x17	1478	229
5 speed	Telelever Fork	Paralever Swingarm	110/80x19	150/70x17	1509	249
5 speed	Telelever Fork	Paralever Swingarm	120/70x17	160/60x17	1633 (1627)	378 (387)
6 speed	Telelever Fork	Paralever Swingarm	110/80x19	150/70x17	1509 (1501)	249 (253)
5 speed	Telelever Fork	Paralever Swingarm	110/90x18	170/80x15	1650	256
5 speed	Telescopic Fork	Rising rate Swingarm	100/90x19 (90/90x21)	130/80x17	1479 (1489)	193 (192)
6 speed	Telelever Fork	Paralever Swingarm	120/70x17	170/60x17	1487	238
Auto 2 stage	Telelever Fork	Swingarm	120/70x13	140/70x12	1488	185
6 speed	Telelever Fork	Paralever Swingarm	120/70x17	170/60x17	1485	279
Auto 2 stage	Telelever Fork	Swingarm	120/70x13	140/70x12	1488	185
6 speed	Telelever Fork	Paralever Swingarm	120/70x17	170/60x17	1473	248

Model	Years	Engine	Bore (mm)	Stroke (mm)	Displ (cc)	Comp ratio	Carburettor	HP
F650CS	2002-05	Single Cyl DOHC 4v	100	83	652	11.5:1	BMS	50 (34) @ 6,800 rpm
K1200GT	2003-05	Four Cyl DOHC 4v	70.5	75	1171		Bosch Motronic Injection	130 (98) @ 8,750 rpm
R1200CL (Montauk)	2003-04	Twin Cyl OHV 4v	101	73	1170	10.0:1	Bosch Motronic Injection	61 @ 5,000 rpm
R850R	2003-06	Twin Cyl OHV 4v	87.5	70.5	848	10.3:1	Bosch Motronic Injection	70 (34) @ 7,000 rpm
R1200GS (Adventure)	2004-07	Twin Cyl OHV 4v	101	73	1170	11.0:1 (12:1)	BMS-K electronic Injection	100 (105) @ 7,000 rpm
K1200S (K1200R) (K1200R Sport)	2004-08	Four Cyl DOHC 4v	79	59	1157		BMS-K electronic Injection	167 (163) @ 10,250 rpm
R1200RT (R1200ST) (2007)	2005-09	Twin Cyl OHV 4v	101	73	1170	12.0:1	BMS-K electronic Injection	110 @ 7,500 rpm
HP2 Enduro	2006-07	Twin Cyl OHV 4v	101	73	1170	11.0:1	BMS-K electronic Injection	105 @ 7,000 rpm
R1200S	2006-07	Twin Cyl OHV 4v	101	73	1170	12.5:1	BMS-K electronic Injection	122 @ 8,250 rpm
K1200GT	2006-08	Four Cyl DOHC 4v	79	59	1157		BMS-K electronic Injection	152 @ 9,500 rpm
F800S/ST	2006-12	Two Cyl DOHC 4v	82	75.6	798		BMS-K electronic Injection	85 @ 8,000 rpm (34 @ 7,000 rpm)
HP2 Megamoto	2007-08	Twin Cyl OHV 4v	101	73	1170	12.0:1	BMS-K electronic Injection	113 @ 7,500 rpm
R1200R	2007-10	Twin Cyl OHV 4v	101	73	1170	12.0:1	BMS-K electronic Injection	109 @ 7,500 rpm
G650X challenge Xmoto Xcountry	2007-09	Single Cyl DOHC 4v	100	83	652	11.5:1	BMS-C II electronic injection	53 @ 7,000 rpm
R1200GS (Adventure)	2008-09	Twin Cyl OHV 4v	101	73	1170		BMS-K electronic Injection	105 @ 7,000 rpm
HP2 Sport	2008-11	Twin Cyl DOHC 4v	101	73	1170	12.5:1	BMS-K electronic Injection	128 @ 8,750 rpm
F800GS (F650GS)	2008-12	Twin Cyl DOHC 4v	82	75.6	798		BMS-KP electronic Injection	85 @ 7,500 rpm (71 @ 7,000 rpm)
G450X	2008-11	Single Cyl DOHC 4v	98	59.6	449		Keihin electronic injection	52 @ 9,000 rpm (41 @ 7,000 rpm)
K1300S (K1300R) (K1300GT)	2009-16	Four Cyl DOHC 4v	80	64.4	1293		BMS-K electronic Injection	175 (173) @ 9,250 rpm (160 @ 9,000 rpm)
F800R	2009-14	Twin Cyl DOHC 4v	82	75.6	798		BMS-KP electronic Injection	87 @ 8,000 rpm
S1000RR (HP4)	2010-14	Four Cyl DOHC 4v	80	49.7	999		BMS-KP electronic Injection	193 @ 13,000 rpm
R1200GS (Adventure)	2010-12 (13)	Twin Cyl DOHC 4v	101	73	1170		BMS-K+ electronic Injection	110 @ 7,750 rpm
R1200RT	2010-13	Twin Cyl DOHC 4v	101	73	1170		BMS-K+ electronic Injection	110 @ 7,750 rpm
K1600GT (K1600GTL) (K1600B) (Grand America)	-2011	Six Cyl DOHC 4v	67.5	72	1649	12.2:1	BMS-X electronic Injection	160.5 @ 9,250 rpm
R1200R	2011-14	Twin Cyl DOHC 4v	101	73	1170		BMS-K+ electronic Injection	110 @ 7,750 rpm
G650GS (Sertão)	2011-16	Single Cyl DOHC 4v	100	83	652	11.5:1	BMS-CII	48 (34) @ 6,500 rpm
C600 Sport (C650GT)	2012-15	Twin Cyl DOHC 4v	79	66	646	11.6:1	BMS-E	60 @ 7,500 rpm
R1200GS (Adventure)	2013-18	Twin Cyl DOHC 4v	101	73	1170	12.5:1	BMS-X electronic Injection	125 @ 7,700 rpm
F800GS (F700GS) (Adventure)	2013-17	Twin Cyl DOHC 4v	82	75.6	798		BMS-KP electronic Injection	85 @ 7,500 rpm (75 @ 7,300 rpm)
F800GT	2013-	Two Cyl DOHC 4v	82	75.6	798		BMS-K Pelectronic Injection	90 @ 8,000 rpm
R nineT (Scrambler) (Racer) (Pure) (Urban G/S)	2014-	Twin Cyl DOHC 4v	101	73	1170		BMS-K+ (MP) electronic Injection	110 @ 7,750 rpm
S1000R	2014-	Four Cyl DOHC 4v	80	49.7	999		BMS-X electronic Injection	160 @ 11,000 rpm (165)
R1200RT	2014-	Twin Cyl DOHC 4v	101	73	1170	12.5:1	BMS-X electronic Injection	125 @ 7,700 rpm
C evolution	2014-	Electric	NA	NA	NA	NA	NA	15/47.5 4650 rpm
R1200R (R1200RS)	2015-	Twin Cyl DOHC 4v	101	73	1170	12.5:1	BMS-X electronic Injection	125 @ 7,700 rpm
S1000XR	2015-	Four Cyl DOHC 4v	80	49.7	999		BMS-X electronic Injection	160 @ 11,000 rpm (165)
F800R	2015-	Twin Cyl DOHC 4v	82	75.6	798		Electronic Injection	90 @ 8,000 rpm (48)
S1000RR	2015-18	Four Cyl DOHC 4v	80	49.7	999		BMS-X electronic Injection	199 @ 13,500 rpm
C650 Sport (C650GT)	2016-	Twin Cyl DOHC 4v	79	66	646	11.6:1	BMS-E2	60 @ 7,500 rpm
G310R (G310GS)	2016-	Single Cyl DOHC 4v	80	61.3	313	10.6:1	BMS-CE2	34 @ 9,500 rpm
HP4 Race	2017-	Four Cyl DOHC 4v	80	49.7	999	13.7-13.9:1	BMS-X electronic Injection	215 @ 13,900 rpm
F850GS (F750GS) (Adventure)	2018-	Twin Cyl DOHC 4v	84	77	853	12.7:1	BMS-M electronic Injection	95 @ 8,250 rpm (77 @ 7,500 rpm)
C400X (C400GT)	2018-	Single Cyl OHC 4v	80	69.6	350	11.5:1	BMS-E2	34 @ 7,500 rpm
S1000RR	2019-	Four Cyl DOHC 4v	80	49.7	999	13.3:1	BMS-0 electronic Injection	207 @ 13,500 rpm
R1250GS (Adventure)	2019-	Twin Cyl DOHC 4v	102.5	76	1254	12.5:1	BMS-O electronic Injection	136 @ 7,750 rpm
R1200RT	2019-	Twin Cyl DOHC 4v	102.5	76	1254	12.5:1	BMS-O electronic Injection	136 @ 7,750 rpm
R1250R (R1250RS)	2019-	Twin Cyl DOHC 4v	102.5	76	1254	12.5:1	BMS-O electronic Injection	136 @ 7,750 rpm

Trans	Front Suspension	Rear Suspension	Front tyre	Rear tyre (mm)	Wheelbase (kg)	Weight
5 speed	Telescopic Fork	Rising rate Monolever	110/70x17	160/60x17	1493	189
6 speed	Telelever Fork	Paralever Swingarm	120/70x17	180/55x17	1555	300
6 speed (5 speed)	Telelever Fork	Monolever Swingarm	150/80x16	170/80x15	1641	308 (265)
6 speed	Telelever Fork	Paralever Swingarm	120/70x17	170/60x17	1487	238
6 speed	Telelever Fork	Paralever Swingarm	110/80x19	150/70x17	1519 (1511)	225 (256)
6 speed	Duolever Fork	Paralever Swingarm	120/70x17	190/50x17	1571	248 (237) (241)
6 speed	Telelever Fork	Paralever Swingarm	120/70x17	180/55x17	1485 (1502)	259 (229)
6 speed	USD 45mm Fork	Paralever Swingarm	90/90x21	140/80x17	1610	196.5
6 speed	Telelever Fork	Paralever Swingarm	120/70x17	180/55x17 (190/50x17)	1487	213
6 speed	Duolever Fork	Paralever Swingarm	120/70x17	180/55x17	1571	282
6 speed	Telescopic Fork	Monoshock Swingarm	120/70x17	180/55x17	1466	182 (187)
6 speed	USD 45mm Fork	Paralever Swingarm	120/70x17	180/55x17	1615	199s
6 speed	Telelever Fork	Paralever Swingarm	120/70x17	180/55x17	1495	223
5 speed	USD 45mm Fork	Rising rate Swingarm	90/90x21 (120/70x17) (100/90x19)	140/80x18 (160/60x17) (130/80x17)	1500 (1500) (1498)	156 (159) (160)
6 speed	Telelever Fork	Paralever Swingarm	110/80x19	150/70x17	1507 (1511)	229 (256)
6 speed	Telelever Fork	Paralever Swingarm	120/70x17	190/55x17	1487	199
6 speed	USD 45mm Fork (Telescopic 43mm)	Monoshock Swingarm	90/90x21 (110/80x19)	150/70x17	1578 (1575) (140/80x17)	207 (199)
5 speed	USD 45mm Fork	Monoshock Swingarm	90/90x21	140/80x18	1475	121
6 speed	Duolever Fork	Paralever Swingarm	120/70x17	190/55x17 (180/55x17)	1585 (1572)	254 (243) (288)
6 speed	Telescopic Fork 43mm	Monoshock Swingarm	120/70x17	180/55x17	1520	199
6 speed	USD 46mm Fork	Monoshock Swingarm	120/70x17	190/55x17 (200/55x17)	1432 (1423)	204 (199)
6 speed	Telelever Fork	Paralever Swingarm	110/80x19	150/70x17	1507 (1510)	229 (256)
6 speed	Telelever Fork	Paralever Swingarm	120/70x17	180/55x17	1484.6	259
6 speed	Duolever Fork	Paralever Swingarm	120/70x17	190/55x17	1618	319 (348) (336) (364)
6 speed	Telelever Fork	Paralever Swingarm	120/70x17	180/55x17	1495	223
5 speed	Telescopic Fork	Rising rate Swingarm	110/80x19 (90/90x21)	140/80x17 (130/80x17)	1477 (1484)	192 (193)
CVT	USD 40mm Fork	Monoshock Swingarm	120/70x15	160/60x15	1591	249 (261)
6 speed	Telelever Fork	Paralever Swingarm	120/70x19	170/60x17	1507 (1510)	238 (260)
6 speed	USD 45mm Fork (Telescopic 43mm)	Monoshock Swingarm	90/90x21 (110/80x19)	150/70x17 (140/80x17)	1578 (1562)	214 (209) (229)
6 speed	Telescopic Fork	Monoshock Swingarm	120/70x17	180/55x17	1514	213
6 speed	USD 46mm Fork (Telescopic 43mm)	Paralever Swingarm	120/70x17 (120/70x19)	180/55x17 (170/60x17)	1476 (1527) (1491) (1493)	222 (220) (219) (221)
6 speed	USD 46mm Fork	Monoshock Swingarm	120/70x17	190/55x17	1439	207 (205)
6 speed	Telelever Fork	Paralever Swingarm	120/70x17	180/55x17	1485	274
NA	USD 40mm Fork	Monoshock Swingarm	120/70x15	160/60x15	1594 (1610)	265 (275)
6 speed	USD 45mm Fork	Paralever Swingarm	120/70x17	180/55x17	1515 (1530)	231 (236)
6 speed	USD 46mm Fork	Monoshock Swingarm	120/70x17	190/55x17	1548	228
6 speed	USD 43mm Fork	Monoshock Swingarm	120/70x17	180/55x17	1526	202
6 speed	USD 46mm Fork	Monoshock Swingarm	120/70x17	190/55x17	1438	204
CVT	USD 40mm Fork	Monoshock Swingarm	120/70x15	160/60x15	1591	249 (261)
6 speed	USD 41mm Fork	Monoshock Swingarm	110/70x17 (110/80x19)	150/60x17 (150/70x17)	1374 (1420)	158.5 (169.5)
6 speed	USD 43mm Fork	Monoshock Swingarm	120/70x17	200/60x17	1440	171.4
6 speed	USD 43mm Fork (Telescopic 41mm)	Monoshock Swingarm	90/90x21 (110/80x19)	150/70x17	1593 (1559)	229 (224) (244)
CVT	USD 35mm Fork	Twin shock Swingarm	120/70x15	150/70x14	1565	204 (212)
6 speed	USD 45mm Fork	Monoshock Swingarm	120/70x17	190/55x17	1441	197
6 speed	Telelever Fork	Paralever Swingarm	120/70x19	170/60x17	1525 (1504)	249 (268)
6 speed	Telelever Fork	Paralever Swingarm	120/70x17	180/55x17	1485	279
6 speed	USD Fork	Paralever Swingarm	120/70x17	180/55x17	1515 (1530)	239 (243)

ALSO FROM VELOCE PUBLISHING –

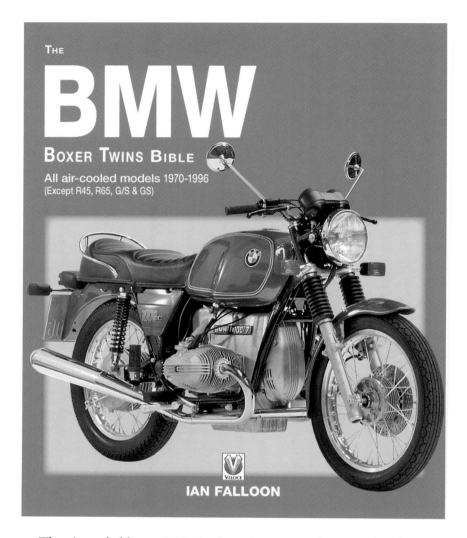

The air-cooled boxer BMW twins were among the most significant motorcycles of the 1970s through the 1980s, providing an unparalleled combination of comfort, reliability, and performance. From the /5 series, a complete series of sport and touring motorcycles evolved that earned a huge following and which was never emulated by other manufacturers.

ISBN: 978-1-845849-99-3
Paperback • 25x20.7cm • 160 pages • 190 colour and b&w pictures

For more information and price details, visit our website at www.veloce.co.uk • email: info@veloce.co.uk • Tel: +44(0)1305 260068

Many books have been published about BMW motorcycles, but this is the first to cover the evolution of the BMW sportsbike to the BMW café racer. A marque not commonly associated with the café racer scene, the growing trend of custom BMW café conversions is illustrated in detail with stunning images of sporting, racing, and 'caféd' BMWs. From Airheads to Oilheads, modified singles to parallel twins, Fours and Concept 6s – see the 'caféd' side of BMW.

ISBN: 978-1-845845-29-2
Hardback • 25x25cm • 128 pages • 205 colour pictures

For more information and price details, visit our website at www.veloce.co.uk • email: info@veloce.co.uk
• Tel: +44(0)1305 260068

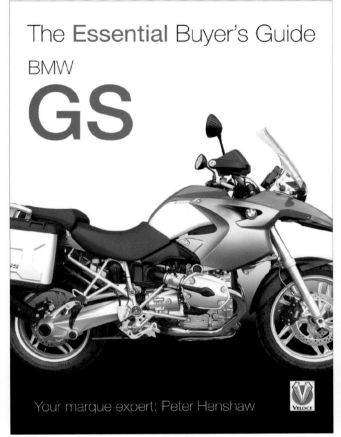

The Essential Buyer's Guide

BMW

GS

Your marque expert: Peter Henshaw

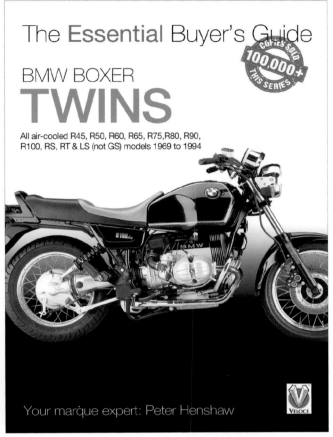

The Essential Buyer's Guide

100,000+ COPIES SOLD THIS SERIES

BMW BOXER

TWINS

All air-cooled R45, R50, R60, R65, R75,R80, R90, R100, RS, RT & LS (not GS) models 1969 to 1994

Your marque expert: Peter Henshaw

ISBN: 978-1-84584-135-5
Paperback • 19.5x13.9cm • 64 pages
• 100 colour pictures

ISBN: 978-1-78711-005-2
Paperback • 19.5x13.9cm • 64 pages
• 101 colour pictures

Having these books in your pocket is just like having
a real marque expert by your side. Benefit from the
authors' years of experience, learn how to spot a bad
BMW quickly, and how to assess a promising one like
a true professional. Get the right bike at the right price!

For more information and price details, visit our website at www.veloce.co.uk • email: info@veloce.co.uk
• Tel: +44(0)1305 260068

INDEX